THE KLEINMAN EDITION

לִימּוּד יוֹמִי

A Daily Dose of Torah

A Torah theme for every day of every week, blending profound perspectives from all areas of Torah literature – Scripture, Mishnah, Jewish Law, Mussar/Ethics, Tefillah/Prayer, and Hashkafah/Jewish Thought – collected for daily study.

ArtScroll Series®

THE KLEINMAN EDITION

A Daily Dose

A TORAH THEME FOR EVERY DAY OF EVERY WEEK
FROM ALL AREAS OF TORAH LITERATURE —
COLLECTED FOR DAILY STUDY.

Rabbi Yosaif Asher Weiss
General Editor

לימוד יומי
OF TORAH

VOLUME 2

DAILY STUDY FOR THE WEEKS OF
CHAYEI SARAH-VAYISHLACH

Published by
ArtScroll ❖ Mesorah Publications, ltd

FIRST EDITION
First Impression … October 2006

Published and Distributed by
MESORAH PUBLICATIONS, LTD.
4401 Second Avenue / Brooklyn, N.Y 11232

Distributed in Europe by
LEHMANNS
Unit E, Viking Business Park
Rolling Mill Road
Jarow, Tyne & Wear, NE32 3DP
England

Distributed in Australia and New Zealand by
GOLDS WORLDS OF JUDAICA
3-13 William Street
Balaclava, Melbourne 3183
Victoria, Australia

Distributed in Israel by
SIFRIATI / A. GITLER — BOOKS
6 Hayarkon Street
Bnei Brak 51127

Distributed in South Africa by
KOLLEL BOOKSHOP
Ivy Common
105 William Road
Norwood 2192, Johannesburg, South Africa

ARTSCROLL SERIES®
THE KLEINMAN EDITION — LIMUD YOMI / A DAILY DOSE OF TORAH
VOL. 2: CHAYEI SARAH– VAYISHLACH
© *Copyright 2006, by* MESORAH PUBLICATIONS, Ltd.
4401 Second Avenue / Brooklyn, N.Y. 11232 / (718) 921-9000 / www.artscroll.com

---

ALL RIGHTS RESERVED
*The text, prefatory and associated textual contents and introductions
— including the typographic layout, cover artwork and ornamental graphics —
have been designed, edited and revised as to content, form and style.*

**No part of this book may be reproduced
IN ANY FORM, PHOTOCOPYING, OR COMPUTER RETRIEVAL SYSTEMS
— even for personal use without written permission from
the copyright holder, Mesorah Publications Ltd.**
*except by a reviewer who wishes to quote brief passages
in connection with a review written for inclusion in magazines or newspapers.*

THE RIGHTS OF THE COPYRIGHT HOLDER WILL BE STRICTLY ENFORCED.

ISBN:
ISBN 10: 1-4226-0140-4 (hard cover)
ISBN 13: 978-1-4226-0140-2 (hard cover)

Typography by CompuScribe at ArtScroll Studios, Ltd.
Printed in the United States of America by Noble Book Press Corp.
Bound by Sefercraft, Quality Bookbinders, Ltd., Brooklyn N.Y. 11232

With gratitude for the past and resolve for the future, we dedicate this volume in memory of the parents and grandparents who are no longer with us, and in tribute to our mother and grandmother תחי׳.

Yidel Klein ז״ל
ר׳ יהודה ב״ר דוד הלוי ז״ל
נפ׳ כ״ז אדר ב׳ תשס״ג

He survived the War with nothing and — with our mother תחי׳ — began from scratch to create a new world of Torah, mitzvos, chesed — and generations loyal to everything that was precious to them.

Settling in Far Rockaway in the 1950's, they worked to build a strong Jewish infrastructure. The major institutions of Torah life in our community are a tribute to their vision and effective labor. Our father planted the seeds that flourished and made this dedication possible. Like his legacy in Far Rockaway and Lawrence, this volume is a force for daily Torah study.

❦ ❦ ❦

We pay tribute to our mother
Suri Klein תחי׳

She was his partner in longing, vision, priorities, and determination to fulfill their joint dreams for their family and neighbors. May she have many healthy years of boundless nachas from her adoring family and be able to enjoy the continued growth of the community she nurtured.

❦ ❦ ❦

We honor the memory of our parents and grandparents

Anchel and Suri Gross ז״ל
אשר אנשיל ב״ר משה יוסף ז״ל   שרה בת ר׳ חיים אליהו ע״ה
נפ׳ ג׳ שבט תשנ״ט   נפ׳ כ״ד סיון תשס״א

They came to America after the War with an uncompromising conviction that their values would be the same in the New World as in the Old, that they would retain their faith and raise their children in the image of their forebears. They epitomized the ideal that "wealth" means a home loyal to Torah, and they imbued us with the resolve that "nachas" means children whose lives revolve around Torah and mitzvos.

❦ ❦ ❦

We honor the memory of our grandparents who perished in the Holocaust:

ר׳ דוד ב״ר יעקב הלוי ע״ה ופעזל בת ר׳ צבי ע״ה הי״ד – קליין
ר׳ מרדכי ב״ר דוד הלוי ע״ה ולאה בת ר׳ יעקב הלוי ע״ה הי״ד – קליין
ר׳ משה יוסף ב״ר בנימין צבי ע״ה ומלכה בת ר׳ יחיאל מיכל ע״ה הי״ד – גראס
ר׳ חיים אליהו ב״ר מרדכי ע״ה וויטא בת ר׳ שלמה אליעזר ע״ה הי״ד – גארטענבערג

תנצב״ה

Motty and Malka Klein
Esther and Chaim Baruch Fogel, Dovid and Chavie, Binyomin Zvi,
Elana Leah and Natan Goldstein, Moshe Yosef, Yaakov Eliyahu

To our fathers and grandfathers, daily Torah study was the first priority.
It is fitting, therefore, that we dedicate this Limud Yomi Series in their memory

Avrohom Kleinman ז״ל
ר' אברהם אייזיק ב״ר אלכסנדר ז״ל
נפ' י״ב שבט תשנ״ט

After years of slave labor and concentration camps — years when he risked his life to put on *tefillin* every day! — he courageously rebuilt. Wherever he was — in DP camps, Poughkeepsie, Borough Park, or Forest Hills — he was a one-man *kiruv* movement, before "*kiruv rechokim*" was a familiar phrase. Everyone was drawn to his enthusiasm for Yiddishkeit.

His home was open to anyone in need, even when there was barely enough for family.

All his life he felt close to his Rebbe, the Nitra Rav, and to the father-in-law he never knew; their *sefarim*, *Naos Desheh* and *Lechem Abirim*, were part of our Shabbos table. He was a caring and gentle man whose life was defined by his love of learning Torah, *gemillas chasadim*, *kiruv* work, *hachnasas orchim*, *askanus*, and love for his family. He left a noble legacy that we are honored to perpetuate.

Mendel Indig ז״ל
ר' מנחם דוד ב״ר מרדכי שמואל ז״ל
נפ' ט' אדר ב' תשס״ג

"It was as if a *maloch* protected us," he used to say about the dark years of Churban Europa. He lost almost everything — even the *tefillin* that he put on every day until the very end — but he kept his spirit, his *emunah*, his dedication to Torah, and his resolve to rebuild.

He became a living legend of Torah, *chesed*, and service to his Bensonhurst community. His home was open to anyone in need, and there was always enough room for guests. His *succah* was the largest in the neighborhood, and he always found a way to bring endangered relatives to America and help them become established.

After he retired, he devoted himself to learning and bringing others close to Yiddishkeit, especially immigrants from the former Soviet Union, teaching them to put on *tefillin* and reuniting them with the Judaism of their ancestors. It is our privilege to carry on his glorious legacy.

We pay tribute to our mothers

Ethel Kleinman תחי'
Rose Indig תחי'

To us and our children and grandchildren — and to all who know them — they are role models of *emunah*, *chesed*, love and wisdom.

Our mothers שיחיו and our fathers ז״ל planted seeds of Torah in America and produced magnificent *doros* of children, grandchildren, and great-grandchildren following their example. May Hashem continue to bless our mothers with good health and many nachas-filled years.

Elly and Brochie Kleinman and their children
**Deenie and Yitzy Schuss   Yossie Kleinman   Aliza and Lavey Freedman
and families**

PATRONS OF LIMUD YOMI / A DAILY DOSE OF TORAH

With dedication to the principle that Torah study should always be available,
the following generous and visionary patrons
have dedicated volumes of this series:

VOL. 1: BEREISHIS-VAYEIRA / בראשית-וירא
Elly and Brochie Kleinman and family
In memory of their fathers
ז"ל Avrohom Kleinman – ר' אברהם אייזיק ב"ר אלכסנדר ז"ל
ז"ל Mendel Indig – ר' מנחם דוד ב"ר מרדכי שמואל ז"ל
and יבלח"ט in tribute to their mothers לאוי"ט שתחי'
Ethel Kleinman
Rose Indig

VOL. 2: CHAYEI SARAH-VAYISHLACH / חיי שרה-וישלח
Motty and Malka Klein
for the merit of their children שיחי'
Esther and Chaim Baruch Fogel   Dovid and Chavie   Binyomin Zvi
Elana Leah and Natan Goldstein   Moshe Yosef   Yaakov Eliyahu
In honor of his mother שתחי'
Mrs. Suri Klein לאוי"ט
In memory of his father
Yidel Klein – ר' יהודה ב"ר דוד הלוי ז"ל נפ' כ"ז אדר ב' תשס"ג
In memory of her parents
Anchel Gross – ר' אשר אנשיל ב"ר משה יוסף ז"ל נפ' ג' שבט תשנ"ט
Suri Gross – שרה בת ר' חיים אליהו ע"ה נפ' כ"ד סיון תשס"א
And in memory of their grandparents who perished על קידוש השם in the Holocaust
Klein – ר' דוד ב"ר יעקב הלוי ע"ה ופעריל בת ר' צבי ע"ה הי"ד
Klein – ר' מרדכי ב"ר דוד הלוי ע"ה ולאה בת ר' יעקב הלוי ע"ה הי"ד
Gross – ר' משה יוסף ב"ר בנימין צבי ע"ה ומלכה בת ר' יחיאל מיכל ע"ה הי"ד
Gartenberg – ר' חיים אליהו ב"ר מרדכי ע"ה ויוטא בת ר' שלמה אליעזר ע"ה הי"ד

VOL. 3: VAYEISHEV-VAYECHI / וישב-ויחי
Leon and Agi Goldenberg and family
In memory of their fathers
ז"ל Abba Goldenberg – ר' אברהם אבא ב"ר צבי ז"ל
ז"ל Joseph Brieger – ר' יוסף אליעזר ב"ר יעקב יצחק ז"ל
and יבלח"ט in tribute to their mothers לאוי"ט שתחי'
Chaya (Sicherman) Goldenberg
Monsey (Karfunkel) Brieger
and their aunt
Faiga (Sicherman) Lebovits

PATRONS OF LIMUD YOMI / A DAILY DOSE OF TORAH

VOL. 14: THE FESTIVALS / מועדי השנה

The Teichman Family (Los Angeles)
In memory of their parents and grandparents

Sam Teichman – שמואל ב"ר יששכר דוב ז"ל ז"ל
Lujza Teichman – ליבה בריינדל בת ר' יהושע הלוי ע"ה ע"ה
Rose Teichman – רחל בת ר' אלכסנר סנדר ע"ה ע"ה
Isaac Nae – יצחק אייזיק ב"ר אברהם חיים ז"ל ז"ל

DEDICATION OPPORTUNITIES

We are gratified by the
very enthusiastic response to this
new program for daily Torah study.
It is yet another demonstration
of the strong and growing desire
to make Torah part of every Jew's life,
seven days a week, fifty-two weeks a year.

Each volume of the

KLEINMAN EDITION
A DAILY DOSE OF TORAH

will carry individual dedications.

Many visionary families have already
undertaken to dedicate volumes
in memory or in honor of loved ones.
Additional dedication opportunities are available.

For further information, please call:
718-921-9000,
write to:

ArtScroll • Mesorah Publications, ltd

4401 Second Avenue • Brooklyn, NY 11232
or e-mail: DailyDose@artscroll.com

~§ Publisher's Preface

King David said: גַּל עֵינַי וְאַבִּיטָה נִפְלָאוֹת מִתּוֹרָתֶךָ, *Unveil my eyes that I may perceive wonders from your Torah* (Psalms 119:18).

Shammai said: עֲשֵׂה תוֹרָתְךָ קֶבַע, *Make your Torah study a fixed practice* (Avos 1:15).

Rav Saadiah Gaon said: The Jewish people is a nation only by virtue of the Torah.

The Torah is the essence of the Jewish people, and not a day should go by without Torah study. How much learning should there be? Just as the Torah itself is infinite, there is no limit to the effort to master its contents. The task does not end when one bids farewell to the academy and enters the world of work and business. All over the world, study halls are filled before dawn and after dark with men plumbing the depths of the Talmud and other works. Before and after their workdays, they overcome fatigue with a relentless desire to absorb more and more of God's word.

To such people, **The Kleinman Edition: Limud Yomi / A Daily Dose of Torah** will be a welcome supplement, an enrichment that offers glimpses of additional topics and a means of filling the day's spare minutes with nourishment for the mind and spirit.

To those who as yet have not been able to savor the beauty of immersion in the sea of study, this new series will be a vehicle to enrich their every day with an assortment of stimulating Torah content.

We are gratified that Volume 1 of this new series has been phenomenally well received. Many people have told us how they are filling once-empty gaps in their day with these "daily doses," and how this work has stimulated them to do further research in these subjects. As King Solomon said, תֵּן לְחָכָם וְיֶחְכַּם־עוֹד הוֹדַע לְצַדִּיק וְיוֹסֶף לֶקַח, *Give the wise man and he will become wiser; make known to the righteous and he will add [to his] learning* (Proverbs 9:9).

Each "Daily Dose of Torah" includes selections from a broad spectrum of Torah sources (see below); in combination they provide a multi-dimensional study program. Each selection can stand on its own, or, ideally, serve as a vehicle for further research and enrichment. These components are as follows:

- ❏ ***A Torah Thought for the Day***, focusing on a verse in the weekly *parashah*. The discussion may revolve around various classic interpretations, or it may offer a selection of insights and lessons that are derived from the verse. This section will draw from a wide gamut of early and later commentators, and will enhance the reader's appreciation for the wealth of Torah interpretation and its lessons for life.

- ❏ ***The Mishnah of the Day***, presenting a Mishnah selection every day, with text, translation, and concise commentary, adapted from the classic ArtScroll Mishnah Series and the Schottenstein Edition of the Talmud. This daily dose will begin with Tractate Shabbos, and continue through Seder Moed.

- ❏ ***Gems from the Gemara***, presenting some of the Talmud's discussion of the daily Mishnah. Thus the reader will "join the academy" of the Talmud's question-and-answer clarification of the laws and underlying principles of the Mishnah.

- ❏ ***A Mussar Thought for the Day***, building upon the theme of the *Torah Thought for the Day*, by presenting an ethical or moral lesson drawn from the masters of Mussar, Hashkafah, and Chassidus. This selection will stimulate thought and growth — and be a welcome source of uplifting ideas for times when the reader is called upon to speak at a *simchah*.

- ❏ ***The Halachah of the Day***, presenting a practical, relevant halachic discussion, beginning with the thirty-nine forbidden categories of Shabbos labor. The selections are adapted from Rabbi Simcha Bunim Cohen's popular and authoritative works, which are part of the ArtScroll Series. [These brief discussions are not intended to be definitive. Questions should be directed to a qualified *rav*.]

- ❏ ***A Closer Look at the Siddur***, broadening the reader's understanding of the rich tapestry of *tefillah*/prayer. The Shabbos Daily Dose will focus on the Shabbos prayers. And once a week, this section will discuss such universal themes as the Thirteen Principles of Faith or the Six Constant Commandments.

❑ *A Taste of Lomdus,* a special weekly feature that will present a brief but in-depth discussion of a Talmudic subject, in the tradition of the Torah giants whose reasoning and novellae are the basis of research and study in advanced yeshivas. Every day, there will be a challenging "Question of the Day," related to the theme of the day. The answers for the questions will come at the end of each week.

Each volume of the Daily Dose of Torah Series will present a capsule study program for twenty-eight days. The annual cycle will be comprised of thirteen four-week volumes, covering all fifty-two weeks of the year, and a fourteenth volume devoted to Rosh Hashanah, Yom Kippur, and the festivals. We are confident that the complete series will bring the excitement of Torah study to countless people, and that many of them will use it as a springboard to further learning, both independently and by joining *shiurim*.

The Kleinman Edition: Limud Yomi / A Daily Dose of Torah is dedicated by **ELLY AND BROCHIE KLEINMAN**, in memory of their fathers ז"ל and in honor of their mothers שיחיו. The Kleinmans have long distinguished themselves as generous and imaginative supporters of Torah and *chesed* causes. With warmth and kindness, they have opened their home countless times to help institutions and individuals. They have richly earned the respect and affection of all who know them, and we are honored to count them not only as major supporters of our work, but as personal friends. They and their family bring honor to the legacy of their parents.

This volume is dedicated by our dear friends **MOTTY AND MALKA KLEIN**, who have dedicated volumes of the Hebrew and English Talmud and the Ohel Sarah Women's Siddur. The Kleins are warm and generous supporters of a host of causes, public and private, and have made an indelible imprint on Torah life in their community and beyond. They combine magnanimity with discernment. They choose the causes where they can do the most good. We are proud that they include many of our projects among their choices.

The editor of this new series is **RABBI YOSAIF ASHER WEISS**, Rosh Yeshivas Ohr Hadaas, Staten Island, who is also a distinguished editor of the Schottenstein Editions of the Talmud Bavli and Yerushalmi. Rabbi Weiss' reputation as a noted scholar and educator will be justly embellished by the Daily Dose Series.

We are grateful to **RABBI RAPHAEL BUTLER**, the dynamic and innovative founder and president of the Afikim Foundation, who conceived of this concept and had a significant role in its development. We are proud to enjoy his friendship.

We are grateful to the outstanding *talmidei chachamim* who are contributing to this series: **RABBI YOSEF GAVRIEL BECHHOFER, RABBI REUVEN BUTLER, RABBI ELIYAHU COHEN, RABBI ASHER DICKER, RABBI MAYER GOLDSTEIN, RABBI BERYL SCHIFF, RABBI MORDECHAI SONNENSHEIN, RABBI MOSHE UNGAR, RABBI YISROEL DOV WEISS, AND RABBI ZEV ZIONS.** The quality of their scholarship shines through every page.

The beauty and clarity of the book's design is yet another tribute to the graphics genius of our friend and colleague **REB SHEAH BRANDER**. As someone once said in a different context, "I can't put it into words, but I know it when I see it." It is hard to define good taste and graphics beauty in words, but when one sees Reb Sheah's work, one knows it.

ELI KROEN, a master of graphics in his own right, designed the cover with his typical creativity and good taste. **MOSHE DEUTSCH** had an important hand in the typesetting and general design. **MRS. CHUMIE LIPSCHITZ**, a key member of our staff, paginated the book. **TOBY GOLDZWEIG, SURY REINHOLD, AND SARA RIFKA SPIRA** typed and corrected the manuscript.

MRS. MINDY STERN proofread and made many important suggestions. **AVROHOM BIDERMAN** was involved in virtually every aspect of the work from its inception, and **MENDY HERZBERG** assisted in shepherding the project to completion.

As this new series continues to take shape, we express our great appreciation to our long-time friend and colleague **SHMUEL BLITZ**, head of ArtScroll Jerusalem. His dedication and judgment have been indispensable components of virtually every ArtScroll/Mesorah project.

We are grateful to them all. The contributions of ArtScroll/Mesorah to the cause of Jewish life and Torah study are possible because of the skill and dedication of the above staff members and their colleagues.

It is an enormous privilege to have been instrumental in bringing Torah knowledge to the people of Torah. There are no words to express our gratitude to Hashem Yisbarach for permitting us to disseminate His Word to His children.

Rabbi Meir Zlotowitz/Rabbi Nosson Scherman

Cheshvan 5767 / October 2006

פרשת חיי שרה

Parashas Chayei Sarah

A TORAH THOUGHT FOR THE DAY

פרשת חיי שרה

SUNDAY

PARASHAS CHAYEI SARAH

וַיִּהְיוּ חַיֵּי שָׂרָה מֵאָה שָׁנָה וְעֶשְׂרִים שָׁנָה וְשֶׁבַע שָׁנִים שְׁנֵי חַיֵּי שָׂרָה

And these were the years of Sarah, one hundred years, and twenty years, and seven years; the years of Sarah's life (Bereishis 23:1).

The Midrash (*Bereishis Rabbah* 58:3) relates that R' Akiva was once giving a lecture to his students when he noticed that they were drowsing. In order to rouse them, he asked: "Why did Esther merit to rule over 127 provinces (as the queen of Achashveirosh)? It was because Hashem declared: 'Let the daughter of Sarah, who lived for 127 years, come and reign over 127 provinces.' "

Why did R' Akiva use these words to arouse his students? *Chidushei HaRim* suggests that R' Akiva wished to impress upon his students the importance of every minute, and the obligation to use one's time to its greatest advantage. It was precisely because all of Sarah's years were sin-free and perfect that her descendant Esther reigned over a full 127 provinces. If each year corresponded to a province, then each month might be a city, each week a neighborhood, each day another family. Had Sarah wasted *any* of her time, Esther's kingdom would not have been complete. But Sarah wasted no time; thus, Esther ruled supreme over the full complement of 127 provinces.

This was the lesson R' Akiva wished to impart to his students. Each of us is presented with the fleeting gift of time, and the mission of utilizing it completely and well. Every moment well spent brings reward — but every misspent second comes at a price. The implied admonition in R' Akiva's words was intended to restore R' Akiva's students to full attention.

Yalkut Yehudah finds another dimension in R' Akiva's choice of encouraging words. R' Akiva lived during a time of great persecution, when the Romans forbade the teaching of Torah (indeed, R' Akiva was ultimately executed for doing so). It was almost inevitable that the morale of Torah students would suffer during such times, as they wondered whether they would survive, or whether their Torah learning even made any difference. R' Akiva reminded them that Esther, too, lived in a time when Hashem's ways were not revealed to the world. Yet, she reigned over the 127 provinces of the world — and in what merit? The merit of her ancestress Sarah, who had lived many centuries earlier. R' Akiva thus assured the students that even if they would have difficulty seeing the fruits of their labors, they could be sure that the merits of their studies would indeed be realized eventually.

MISHNAH OF THE DAY: SHABBOS 5:2

פרשת חיי שרה

SUNDAY
PARASHAS CHAYEI SARAH

The Mishnah continues enumerating cases in which a person may let his animal out into a public domain on the Sabbath:

חֲמוֹר יוֹצֵא בְּמַרְדַּעַת בִּזְמַן שֶׁהִיא קְשׁוּרָה בּוֹ — *A donkey may go out with a saddlecloth*[1] *when it is tied onto it;*[2] זְכָרִים יוֹצְאִין לְבוּבִין — *rams may go out strapped;*[3] רְחֵלוֹת יוֹצְאוֹת שְׁחוּזוֹת כְּבוּלוֹת וּכְבוּנוֹת — *ewes may go out exposed,*[4] *tied,*[5] *or covered;*[6] הָעִזִּים יוֹצְאוֹת צְרוּרוֹת — *goats may go out* with their udders *tied.*[7]

A dissenting view:

רַבִּי יוֹסֵי אוֹסֵר בְּכוּלָן חוּץ מִן הָרְחֵלִין הַכְּבוּנוֹת — *R' Yose forbids in all of these* cases, *except for* that of *the ewes that are covered.*[8]

Another dissenting view:

--- NOTES ---

1. A small saddle [made of cushions (*Tiferes Yisrael*)] worn by the donkey throughout the day to keep it warm, since donkeys chronically feel chilled, even during the hottest days of summer (*Rav; Rashi*).

2. By tying the saddlecloth to the donkey before the Sabbath, a person indicates that the donkey needs it to keep warm. It is, therefore, considered a garment, not a burden (*Rav; Rashi*).

3. Rams were strapped with a leather pouch under their genitals to prevent them from copulating with the ewes (*Rav; Tiferes Yisrael* from Gemara 53b). The pouch was heart shaped, to fit properly around the genitals. Hence the word לְבוּבִין from לֵב, *heart* (*Tiferes Yisrael*).

4. Ewes may go out with their tails tied to their backs, exposing their genitals, to encourage copulation with the rams (*Rav* from Gemara 53b).

5. Ewes may go out with their tails tied down to their legs, to prevent copulation with the rams (*Rav* from Gemara 54a).

6. From birth, a cloth is bound around the ewe lambs to protect their wool from becoming soiled (*Rav; Rashi* 54a).

7. A goat's udders are sometimes tied tightly to stop lactation — either to allow the goats to conceive or to cause them to become fatter. At other times, a pouch is tied onto the udders to prevent the milk from dripping and being wasted (*Rav, Rashi*). [The Tanna Kamma permits a goat to go out with her udders tied in both of these cases. Later in the Mishnah, R' Yehudah will disagree with one of the cases.]

8. R' Yose disallows all of the animals listed by the Tanna Kamma to go out to a public domain with their respective gear, since he considers the gear a burden. The sole exception is ewes; they may go out covered up. Since the purpose of the cover is to keep the wool clean, even R' Yose considers it an article of attire rather than a burden. The animal may therefore wear it when walking in the public domain (*Rav*).

SUNDAY
PARASHAS CHAYEI SARAH

פרשת חיי שרה

עִזִּים יוֹצְאוֹת — *R' Yehudah says:* רַבִּי יְהוּדָה אוֹמֵר — *Goats may go out* with their udders צְרוּרוֹת לְיַבֵּשׁ — *tied for* the purpose of *drying* them up, אֲבָל לֹא לֶחָלָב — *but not for* the purpose of *being milked.* [9]

———————————— NOTES ————————————

9. In allowing goats to go out with their udders tied tightly in order to dry up the milk, R' Yehudah agrees with the Tanna Kamma, who considers the pouch an article of attire rather than a burden. He permits this, however, only if the pouch is tied tightly in order to dry up the milk. In the case of a pouch tied on to catch the dripping milk, since the pouch is tied loosely, there is the possibility that the pouch will fall off and the goatherd will carry it. R' Yehudah therefore disallows the animal to go out with a pouch tied on for this purpose (*Rav; Rashi*).

GEMS FROM THE GEMARA

The Gemara (53a) explains the Mishnah's ruling that a donkey may go out with a saddlecloth that is tied onto it. Shmuel clarifies that the saddlecloth in question must be tied onto the donkey since before the onset of the Sabbath.

[According to *Rashi* (54b), although the saddlecloth may be tied onto the donkey on the Sabbath with a permitted knot (see *Ritva; Ran*), in such a case the saddlecloth is treated as a burden, and the donkey may not go out with it. *Rashba* and *Rosh*, however, maintain that a saddlecloth may not be tied onto a donkey during the Sabbath, because the act of tying entails leaning against the animal, thus violating the Rabbinic prohibition against making use of an animal on the Sabbath. And it was to prevent this that the Rabbis prohibited a donkey to go out with a saddlecloth that was tied on during the Sabbath.]

The Gemara then cites Rav Nachman, who provides support for Shmuel's statement, noting that this condition is implicit in the phrasing of the next Mishnah's statement: "A donkey may not go out with a saddlecloth when it is not tied onto it." What does this Mishnah mean to teach us? It cannot mean to teach us only that the saddlecloth must be tied, as it is obvious that a donkey may not go out with the saddlecloth untied, lest it fall off, and one might come to carry it four *amos* in the public domain. There is no need for the Mishnah to teach such an obvious prohibition. Rather, it surely means that the donkey may not go out with a saddlecloth was not tied on since before the Sabbath. This implies that our Mishnah (which states that a donkey *may* go out with a saddlecloth if it is tied on) refers to a case where it was tied on since before the Sabbath, as Shmuel stated. (See the Gemara for further support for Shmuel from a Baraisa.)

פרשת חיי שרה
SUNDAY
PARASHAS CHAYEI SARAH

[Why did the Gemara have to cite the next Mishnah to prove its point? The same inference could have been made from our Mishnah, which states: "A donkey may go out with a saddlecloth *when it is tied onto it."* Here too one could reason: Surely the Mishnah does not need to tell us the obvious fact that the saddlecloth must be tied on. Therefore, the clause, "when it is tied onto it," must mean that it was tied on since the previous day! *Tosafos* answer that one could not make this inference from our Mishnah, because it could be argued that our Mishnah comes to *dispel* the notion that it must be tied on since the previous day. It possibly serves to teach that the donkey may go out even if the saddlecloth was tied on during the Sabbath. Only the next Mishnah — which would be superfluous were it referring to a saddlecloth that is not tied on at all — proves that the saddlecloth must have been tied on before the Sabbath.]

A MUSSAR THOUGHT FOR THE DAY

The lesson of Sarah's life — that every second of one's life must be recognized for the Divine gift that it is, and cherished accordingly — is one that can literally change a person's entire attitude toward living.

R' Moshe Feinstein was once delivering a *shmuess* to his *talmidim* on Chanukah about the importance of not wasting time, when he said, "In America, there is a saying, that one can 'kill time.'" Suddenly, without warning and totally out of character, he leaned forward and banged loudly on his table. Eyes blazing, he stared at his shocked students and declared forcefully, *"Ess is takeh retzichah!"* [That really *is* murder!] His passion left an indelible impression on those who were present.

Chidushei HaRim notes further that every second of one's life has a purpose. In this vein, he explains Hillel's famous dictum: וְאִם לֹא עַכְשָׁו אֵימָתַי, *If not now, when?* (*Avos* 1:14). Simply understood, the Mishnah is warning that time is not forever. No man knows how long he will live, or whether he will be granted the time to perform any good work that he seeks to push off for another time. But *Chidushei HaRim* sees a deeper meaning in Hillel's words. He explains that each *now*, that is, every point in time, has a particular purpose and destiny for every human being. Hashem intends for each person to be doing a specific thing at any given point in time. For some it is Torah study, for others the performance of

SUNDAY

PARASHAS CHAYEI SARAH

a mitzvah. It may be eating, sleeping, or earning a livelihood. But there is always something to be done — and the obligation cannot be postponed to another time, because that time has an obligation of its own.

The result of postponing until tomorrow what must be done today is that what was to be done tomorrow is never accomplished. Every minute of every day has never come before, and, once it departs, will never come again. And there is only one chance to utilize each moment properly. Thus, says *Chidushei HaRim,* Hillel means to ask: If not now, when? If one does not fulfill the obligation of this *now* — an obligation that must be discharged, and can only be properly fulfilled, at this moment — when will it be done? It will be lost forever! These words must serve as a powerful spur to propel us toward a new appreciation of the value of time.

HALACHAH OF THE DAY

The second condition required to facilitate permissible *sorting* is that the selecting must be done by *hand,* not through the use of a utensil that aids the selecting process. This condition precludes the use of almost all utensils, not only specialized utensils that facilitate the act of selecting, such as sieves and strainers. For example, one may not create a narrow opening between a pot and its cover in order to strain and separate soup from its contents. This is because by doing so, one is using a utensil — the pot cover — to separate "food" (the soup) from waste (the contents of the soup) using a utensil — the pot cover.

There are times, however, when the use of a utensil is not forbidden. The prohibition against the use of a utensil applies only when the purpose of the utensil is to enable one to separate the mixture more efficiently. However, if the utensil is being used not as an aid to improve the straining, but only as a matter of convenience, and the degree of straining that will be accomplished is one that could have been done by one's hand alone, then the use of the utensil is permitted. This is because in such cases, the utensil being used is seen only as an extension of the person's hand, not as a utensil that contributes to straining.

To illustrate this rule, let us analyze the following examples: One is permitted to eat fish by separating the fish from the bones with a fork. This is because he is separating the fish, the food portion of the mixture, from the bones, the waste. In this case, although he is using a fork, we must look at the purpose for which the fork is being used. A fork does not do a better job of separating fish from bones than fingers would. The purpose of the fork is simply to allow one to eat while keeping his hands clean. Since it is only a matter of convenience rather than a direct contribution to the act of straining, this activity is permitted on Shabbos.

פרשת
חיי שרה

SUNDAY
PARASHAS
CHAYEI
SARAH

One may also use a utensil in order to remove something from a deep pot. Once again, the utensil does not contribute to an improvement in the act of selecting; it only enables one to more easily make a selection that could have been equally accomplished by hand if the desired object would be within his reach.

A CLOSER LOOK AT THE SIDDUR

We spend much of our *tefillah* in declaring Hashem's praises and greatness. Among the reasons for doing so is that proper service of Hashem includes the emulating of His ways, and by constantly recounting His ways we can train ourselves to follow in His path.

Although time itself is a creation, and thus anything Hashem does is by definition not bound by time, we do find in our prayers the concept of Hashem using every second. For example, in the *berachah* of *Yotzer Ohr* that we recite before the *Shema* of *Shacharis*, we note that Hashem *renews in His Goodness each day, constantly, the works of Creation.* [The source of this statement is the famous Midrash that states that Hashem is constantly providing the power for Creation to exist, and, were He to stop doing so for even an instant, all would revert to emptiness and void.]

With respect to Hashem's interaction with man, we find reference to Hashem's constant beneficence in the *Shemoneh Esrei* prayer, in the *berachah* of *Modim*. We thank Hashem *for Your miracles that are with us every day, and for Your wonders and favors that are at all times. Eitz Yosef* explains that *miracles* refers to extraordinary happenings that all can recognize as Hashem's intervention, while *wonders* refers to "ordinary" miracles like the wonders of the human body, the rain cycle, and all growing things. Hashem causes all of these things to run constantly and uninterruptedly, to provide us with the ability to live and perform His work.

[It is noteworthy that according to *Eitz Yosef,* there are miracles happening *every day* that are extraordinary, and clearly recognizable as

פרשת חיי שרה
SUNDAY
PARASHAS CHAYEI SARAH

Hashem's intervention; we have only to develop the eyes to see them. Others, however, define *miracles* here as the miracles of nature that affect the entire world, and *wonders* as referring to Hashem's interaction with the life of each Jew on a personal level, watching over him and protecting him from harm (see, for example, *Yaaros Devash* 1:1). This interpretation is borne out by the fact that our thanks for Hashem's miracles speaks of the miracles *that are with us,* while the thanks for wonders does not include such a clause.]

Another aspect of Hashem's constant renewal of the world is that every day must be regarded as new and fresh. This is true of our Torah observance as well. In the *Shema,* we are commanded to keep close to our hearts the words of the Torah *that I have commanded you today; Sifri (Devarim* 6:6) teaches that Hashem urges us to always regard the Torah as if it had just been given, and to respond to it with freshness and vigor. When one performs the same mitzvos, and prays the same *tefillos,* every single day, he will all too often fall into the trap of routine — he will pray and learn by rote, without thinking of what he is saying or doing. His actions will become mechanical, without feeling or meaning. The prophet Yeshayah (29:13) describes such service of Hashem as מִצְוַת אֲנָשִׁים מְלֻמָּדָה, *Mitzvos that men have learned to perform.*

This is not the service that Hashem desires. Rather, it is incumbent upon us to delve into the meaning of our prayers and our Torah study and mitzvah performance. To this end, we are bidden to view the Torah with the same excitement as we would, had we just received it *today.* It is human nature to greet something new with enthusiasm and energy — and this energy, properly channeled, will invest our *avodas Hashem* with the freshness it requires and deserves.

QUESTION OF THE DAY:
Why does the verse repeat the words חַיֵּי שָׂרָה, *the life of Sarah, twice?*

For the answer, see page 54.

A TORAH THOUGHT FOR THE DAY

פרשת חיי שרה

MONDAY
PARASHAS CHAYEI SARAH

וַיָּבֹא אַבְרָהָם לִסְפֹּד לְשָׂרָה וְלִבְכֹּתָהּ
*And Avraham came to eulogize Sarah,
and to cry over her* (Bereishis 23:2).

Rashi explained that the death of Sarah is recorded in the Torah immediately following the *Akeidah* to reveal to us that the two events are connected; for when Sarah heard that Avraham had been told to take Yitzchak and slaughter him as a sacrifice, and that this had nearly occurred, her soul departed from her and she died.

There are actually several Midrashic versions of exactly what Sarah was told that caused her death, as well as several different identifications of the narrator of the tale. According to the most well-known version, the perpetrator was the Satan himself, who was determined to avenge himself after failing to dissuade Avraham and Yitzchak from doing Hashem's will. He went to Sarah and said, "Alas, Sarah! Have you not heard what has happened?" When she replied in the negative, he continued, "Your husband has taken your son Yitzchak, and offered him as a sacrifice upon the altar. Yitzchak wept, but there was no one there to save him."

Upon hearing this, Sarah burst into a fit of wailing, crying aloud three times like three *tekiah* blasts of a *shofar*. She then sobbed three times, similar to the *teruah* blasts; her soul then left her, and she died (see *Pirkei D'Rabbi Eliezer*). *Midrash HaGadol* notes that for this reason we sound these notes on the *shofar* on Rosh Hashanah, to recall Sarah's lament so that her cries should be atonement for us.

Vayikra Rabbah (20:2) relates that Sarah was never fooled into thinking Yitzchak had been killed; indeed, according to that Midrash it was Yitzchak himself who told his mother all that had transpired. But when he told her, "Had the angel not called down from heaven at that very moment, I would have been slaughtered," the very thought of that awful possibility was too much for Sarah to bear, and she died. [In *Midrash Tanchuma* the narrator is the Satan, disguised as Yitzchak.]

In yet another version of the story, found in *Sefer HaYashar,* the Satan told Sarah (who was still in Be'er Sheva) that Avraham had taken her son Yitzchak and slaughtered him. Sarah threw herself to the ground and placed ashes upon her head, mourning and wishing that she had been taken in his stead. She exclaimed: "I console myself in that you have performed Hashem's will . . . You are just, Hashem! While my eyes

PARASHAS CHAYEI SARAH — MONDAY

weep bitterly, my heart rejoices." Thus, she accepted Hashem's [supposed] decree. She then frantically tried to find anyone who could tell her of her husband's or son's whereabouts, so she could find out what had truly occurred. Suddenly, the Satan appeared to her in the guise of an old man. He said to her, "That which I told you before was a lie. Avraham did not kill Yitzchak, and he is still alive!"

When Sarah heard this, she was so elated that her soul departed from the joy, and she died.

For further discussion of why the news of the *Akeidah* overcame Sarah, see *A Mussar Thought for the Day*.

MISHNAH OF THE DAY: SHABBOS 5:3

Having previously enumerated cases in which an animal may be allowed to go out while carrying certain items on the Sabbath, the Mishnah now delineates cases in which this is forbidden:

וּבַמֶּה אֵינָהּ יוֹצְאָה — *And with what may* an animal *not go out* on the Sabbath? לֹא יֵצֵא גָמָל בִּמְטוּטֶלֶת — *A camel may not go out with a patch on its tail*,[1] לֹא עָקוּד — *nor* with its forelegs and hind legs *chained together*,[2] וְלֹא רָגוּל — *nor* with its *foreleg bent back* upon itself;[3] וְכֵן שְׁאָר כָּל הַבְּהֵמוֹת — *and so* is the law in regard to *all other animals*. לֹא יִקְשׁוֹר גְּמַלִּים זֶה בָּזֶה וְיִמְשׁוֹךְ — *One may not tie camels to each other and pull* one of them so that the others follow,[4] אֲבָל

---- NOTES ----

1. A camel may not go out into a public domain on the Sabbath with a patch of cloth attached to its tail for the purpose of identification, or for any other purpose, as this is considered a burden (*Rav; Rambam*). For other interpretations of *metulteles*, see *Gems from the Gemara*.

2. A camel's legs are chained together to prevent it from running away (*Rav* from Gemara 54a; *Rashi*). Both this form of restraint, and the following form — bending the foreleg back upon itself and tying it in place — are forbidden because they are excessive restraints for control of the animal, and are therefore considered burdens (*Tiferes Yisrael*).

3. The foreleg was bent back toward the shoulder and tied (*Rav; Tiferes Yisrael* from Gemara ibid.), leaving the animal only three free legs, so as to prevent it from running away (*Rashi* to Gemara 54a).

4. One may not tie camels one behind the other and pull the lead camel so that the others follow, since he appears to be taking them to a fair for sale (*Rav; Tiferes Yisrael* from Gemara 54a).

פרשת חיי שרה
MONDAY — PARASHAS CHAYEI SARAH

מַכְנִיס חֲבָלִים לְתוֹךְ יָדוֹ וְיִמְשׁוֹךְ — *but he may gather* their *ropes into his hand and pull* all of them at once, וּבִלְבַד שֶׁלֹּא יִכְרוֹךְ — *provided that he does not wind* the ropes around his hand.[5]

---- NOTES ----

5. The Gemara explains that the final clause of the Mishnah concerns a person who is holding ropes of linen and ropes of wool in his hand, and the issue involved is not related to the Sabbath; rather, it is related to the prohibition of wearing or covering oneself with *shaatnez,* a combination of wool and linen (see *Leviticus* 19:19 and *Deuteronomy* 22:11). One usually violates this law if he *wears* a garment made of wool and linen. However, even if a person takes two ropes in his hand to lead two animals, and one rope is made of wool while the other is made of linen, he is also in violation of this prohibition — provided the ropes are fastened together in such a way as to be considered one. Thus, if he knots together the ends of the linen and wool ropes, the two become one rope of *shaatnez.* Consequently, he may not hold them in his hand, since by holding them in his hand he tends to warm his hand. This is akin to wearing a glove of *shaatnez,* and hence a violation of the Torah prohibition. However, as long as he does not twist the ropes together in such a fashion that they will remain permanently entwined — i.e., by knotting together the ends of the ropes — the ropes are not considered to be combined as one, and he remains exempt (*Rav;* see also *Shenos Eliyahu* and *Meleches Shlomo*).

GEMS FROM THE GEMARA

In our elucidation of the Mishnah, we followed *Rav,* and translated *metulteles* as a patch on the camel's tail, used for purposes of identification. *Rashi* to the Mishnah offers two other interpretations: (1) a strap that anchors the animal's load to its tail, and prevents the load from sliding forward when the animal is going downhill; (2) a saddlecloth, similar to the מַרְדַּעַת of a donkey. In *Rashi's* own opinion, however (see 54a ד"ה בשלייתה), a *metulteles* is a small cushion that is placed between the tail and the tail strap, to prevent the strap from chafing the animal's skin.

The Gemara (54a) cites a Baraisa that qualifies our Mishnah's ruling that a camel may not go out with a *metulteles.* The Baraisa states that a camel may go out with a *metulteles* that is tied both to its tail and to its hump. *Rashi* explains that since the *metulteles* is tied to both, it will not fall off [even if the animal attempts to shake it off]. This proves that a *metulteles* is not considered a burden, for if it were considered a burden, it would be forbidden for the camel to go out while wearing it even if it were tightly fastened and could not fall off (see the introduction to

פרשת חיי שרה

MONDAY

PARASHAS CHAYEI SARAH

Mishnah 1). The Gemara adds that Rabbah bar Rav Huna said that a camel may go out with the *metulteles* tied to its placenta — i.e., to a placenta that is partially hanging out. *Rashi* explains that this is because the camel will not try to shake off this *metulteles,* because doing so would cause her pain. Hence, it is unlikely to fall off.

The qualification of the Baraisa would seem to support *Rashi's* own explanation of *metulteles,* since it proves that a *metulteles* is not considered a burden, for if it *were* considered a burden, it would be forbidden for the camel to go out while wearing it even if it were tightly fastened and could not fall off (see the introduction to Mishnah 1). See *Sfas Emes* for further discussion of this difficulty.

A MUSSAR THOUGHT FOR THE DAY

The difference between the reactions of Avraham and Sarah to the command to bring Yitzchak as a sacrifice requires explanation. As we see in the Torah, when Avraham was informed that he would have to sacrifice his beloved son, he repressed his natural instinct of mercy and went eagerly to fulfill Hashem's command. Indeed, the Torah testifies that Hashem knew that Avraham did not hold back his son at all — for had the angel not commanded him to cease, he would have actually sacrificed Yitzchak. Sarah, on the other hand, was faced by the news that Hashem had required such a sacrifice and (at least according to some versions of the Midrash — see A Torah Thought for the Day) was unable to bear the very thought, dying as a result. Why was Avraham able to withstand the mental pressure, while Sarah was not?

This question becomes even more difficult if we bear in mind that with respect to prophecy, Sarah's greatness surpassed even that of Avraham (see *Rashi* to *Bereishis* 21:12). If Avraham could withstand the test, why was Sarah unable to do so?

R' Chaim Shmulevitz explains that Hashem, in His kindness, endows human beings with the trait of adaptability. No matter how difficult the circumstances, a person is able to adapt and survive. In our lifetimes, we have seen and heard from people who survived unimaginable horrors of the Nazi Holocaust. Why were they able to do so? Because as their situations worsened, step by step, they found the ability to adapt to their surroundings, eventually surviving the war and rebuilding their lives.

When Hashem told Avraham that he was to bring Yitzchak as a sacrifice, He did so in a gradual manner. First, He simply told Avraham,

Please take your son, then *your only son,* then *whom you love,* and only then did He clarify that He was referring to *Yitzchak. Rashi* there explains: Why did Hashem not reveal that Yitzchak would be the sacrifice from the beginning? So as not to confuse Avraham and disorient him, causing him to lose his mind.

פרשת
חיי שרה

MONDAY

PARASHAS CHAYEI SARAH

From this *Rashi* we see that even Avraham, had he been confronted suddenly with the awareness that he must sacrifice Yitzchak, would not have survived. Thus, Hashem informed him gradually, allowing his feelings and emotions to adapt to the command. It was only the gradual realization of his duty that enabled him to assimilate this obligation gradually, and consequently perform Hashem's command with equanimity. Such was not the case, however, with Sarah. Brusquely informed of the news by the Satan, she was overwhelmed by the realization of what has transpired, and she died from the sudden shock.

For another possible explanation, see *A Closer Look at the Siddur.*

HALACHAH OF THE DAY

The third and final condition required for *sorting* to be permitted is that the selecting must be done *for immediate use.* How are we to quantify the meaning of *immediate* in this context? Let us now try to clarify this final condition.

The underlying concept responsible for the permissibility of selecting done in a manner incorporating these three conditions is this: This type of selection is considered an intrinsic part of the natural eating process. Since the Torah does not prohibit one from eating on Shabbos, it also, perforce, allows one to engage in the typical activities associated with normal eating.

Selecting from among the foods placed before a person immediately prior to eating them is considered a normal and expected part of the eating process. It is therefore (when joined by the other two conditions mentioned above) permissible. In accordance with this explanation, the term *immediate use* may be understood as the normal amount of time it routinely takes a person to select a food and eat it. However, *sorting* is also an intrinsic and necessary part of the preparation that takes place immediately prior to the serving of a meal. For this reason, the *poskim* extend this period of permissiblity even further. They explain that "immediate use" in the context of this *melachah* also includes the period of

פרשת חיי שרה

MONDAY

PARASHAS CHAYEI SARAH

time immediately prior to the meal that is necessary for the preparation of the entire meal. Therefore, selecting done while preparing for a meal is permitted during the time required for this preparation immediately prior to the serving of the meal.

This period of time cannot be represented as an absolute. It will vary according to the size and nature of the meal that is being prepared. A simple meal for two people may require only 15 minutes of preparation time. By contrast, a lavish Shabbos meal to be served to a large family with guests may require lengthy preparation time of an hour or more. Whatever the particular case in question may be, the time period of immediate use must be adjusted accordingly.

During this period of time, one is not required to delay any activities entailing selecting to the last possible moment before the meal; selecting is permitted throughout the preparation time. Thus, for example, if a lavish Shabbos *Kiddush* necessitates five hours of preparation, one may begin selecting food from waste by hand a full five hours before the *Kiddush* begins.

It must be noted, however, that the period during which selecting is permitted in preparation of a meal includes only time immediately prior to the meal. One may not decide to prepare for a meal in advance even if the amount of preparation time remains the same. To illustrate: A housewife planning to attend shul on Shabbos morning may not peel vegetables for the meal prior to her going out to shul. Since she will be going out after her preparations are done, this is clearly not a case of immediate use. Upon returning home, however, she may commence her preparations for the meal and peel vegetables immediately, even if the preparations for the meal are only beginning.

A CLOSER LOOK AT THE SIDDUR

In the *Yehi Ratzon* prayer that we recite after the morning blessings are said at the beginning of *Shacharis,* we ask: וְאַל תְּבִיאֵנוּ . . . וְלֹא לִידֵי נִסָּיוֹן — *and do not let us come . . . into the hands of nisayon.* We pray that Hashem not subject us to *nisyonos,* tests of our moral commitment. This sentiment is echoed by the Gemara in *Sanhedrin* (107a), which cites R' Yehudah who states in the name of Rav: A person should never bring himself to a test, for even King David brought himself to a test (in the matter of Batsheva), and he stumbled (see further in the Gemara there).

פרשת חיי שרה

MONDAY

PARASHAS CHAYEI SARAH

One might ask: Do we not find that the path to growth is through *nisyonos*? We know that Avraham was tested many times, and the righteous men of the ages faced many trials. Do we not wish the opportunity to grow?

R' Chaim Shmulevitz explains that a test that is put to a person *by Hashem* is different, for Hashem then assists the person by providing him with the ability to withstand the trial; the person has only to apply himself to the task (see *Kiddushin* 30b). However, when one brings a test upon *himself,* as David did, he is not necessarily granted this assistance, and the test is therefore much harder to pass.

R' Chaim notes that this distinction can be used to explain why Avraham was able to withstand the trial of the *Akeidah,* while Sarah could not (see *A Mussar Thought for the Day*). Avraham was put to the test by Hashem, and he was therefore endowed with the incredible mental strength and resolve he needed to withstand the emotional upheaval. Sarah, on the other hand, was not given this test, and was not endowed with these special abilities. She therefore could not withstand the accompanying emotions, although she was Avraham's superior in prophecy.

According to this approach, when we pray that Hashem not bring us to the hands of *nisayon,* we do not mean to ask that Hashem should not test us and raise our spiritual level thereby. Rather, we ask that Hashem grant us the wisdom to realize that we must not bring such *nisyonos* upon ourselves, when we are not prepared to withstand the pressures that accompany them.

R' Shimon Schwab proposes a different understanding of this prayer. He notes that while it is true that Hashem does not test a person without endowing him with the ability to succeed in passing the test, this alone does not ensure that the test will actually be passed. It is one thing to possess the *ability* to do something, and quite another to actually *do* it. Thus, he explains that in this prayer we ask Hashem to give us the will power and fortitude to make use of the strength within us to overcome our tests.

QUESTION OF THE DAY:
Why was the Cave of Machpelah so named?

For the answer, see page 54.

A TORAH THOUGHT FOR THE DAY

TUESDAY
PARASHAS CHAYEI SARAH

וַיִּשְׁמַע אַבְרָהָם אֶל־עֶפְרוֹן וַיִּשְׁקֹל אַבְרָהָם לְעֶפְרֹן אֶת־הַכֶּסֶף אֲשֶׁר דִּבֶּר בְּאָזְנֵי בְנֵי־חֵת אַרְבַּע מֵאוֹת שֶׁקֶל כֶּסֶף עֹבֵר לַסֹּחֵר

Avraham listened to Ephron; and Avraham weighed out to Ephron the silver that he had mentioned in the hearing of the children of Cheis — four hundred silver shekels, in fully negotiable currency (Bereishis 23:16).

This verse marks the conclusion of the negotiations that culminated in Avraham's purchase of the Cave of Machpelah from Ephron. Although Ephron protested loudly that he would be honored to present Avraham with the field as a gift, he also made very sure that he included a valuation in his protestations — *what is a land worth four hundred shekels between myself and you?* (v. 15). Our verse states that Avraham was quick to read the hint implicit in Ephron's posturing, and instantly agreed to pay the full amount that had been mentioned *in the hearing of the children of Cheis.* Indeed, *Rashbam* comments that to this verse we may apply the well-known aphorism, דַּי לְחַכִּימָא בִּרְמִיזָא, *a hint to the wise is sufficient.*

But Ephron was not merely disingenuous — he was greedy as well. The verse states that Avraham paid Ephron in silver that was עֹבֵר לַסֹּחֵר, *fully negotiable currency.* The Gemara in *Bava Metzia* (87a) explains that Ephron insisted upon payment consisting of the most expensive coinage in the world — *shekels* known as *centenaria. Rashi* there explains that each one of these special *shekels* was worth 2,500 ordinary *shekels.* Thus, instead of paying 400 *shekels* for the cave, Avraham actually paid *one million shekels!* The Midrash (cited by *Rashi* here) notes further that the name Ephron in the phrase *and Avraham weighed out to Ephron* is spelled in a deficient manner — עֶפְרֹן instead of עֶפְרוֹן. This, explains the Midrash, is because by taking so large a sum of money after claiming that he would take none at all, Ephron indeed exhibited a deficiency. Instead of being like the righteous man, who says little and does much, Ephron said much and did not do even a little.

One might ask: Why did Avraham so readily agree to what was essentially extortion on Ephron's part? *R' Yehezkel Danziger* suggests that Avraham was aware that the burial place of the *Avos* would not always remain in Jewish hands, and he was afraid that in later generations, the sale would be forgotten or denied. He therefore sought to make the purchase so sensational that it would become legend, ensuring that no one could deny that it had been purchased by the Jews. And the stratagem worked — for even today, no one denies that the *Avos* are buried there.

In a similar vein, the Midrash (*Bereishis Rabbah* 79:7) notes that there are three sites that the nations of the world cannot deny were rightfully purchased by the Jews, for the transactions are clearly recorded in Scripture. They are: (1) the Cave of Machpelah (in our verse); (2) the site of the *Beis HaMikdash* (which David bought from Ornan the Jebusite, as recorded in *I Chronicles* 21:25); and (3) the tomb of Yosef (see *Bereishis* 33:19 and *Yehoshua* 24:32). In all of these cases, payment was made in uncontestable currency, and the first asking price was agreed to, with no haggling; no claim could therefore ever be made that the sales were invalid.

פרשת
חיי שרה

TUESDAY

PARASHAS CHAYEI SARAH

MISHNAH OF THE DAY: SHABBOS 5:4

The Mishnah continues to enumerate cases in which an animal may not be allowed out into a public domain on the Sabbath:

אֵין חֲמוֹר יוֹצֵא בַּמַּרְדַּעַת בִּזְמַן שֶׁאֵינָהּ קְשׁוּרָה לוֹ — *A donkey may not go out with a saddlecloth if it is not tied onto [the donkey]*,[1] וְלֹא בַזּוּג אַף עַל פִּי שֶׁהוּא פָקוּק — *nor with a bell even if it is stopped up*;[2] וְלֹא בְסוּלָם שֶׁבְּצַוָּארוֹ — *nor with a "ladder"*[3] *on its neck;*[4] וְלֹא בִרְצוּעָה שֶׁבְּרַגְלוֹ — *nor with a strap on its leg.*[5] וְאֵין הַתַּרְנְגוֹלִים

— NOTES —

1. This is a saddlelike cushion worn by the donkey to keep it warm, and if it was not tied onto the donkey before the Sabbath, the animal may not go out with it, as was explained in mishnah 2 (see notes 1-2 there).

2. Even though the inside of the bell is stuffed with wool or cotton so that it cannot ring, the animal still may not go out with it, since it appears as though one is leading the donkey to the fair to sell it (*Rashi; Rambam; Rav*). [It was customary to hang a bell on an animal one wished to sell, in order to attract prospective customers (*Tiferes Yisrael*).]

3. When an animal had a wound on its foreleg or on its neck, a ladderlike wooden frame was attached around its head to prevent it from turning its head to scratch at the wound with its teeth (*Rav* from Gemara 54b).

4. The reason for this prohibition is that the "ladder" may fall off the animal. Since it is valuable, we are concerned that the owner, forgetting the Sabbath, may come to pick it up and carry it in the public domain (*Rashi*; cf. *Rambam Commentary*).

5. An animal whose strides were short, causing its feet to knock against each other, would wear a strap around its feet to prevent them from becoming bruised (*Rav; Rashi*). This strap would often fall off. Therefore, in this case as well, we are concerned

PARASHAS CHAYEI SARAH — TUESDAY

יוֹצְאִין בַּחוּטִין — **And chickens may not go out with cords;**[6] וְלֹא בִרְצוּעָה שֶׁבְּרַגְלֵיהֶם — **nor with a strap on their legs.**[7] וְאֵין הַזְּכָרִים יוֹצְאִין בַּעֲגָלָה שֶׁתַּחַת הָאַלְיָה שֶׁלָּהֶן — **And rams may not go out with a wagonette under their tails.**[8] וְאֵין הָרְחֵלִים יוֹצְאוֹת חֲנוּנוֹת — **And ewes may not go out with henna chips in their noses.**[9] וְאֵין הָעֵגֶל יוֹצֵא בַגִּימוֹן וְלֹא — **And a calf may not go out with a little yoke;**[10] פָּרָה בְּעוֹר הַקּוּפָּר — **nor a cow with a hedgehog skin** on its udders;[11] וְלֹא בִרְצוּעָה שֶׁבֵּין קַרְנֶיהָ — **nor with a strap between her horns.**[12] פָּרָתוֹ שֶׁל רַבִּי אֶלְעָזָר בֶּן עֲזַרְיָה הָיְתָה יוֹצְאָה בִּרְצוּעָה שֶׁבֵּין קַרְנֶיהָ — **The cow of R' Elazar ben Azaryah used to go out with a strap between her horns,** שֶׁלֹּא בִּרְצוֹן חֲכָמִים — **against the will of the Sages.**[13]

NOTES

that the owner, forgetting the Sabbath, may come to pick it up and carry it in the public domain (*Meiri*).

6. These were attached for identification (*Rav* from Gemara 54b).

7. These were attached to shorten their stride and prevent them from jumping and breaking utensils (*Rav* from Gemara ibid.).

8. It was customary to tie a small wagon under the fat tails of sheep to protect them from becoming lacerated by stones and boulders (*Rav*).

9. Chips from the henna tree, known in Hebrew as חֲנוּן or יַחְנוּן, were inserted into the nostrils of the ewes, to induce sneezing that would rid them of worms in their head. [Rams did not require this treatment, since they would habitually butt each other and the butting would dislodge the worms (Gemara ibid.).] Since the worms produced only mild discomfort, this remedy was prohibited on the Sabbath (*Tiferes Yisrael*). Alternatively, as in the previous cases, the reason for this prohibition was that the chips may fall out and come to be carried (*Meiri*).

10. This yoke was placed on the calf's neck to accustom it to bend its head in order that it be amenable to bearing a yoke when it grows up (*Rashi* on Gemara 54b). The training yoke was called גִּימוֹן because it trained the calf to bend its head like an אַגְמוֹן, *a reed* (Gemara 54b).

11. It was customary to cover a cow's udders with hedgehog skin to prevent leeches from sucking the cow's milk while it was asleep. When leeches, snakes, or other reptiles would attempt to suck at the udders, they would be repelled by the sharp spines of the hedgehog skin (*Rav, Rambam* from Gemara ibid.).

12. This is prohibited regardless of whether the strap is intended as an ornament or to control the cow. Since it is excessive restraint, it is considered a burden (*Rav* from Gemara 55a).

13. The Gemara explains that in reality, it was not R' Elazar's cow, but his neighbor's. However, since he did not prevent this neighbor from letting her cow go out with the strap between its horns, he was considered responsible, and the cow was therefore referred to as his (*Rav, Rambam* from Gemara 54b).

GEMS FROM THE GEMARA

פרשת
חיי שרה

TUESDAY
PARASHAS
CHAYEI
SARAH

As we noted in the Mishnah (note 13), the Gemara on 54b (citing a Baraisa) states that the cow that went out with a strap between its horns was not R' Elazar ben Azaryah's own cow, but that of a female neighbor of his. However, because he did not protest against her, it was called his cow.

The Gemara then goes on to cite a statement of the Sages on the importance of protesting against the transgressions of fellow Jews: Rav and R' Chanina and R' Yochanan and Rav Chaviva taught that whoever has the ability to protest (and thus prevent) the misdeeds of members of his household, but does not protest, is punished for the transgressions of the members of his household. Similarly, one who can protest the misdeeds of the people of his town, but does not do so, is punished for the transgressions of the people of his town. Further, one who can protest the misdeeds of the entire world, but does not protest, is punished for the transgressions of the entire world. As an example of this teaching, Rav Pappa said that the officials of the house of the Exilarch (whose authority was such that their protests could have borne fruit) are punished for the transgressions of the entire Jewish world, if they fail to protest.

R' Chanina adduces Scriptural support for this teaching, from the verse that states (*Isaiah* 3:14): *Hashem will enter into judgment with the elders of His people and its rulers.* R' Chanina asks: If the rulers sinned, still, what sin did the elders commit? Rather, Scripture refers to elders who did not protest against the sinful actions of the leaders, and were therefore brought to judgment by Hashem.

A MUSSAR THOUGHT FOR THE DAY

Above, in *A Torah Thought for the Day,* we offered one explanation for Avraham's willingness to pay such a high price for the Cave of Machpelah without any bargaining or haggling. In the *sefer Yeitiv Leiv,* another possible reason is offered, based on the Mishnah in *Avos* (4:7). The Mishnah states that one should not use one's Torah greatness as a crown with which to attain glory, or as a tool to acquire favors. For this reason, he explains, righteous people are extremely vigilant never to benefit materially from their righteousness and their Torah knowledge, refusing preferential treatment when it is offered them because of their exalted status.

Chovos HaLevavos (*Shaar Yichud HaMaaseh* Ch. 5) relates the story of

פרשת חיי שרה

TUESDAY

PARASHAS CHAYEI SARAH

a *tzaddik* who came into a store to buy a certain item from a shopkeeper who did not know him. He overheard the neighbor of the shopkeeper saying, "Be sure to give this man a discount, for he is a God-fearing man and a Torah scholar." Upon hearing this, the *tzaddik* said to the shopkeeper, "I am not interested in receiving a discount from you! I came here to buy the item with my money, not with my Torah knowledge!" Ultimately, the *tzaddik* did not purchase the item in that store, and went instead to another shop where his identity was not known, so he could purchase it without fear of the price being adjusted in recognition of his stature.

Avraham, too, was loath to accept any discount or preferential treatment due to his righteousness. Therefore, once the children of Cheis said to him, *Hear us, my master; you are a prince of* Hashem *in our midst; in the choicest of our graves you may bury your dead* (Bereishis 23:6), he realized that any special consideration would be due to their recognition of his special closeness to Hashem. As he was not willing to receive such favors, he resolved to pay the full price for the burial site, whatever would be asked. The greedy Ephron realized that Avraham was not disposed to bargain, and took advantage of this to extract an inflated price.

HALACHAH OF THE DAY

At this point in our discussion, a brief summary of the permissible method of *selecting* or *sorting* on Shabbos is in order.

In order for *selecting* to be permitted, one must select *food from waste, by hand, for immediate use.*

Food from waste: In any mixture, one must select the object that is desired, and leave behind the unwanted items.

By hand: A utensil may not be used to select more efficiently. It is, however, permissible to use a utensil as a matter of convenience — for example, so as not to soil one's hands, or to help reach a desired object. The use of specialized sorting or selecting implements, e.g. strainers, is always forbidden.

For immediate use: Selecting may be done only immediately before eating, or during the period of preparation immediately prior to the start of the meal.

While as a rule it is only permissible to select food from waste, there are circumstances where it becomes permissible to separate waste from food. [We must note that even in these cases, the other two prerequisites of permissible selecting — by hand and for immediate use — must still be met.] In situations where it is extremely difficult or impossible to select the food from the waste, one is permitted to remove the waste material and leave the food behind. For example, one may peel fruits and vegetables on Shabbos, even though this is clearly a case of removing the waste from the food. Since it is, for all practical purposes, not possible to gain access to the food without removing the waste, one may peel away the waste while leaving behind the food. Some other applications of this rule are as follows: One may peel an egg or shell nuts for immediate consumption. After cutting open a melon, one is permitted to scoop out the seeds from the cavity. Since there is no practical way to remove the food from the waste in these cases, separating the waste is permitted for immediate use.

If one has before him a mixture in which one item is desired immediately, while the other will be eaten later on in the same meal, it is permissible to remove the item desired later. This is not considered selecting waste from food. Since the selected item is desired for later on in the same meal, it cannot be seen as waste in the context of the current meal. Of course, if the unwanted item will not be used until a later meal, it is considered "waste" for the purposes of the current meal, and may not be removed.

A CLOSER LOOK AT THE SIDDUR

This week, we will discuss the fifth of the Thirteen Fundamental Principles (י״ג עיקרים) enumerated by *Rambam*.

The Fifth Principle states:

אֲנִי מַאֲמִין בֶּאֱמוּנָה שְׁלֵמָה שֶׁהַבּוֹרֵא יִתְבָּרַךְ שְׁמוֹ לוֹ לְבַדּוֹ רָאוּי לְהִתְפַּלֵּל וְאֵין לְזוּלָתוֹ רָאוּי לְהִתְפַּלֵּל.

I believe with perfect faith that it is only to the Creator, blessed be His Name, that one must pray, and that one must not pray to anyone or anything else besides Him.

This principle teaches us to always remember that Hashem is the sole source for all of our requirements. Everything comes from Hashem; it is thus improper to pray to any other entity or force to provide that which only Hashem can provide if He so chooses. In addition, the praises that we include in our prayers to Hashem as the Master of the world may never be directed toward any other entity.

פרשת חיי שרה

TUESDAY

PARASHAS CHAYEI SARAH

This applies not only to idols and the like, but even to those creations such as angels, or the heavenly bodies such as the sun and the moon. Although these creations have great power and function in the world, they are still creations, and may function only as Hashem wishes. They do not have the ability to determine their own future or destiny. Only Hashem has the ability to do these things, and therefore it is only to Him that we must direct our prayers and praises.

Rambam (in *Hilchos Avodas Kochavim*) explains that mankind originally erred during the generation of Enosh, and strayed toward idolatry in their belief that the sun and stars, as faithful servants of Hashem, deserved to be accorded respect and worship. From this mistake they eventually strayed further to the point where they began to view the heavenly bodies themselves as divine, and would worship them and even build temples to them. Thus, we see that idolatry can stem from the mistaken belief that there is more than one entity to whom one may pray. Even one who acknowledges that Hashem is the true God, but worships any of His creations in the manner that Enosh and his generation did, is considered to be an idolater.

Similarly, it is forbidden to pray to angels or to any other heavenly beings, to ask them to intercede before Hashem on one's behalf. [There are several instances that can be found in our prayers, particularly several of the *Selichos* prayers, where we *do* seem to be addressing angels. For further discussion of this subject, see *Maharal, Nesivos Olam, Nesiv HaAvodah* §12, and Responsa of *Chasam Sofer, Orach Chaim* §166.]

QUESTION OF THE DAY:
What law pertaining to kiddushin (the first stage of Jewish marriage) do we derive from the sale of the Cave of Machpelah?

For the answer, see page 55.

A TORAH THOUGHT FOR THE DAY

פרשת חיי שרה

WEDNESDAY
PARASHAS CHAYEI SARAH

וַיִּקַּח הָעֶבֶד עֲשָׂרָה גְמַלִּים מִגְּמַלֵּי אֲדֹנָיו וַיֵּלֶךְ וְכָל־טוּב אֲדֹנָיו בְּיָדוֹ וַיָּקָם וַיֵּלֶךְ אֶל־אֲרַם נַהֲרַיִם אֶל־עִיר נָחוֹר

Then the servant took ten camels of his master's camels, and set out with all the bounty of his master in his hand; and he made his way to Aram Naharaim, to the city of Nachor (Bereishis 24:10).

Why was it necessary to state that the camels that Eliezer took belonged to his master? Certainly he would not have taken anyone else's camels! *Rashi*, citing *Midrash Rabbah*, explains that the intent of the verse is to indicate that it was evident to all that they were Avraham's camels, for they were muzzled as they walked, so they should not graze in others' fields and be guilty of robbery.

The verse below (24:32) states that when Eliezer arrived at the house of Lavan, וַיְפַתַּח הַגְּמַלִּים. *Rashi*, in line with his interpretation here, explains this to mean that Eliezer *unmuzzled* the camels, which had been muzzled until this point to prevent them from grazing in others' fields.

Ramban, however, takes issue with this interpretation. He maintains that Avraham would not have needed to muzzle his camels to prevent them from eating food forbidden to them; indeed, the Gemara (*Chullin* 7a) states that the donkey of R' Pinchas ben Yair would not eat untithed grain. [This phenomenon stems from the fact that it is considered demeaning for a supremely righteous individual to be tainted by any connection, no matter how tenuous, to consumption of forbidden items.] Surely, asks *Ramban*, the camels of Avraham were equal to the donkey of R' Pinchas ben Yair! *Ramban* therefore explains that indeed, the camels were *not* muzzled; and the word וַיְפַתַּח means simply that Eliezer *unharnessed* the camels, which had previously been traveling while tied together in a train.

In defense of *Rashi*, several approaches have been suggested. *Sifsei Chachamim* states that Avraham was even more scrupulous than required by law, and did not allow the camels to graze even from the grass found at the very edges of the road, areas where the owners would generally surrender their rights to the public. Although legally such grazing would have been allowed (and therefore even the camels of a righteous man such as Avraham would not hesitate to graze), Avraham wished to be an inspiration to his descendants, and went beyond the letter of the law. *Mizrachi* explains that although the camels would probably not have eaten anything forbidden, Avraham still was accustomed to keeping them muzzled, because he did not wish to rely upon miracles to avoid misdeeds

WEDNESDAY

PARASHAS CHAYEI SARAH

פרשת חיי שרה

MISHNAH OF THE DAY: SHABBOS 6:1

Having dealt in the previous chapter with those items that animals may and may not go out with on the Sabbath, the Mishnah turns its attention to the items that *people* may and may not go out with on the Sabbath:[1] בַּמֶּה אִשָּׁה יוֹצְאָה — *With what* accessories *may a woman go outside* on the Sabbath, וּבַמֶּה אֵינָהּ יוֹצְאָה — *and with what* accessories *may she not go outside* on the Sabbath?[2] לֹא תֵצֵא אִשָּׁה — *A woman may not go out* לֹא בְחוּטֵי צֶמֶר וְלֹא בְחוּטֵי פִשְׁתָּן וְלֹא בִּרְצוּעוֹת שֶׁבְּרֹאשָׁהּ — *neither with woolen strands, nor with linen strands, nor with straps that are on her head;*[3] וְלֹא תִטְבּוֹל בָּהֶן עַד שֶׁתְּרַפֵּם — *and she may not immerse herself* in a *mikveh while wearing them, until she loosens them.*[4] וְלֹא בְטוֹטֶפֶת וְלֹא בְסַרְבִּיטִין — *Nor* may

---
NOTES
---

1. The preceding chapter, which discusses what gear animals may wear outside on the Sabbath, was taught before this chapter, which deals with people's accessories, because it was common in agricultural societies for animals to go out earlier in the morning than most people (*Tiferes Yisrael;* see also *Melecheth Shlomo*). [This follows the observation of *Tosafos* (to 2a השבת יציאות ד״ה) that the early chapters of our tractate are arranged in chronological sequence, beginning with things forbidden on Friday afternoon in preparation for the Sabbath, and moving on to the laws governing the Sabbath day itself.]

2. The Mishnah is speaking of accessories worn as ornaments — viz., jewelry — not those that are carried, such as a purse or handbag. Thus, there is certainly no Torah prohibition to go out while wearing them. However, out of concern that a woman might remove one of them while outside in order to show it to a friend, and unwittingly carry it four *amos* in a public domain — which *is* a Torah prohibition — the Rabbis prohibited the wearing of certain accessories on the Sabbath (*Rashi,* from Gemara 59b). [See below, note 9, for the extent of this prohibition.]

3. The expression, *that are on her head,* describes all three items mentioned — i.e., a woman may not go out on the Sabbath, neither with woolen nor with linen threads on her head, nor with straps on her head, even if these ornaments are braided into her hair (*Rav; Rashi;* cf. *Tosafos*). Although according to Torah law a woman may go out with any of these ornaments braided into her hair, the Rabbis forbade this practice, for the reason explained below (see next note).

4. Following the cessation of her menstrual period, a woman is still considered a נִדָּה, a *menstruant,* until she immerses herself in a *mikveh.* Such immersion is not valid if any חֲצִיצָה, *interposition,* prevents the water of the *mikveh* from reaching any part of her body. Since the straps and threads of our Mishnah prevent the *mikveh* water from reaching those hairs that they bind, they are considered interpositions. Therefore, they must be loosened before her immersion, so as to allow the water to pass between them and the hair. Often, however, rather than merely loosening the straps or threads, a woman will find it more convenient to remove them entirely. Should the

פרשת חיי שרה
WEDNESDAY
PARASHAS CHAYEI SARAH

she go out **with a frontlet,** [5] **nor with head bangles,** [6] בִּזְמַן שֶׁאֵינָן תְּפוּרִים — **as long as they are not sewn to her hat.** [7] וְלֹא בְּכָבוּל לִרְשׁוּת הָרַבִּים — **Nor** may she go out **with a forehead pad** [8] **into the public domain;** [9]

— NOTES —

time of her immersion occur on the Sabbath, she might forget to retie them in her hair (especially since her hair is still somewhat wet) and carry them home. To avoid such an unintentional desecration of the Sabbath, the Rabbis prohibited the wearing of such ties on the Sabbath (*Rav* from Gemara 57a).

This rule applies to all accessories that: (a) must be removed before immersion; and, (b) that a woman will sometimes carry with her rather than put on. Moreover, once the Rabbis prohibited wearing these hair ties, they did not differentiate between younger women (who must go to the *mikveh*) and older women (who, having experienced menopause, no longer need to go to the *mikveh*). This follows the general rule of לא פלוג, *non-differentiation* (in Rabbinic ordinances) — i.e., that where Rabbinic ordinances are instituted, the Rabbis do not distinguish between individual differences of circumstances or people (*Turei Zahav* 303:2). [Garments are not included in this prohibition, since a woman would obviously not walk through the streets without wearing her clothing (*Tosafos*).]

5. This is an ornament worn on the forehead that stretches from ear to ear [resembling the golden ציץ, *forehead plate,* worn by the Kohen Gadol (see *Yoma* 7:5)] (*Rav; Tiferes Yisrael* from Gemara 57b).

6. Ribbons were sometimes attached to the frontlet. These ribbons hung over the temples, reaching down to the cheeks. They were made either of gold, silver or colored cloth, depending upon the wearer's financial status (*Rav* from Gemara 57b).

7. As we have seen, the Rabbis prohibited wearing ornaments outside because of the concern that a woman might remove them there to show to a friend. Accordingly, this decree applies only to those items that a woman might conceivably remove in the street. Therefore, it is forbidden to wear frontlets and head bangles only if they are not attached to a hat that covers a woman's head. However, if they are attached to a hat, they may be worn, for then a woman cannot remove them without removing her hat as well — and she would not uncover her hair in public (*Rav; Rashi*).

8. A cloth pad — usually worn under the frontlet — was generally used to protect the forehead from irritation, but sometimes it was worn as an ornament, even without the frontlet (*Rav*).

9. A woman may not wear a forehead pad when going out to a public domain, but she may wear it in a courtyard. However, the wearing of the other ornaments mentioned in this Mishnah is prohibited even inside a courtyard (where one is ordinarily permitted to carry), so that a woman will refrain completely from adorning herself with these items on the Sabbath. In this way, she will not come to wear them in the public domain, where she might take them off to show her companions. However, since the Rabbis did not want to leave women completely unadorned (lest they become plain and unattractive in the eyes of their husbands), they did not prohibit the wearing of the forehead pad in a courtyard (*Rav* from Gemara 64h)

WEDNESDAY

PARASHAS CHAYEI SARAH

וְלֹא בְעִיר שֶׁל זָהָב — *nor may she go out with a "city of gold";*[10] וְלֹא בְקַטְלָא — *nor with a choker;*[11] וְלֹא בִּנְזָמִים — *nor with nose rings;* וְלֹא בְטַבַּעַת שֶׁאֵין עָלֶיהָ חוֹתָם — *nor with a ring that bears no signet;*[12] וְלֹא בְמַחַט שֶׁאֵינָהּ נְקוּבָה — *nor with a needle that is not pierced.*[13] וְאִם יָצָאת — *But if she went out* wearing any of these on the Sabbath, אֵינָהּ חַיֶּיבֶת חַטָּאת — *she is not liable to a chatas offering.*[14]

NOTES

10. A golden crown engraved with a likeness of Jerusalem and its walls (*Rav; Rambam Commentary; Tos.* 59a; cf. *Rashi*).

11. An ornament tied tightly around the neck to give the impression that the wearer is plump (which was fashionable in Talmudic times). This was accomplished by forcing forward the skin under the chin, giving the impression of a double chin (*Rav; Rashi* 57b).

12. A signet ring was used by men to seal letters and packages. Women would wear ornamental rings bearing no signet. Our Mishnah teaches us that it is *Rabbinically* forbidden to wear an ornamental ring outside on the Sabbath, lest a woman take one off to show to her companions. This is not to imply that a woman is permitted to go out wearing a *signet* ring on the Sabbath; on the contrary, the Mishnah speaks only of a ring without a signet because it is *Biblically* forbidden for a woman to go out with a signet ring on the Sabbath. Such a ring is not an ornament for a woman, and is thus considered merely an item being carried on the finger, as Mishnah 3 states below (*Rav; Rashi*).

13. This is a pin to which a gold plate was attached. On weekdays, a woman uses the pointed end to part the hair. On the Sabbath, she inserts the pin into her turban, and the gold plate adorns her forehead. The Mishnah states that even though this accessory is an ornament, a woman may not go out with it on her head (Gemara 60a). [Here, as in the previous case, our Mishnah teaches the Rabbinic prohibition. Mishnah 6:3 will teach that if she goes out with a needle that has an eye, she violates a Biblical prohibition.]

14. Since these restrictions are Rabbinic in nature, enacted lest a woman take off her jewelry to show her friends, no *chatas* offering is required (*Rav*).

QUESTION OF THE DAY:
Why was Charan known as the city of Nachor?

For the answer, see page 55.

GEMS FROM THE GEMARA

פרשת
חיי שרה

WEDNESDAY
PARASHAS CHAYEI SARAH

The Gemara (59a) discusses another ornament, a tiara, and whether it may be worn outside on the Sabbath. This is a matter of dispute: Rav prohibits it, while Shmuel permits it.

The Gemara qualifies the dispute: Concerning a tiara fashioned of a hammered plate of gold or silver, there is no dispute; all agree that wearing it is prohibited. [Since this tiara is a significant ornament, the Rabbis prohibited wearing it outside on the Sabbath, lest a woman remove it to show it to her friend and come to carry it four *amos* in the public domain (*Rashi*).] The argument concerns a tiara made of fabric studded with gold pieces and precious stones: Rav holds that the gold pieces in the tiara are the primary part of the ornament, and thus it is a significant item that a woman would wish to show to a friend; accordingly, he rules that wearing it is prohibited. Shmuel, however, holds that the fabric is the main part of the ornament, and therefore it is not considered a significant ornament; accordingly, it may be worn on the Sabbath. [A woman will only show her friend an ornament that she considers to be worthy of showing off. According to Shmuel, a tiara that consists of jewel-studded fabric is not considered a fancy ornament, and a woman is not likely to remove it in the public domain; thus, it is not included in the Rabbinic edict against wearing an ornament outside on the Sabbath (see *Rashi*).]

Rav Ashi then teaches a more lenient interpretation of the dispute. In his opinion, there is also no dispute concerning a tiara made of fabric studded with gold and stones; all agree that wearing it is permitted. When do they argue? Concerning a tiara fashioned of a hammered metal plate: Rav holds that a woman might remove such a tiara in the street and show it to a friend, and come to carry it four *amos* in the public domain — hence, wearing it is prohibited. Shmuel, on the other hand, holds that wearing it is permitted — for who is accustomed to go out wearing such a tiara? Only a distinguished woman, and a distinguished woman is not likely to remove her tiara and show it to another woman in the street.

Subsequently, the Gemara recounts that Levi taught in Nehardea that wearing a tiara on the Sabbath is permitted, and twenty-four tiaras emerged from all of Nehardea and were worn outside on the Sabbath. Years later, Rabbah bar Avuha taught in Mechoza that wearing a tiara on the Sabbath is permitted, and eighteen tiaras emerged from a single alley in the town, as Mechoza was a much wealthier town than Nehardea.

פרשת חיי שרה

A MUSSAR THOUGHT FOR THE DAY

WEDNESDAY
PARASHAS CHAYEI SARAH

One opinion mentioned in the Gemara (*Bava Kamma* 30a) states that one who wishes to become a *chassid* — a truly pious individual — should be scrupulous with respect to *mili d'nezikin*, "matters of damages," just as we find that Avraham took care to muzzle his camels so they would not graze in others' property (see *A Torah Thought for the Day*.) While avoiding *nezikin* is undoubtedly important, we must understand what is so central about the need for a person to safeguard himself and his property from damaging others that makes this a central pillar upon which *chassidus*, "righteousness," is based.

This question is strengthened when the Gemara's statement is viewed in the perspective of one of the *Mesillas Yesharim's* definitions of a *chassid* as a person whose life is based on performing acts of *chesed*, and living a life based on the providing of benefit for others. How does refraining from damaging others — which one must do even according to the *strict* letter of the law — fit into this definition?

R' Yerucham Levovitz (*Daas Torah*, Shemos p. 234) explains that a person can acquire *chassidus* through being scrupulous in *mili d'nezikin* because taking precautions not to damage another person forces a person to consider why he is doing so. He will then realize that the Torah teaches us that in addition to being forbidden to steal another's items, a person must take every possible preventive measure to avoid damaging his fellow, such as by muzzling his animals before they set out on a journey, and not leaving heavy items in a place where they may fall and cause damage. Upon looking further, he will realize that it is not only *physical* damage that one is forbidden to inflict — the Torah also forbids one from embarrassing his fellow, speaking *lashon hara* about him, or otherwise hurting his reputation or feelings.

When a person studies and lives according to the standards of *mili d'nezikin*, explains R' Yerucham, he will become cognizant of the fact that with these laws, the Torah is teaching us about the relationships that we are expected to have with others. Why can I not destroy another's possessions? Because he worked hard for them — how will he feel if, after all his toil, he is left with nothing? We see from the *mili d'nezikin* that the Torah does not want him to have to suffer in this way. Why not? Clearly, the Torah is sending a message that as part of a person's life, he must consider the feelings of others; he is not the only one who is important. When one realizes that the Torah — by teaching the prohibition against damaging, and the need to take protective measures ensuring that no harm will occur to another — is sending a message stressing the need to include another person's intrinsic importance into one's life, this will propel him toward the path of *chassidus*, a lifestyle whose focus is helping others.

פרשת חיי שרה

WEDNESDAY

PARASHAS CHAYEI SARAH

HALACHAH OF THE DAY

We closed our discussion yesterday with instances where selecting "waste" from food is permissible, despite the general rule which permits only the opposite manner of selection.

Another scenario where it is permissible to remove waste from food is where the removal of the waste takes place after the food has already been placed in the mouth. This is especially helpful in cases where the removal of the waste material is difficult. For example, when eating watermelon, one may avoid the question of how to remove the seeds from the melon by placing a piece in his mouth and subsequently spitting out the seeds. Similarly, when eating fish that contains bones, one is permitted to pull the bones out of a piece of fish that has already been placed in his mouth. [Note that pits and bones are generally *muktzeh*, and care must be taken to handle them in a halachically permissible manner.]

It is permissible to remove waste from food if one removes some of the food along with the waste. For example, one may remove watermelon pits if, when selecting the seeds for removal, he is careful to include some of the melon with the seeds. Similarly, fish bones may be removed by taking a bit of fish along with each bone. If a particle of dirt or an insect falls into a drink, one may not remove the particle or bug by itself; he may, however, scoop it out together with a spoonful of liquid. As long as the food and the waste are removed as a single unit, this method of taking is not an act of *sorting* at all; since he is actually removing some of the *combined mixture*, there is no act of selection taking place and it is therefore permitted even for later use.

In instances where the food and the waste are not mixed, but are rather attached (such as is the case with meat and its attached fats), there is an additional leniency. As we have previously mentioned, this type of combination is considered to be "mixed" only at the point of contact between the two diverse components. Since this is the case, one

פרשת חיי שרה

WEDNESDAY

PARASHAS CHAYEI SARAH

may remove part of the fat as long as he leaves intact a minute sliver of the fat still touching the meat; in this way he has not separated the mixture, as the two components are still combined at the point of contact.

Mixtures of large items that have been stacked upon one another also have a unique leniency. In this case, one may remove unwanted items from the top of the pile in order to reach a desired item at the bottom. For example, if one has a stack of various linens, and he requires the item at the bottom, he may remove the upper items in order to reach the required one at the bottom. [This ruling does not apply to any other type of mixture.]

A CLOSER LOOK AT THE SIDDUR

The Gemara in *Maseches Shabbos* (31a) refers to the Mishnaic order of *Nezikin* (Damages) as *yeshu'os* — literally, *salvations* — because it is only by taking meticulous, often inconvenient precautions — such as muzzling animals when traveling or always hiring appropriate watchmen to guard dangerous oxen or open fires — that a person will ultimately be saved from transgressing a Torah prohibition (in addition to being saved from having to pay for the damage). Although this point is not directly addressed in our prayers, the message of *nezikin* — that there is sometimes a need for severe standards to ensure that a greater harm does not take place — is a powerful example for a phrase that we find in the prayer of בָּרוּךְ שֶׁאָמַר, the blessing with which we open the section of *Pesukei D'Zimrah* during *Shacharis*. In this prayer, we find the words: בָּרוּךְ גּוֹזֵר וּמְקַיֵּם — whose literal translation is, *Blessed is He Who decrees and upholds*. Although this is usually explained to mean that Hashem is blessed for making decrees and then upholding them by carrying them out, *Maharal* (*Derech Chaim* 1:18) offers a different approach. He translates the phrase as meaning: *Blessed is He Who upholds the world through decrees;* that is, through a rigid system of exacting standards of justice that, although at times seems to be inconvenient, is truly the only way the greater good may be attained.

Although he translates the words בָּרוּךְ גּוֹזֵר וּמְקַיֵּם differently, *Maggid Tzedek* sees a message similar to that of *Maharal* in this praise of Hashem. He bases his explanation on the *Abudraham's* comment that the ten mentions of *Baruch* (*Blessed*) in *Baruch She'amar* that follow the introductory phrase בָּרוּךְ שֶׁאָמַר וְהָיָה הָעוֹלָם, *Blessed is He Who spoke and the world came into existence,* are meant to correspond to the *Asarah*

פרשת חיי שרה

WEDNESDAY
PARASHAS CHAYEI SARAH

Maamaros, the Ten Utterances of Hashem through which the world was created. According to this approach, the phrase בָּרוּךְ גּוֹזֵר וּמְקַיֵּם corresponds to Hashem's third declaration, that was stated on the second day: וַיֹּאמֶר אֱלֹהִים יְהִי רָקִיעַ בְּתוֹךְ הַמָּיִם וִיהִי מַבְדִּיל בֵּין מַיִם לָמָיִם, *And HASHEM said: "Let there be a firmament between the waters, which will be a separation between the waters"* (*Bereishis* 1:6). *Maggid Tzedek* explains that since in the context of water גּוֹזֵר means to *cut* or *divide* (see, for example, *Tehillim* 136:13), the literal translation of בָּרוּךְ גּוֹזֵר וּמְקַיֵּם is: *Blessed is He Who divides to maintain (the world)*. This, too, is an example of seeming harshness that is necessary — for the splitting of the waters was essential for the continued existence of dry land.

This praise of Hashem, explains *Maggid Tzedek* further, may be better understood in the context of the Midrash that comments that while it was unquestionably necessary to divide the waters into two, a declaration of Hashem's satisfaction (וַיַּרְא אֱלֹהִים כִּי־טוֹב, *And HASHEM saw that it was good*) is *not* written after the second day of Creation, for *any* division or argument, for *any* reason, no matter how noble, cannot be called "good." Nevertheless, Hashem used even this negative quality of division for the sake of the world's ultimate growth. [Indeed, *Maggid Tzedek* concludes by citing *Olelos Ephraim*, who considers the division of the waters as the paradigm of *machlokes l'sheim Shamayim*, "a division for the sake of Heaven," concerning which the Mishnah in *Pirkei Avos* promises that both sides will ultimately flourish — for it was only because of the water's division that the entire world was able to endure.]

Yet another insight into Hashem's Creation of the world revealed by the words בָּרוּךְ גּוֹזֵר וּמְקַיֵּם can be found in the *sefer Toras HaOlah* (written by the *Rama*). He notes that when relating the process of Creation, the Torah first relates what it was that Hashem said should be created, and afterward, the Torah writes וַיְהִי כֵן, *and it was so*. *Rama* explains the purpose of these two steps: First, Hashem created the item in question, and then He endowed it with permanence — the ability to endure over time, without being destroyed or ceasing to exist. According to *Rama*, Hashem's initial statement (וַיֹּאמֶר אֱלֹהִים) refers to the actual creation, while *and it was so* is a reference to the command that the created item be permanent.

These two steps of Creation are alluded to in the words of the בָּרוּךְ שֶׁאָמַר prayer. We thank Hashem first for being גּוֹזֵר — for *decreeing* by His statements that the world should come into being. Then, we thank him for being מְקַיֵּם — for endowing Creation with the ability to be lasting and permanent.

פרשת חיי שרה

A TASTE OF LOMDUS

WEDNESDAY

PARASHAS CHAYEI SARAH

The Gemara in *Bava Kamma* (3a) puts the damage that occurs when a person's animal grazes in another's field into the category of damage called *shein* (literally, *tooth*), a category that includes all damages done by an animal seeking enjoyment. The Gemara includes *shein* in its list of those *nezikin* (*damages*) which require the owner to pay restitution. The Torah obligates a person to pay for all damage done by his person or his property, such as his animals, or faulty roofs or walls, as long as the damage came about because of his failure to take sufficient precautions. In other words, a person is responsible under Torah law to guard himself and his property from becoming damagers.

Although the Gemara cites the specific Scriptural sources for the prohibitions of many subcategories of damages, a number of major prohibitions seem to remain, uncharacteristically, unaccounted for. For example, the Torah considers taking a person's belongings without permission — even with the intent to pay for them — tantamount to theft, and prohibits this with the verses (*Vayikra* 19:11 and 19:13) of *lo signovu*, "you shall not steal," and *v'lo sigzol*, "and you shall not rob." We find no obvious source in Scripture, however, for the law forbidding a person from *damaging* another's property without actually *stealing* it. We may thus ask: How do we know that the Torah obligates a person to pay for breaking his friend's vase? From where do we derive the rule that a person must muzzle his animals, in the tradition of Avraham Avinu, to prevent them from destroying another person's fields (even if he is willing to pay for the damage caused)? [This question is discussed extensively by the commentators to *Maseches Bava Kamma*.]

Rashi (cited above, in *A Torah Thought for the Day*) explains that Avraham muzzled his animals *mipnei hagezel,* because of robbery. At first glance, this statement seems rather puzzling. As explained above, the Torah classifies *shein,* damages done by an animal seeking enjoyment, as a kind of "damage," not robbery. This seems to be the correct way to describe the animal's action — after all, the animal does not take the grass out of the original owner's possession; rather, it destroys it on site, by eating it. Furthermore, even if an animal somehow managed to snatch some produce and carry it home intact, the owner of this animal would not be liable for theft until he tried to retain the "stolen" item, which Avraham Avinu clearly would not have done! Why does *Rashi* introduce the concept of robbery here, when seemingly the issue is one of *nezikin,* damages? [Moreover, the Midrash cited by *Rashi* simply

פרשת חיי שרה

**WEDNESDAY
PARASHAS CHAYEI SARAH**

states that Avraham muzzled his camels so they would not eat in the fields of others, without mentioning robbery. However, in defense of *Rashi*, it must be noted that with regard to the argument between the shepherds of Avraham and the shepherds of Lot, the Midrash *does* refer to grazing from others' fields as robbery.]

One possible answer is that *Rashi* does not mean to speak of robbery to the exclusion of *shein*. Rather, he is trying to instruct us regarding the source for the law against damaging another's property through *shein; Rashi* is explaining that it is included in the Torah's prohibition against theft. Indeed, *Rashi* is not alone among the commentators in connecting *nezikin* to robbery. *Rabbeinu Yonah*, at the beginning of his commentary to *Pirkei Avos*, also mentions that the prohibitions against all forms of damages have their legal roots in the Torah's instruction of *v'lo sigzol*, "and you shall not rob."

R' Shlomo Fisher (see also *Chidushei Rabbeinu Chaim HaLevi al HaRambam, Hilchos Geneivah* 1:15, and *Ketzos HaChoshen* 354:2) explains that *Rashi* and *Rabbeinu Yonah* must understand the command *v'lo sigzol*, "and you shall not rob," as prohibiting causing another person a loss, regardless of the form — whether by taking the object, depriving the owner of its value or of the ability to use it. From the owner's perspective, it makes very little difference if another person breaks his vase or steals it. Either way, it is gone. Thus, the Torah's prohibition against robbery can include any action that ultimately prevents a person from being able to use and enjoy his possessions. *Rashi*, in explaining that Avraham muzzled his camels so they would not "rob," thus provides us with an insight into the essence of the prohibition against damaging another's property.

פרשת חיי שרה — A TORAH THOUGHT FOR THE DAY

THURSDAY
PARASHAS CHAYEI SARAH

וְהָיָה הַנַּעֲרָ אֲשֶׁר אֹמַר אֵלֶיהָ הַטִּי־נָא כַדֵּךְ וְאֶשְׁתֶּה וְאָמְרָה שְׁתֵה וְגַם־גְּמַלֶּיךָ אַשְׁקֶה אֹתָהּ הֹכַחְתָּ לְעַבְדְּךָ לְיִצְחָק וּבָהּ אֵדַע כִּי־עָשִׂיתָ חֶסֶד עִם־אֲדֹנִי

Let it be that the maiden to whom I shall say, "Please tip over your jug so I may drink," and she will say, "Drink, and I will also water your camels" — it is she whom You will have designated for Your servant, for Yitzchak, and through her I will know that you have done kindness with my master (Bereishis 24:14).

Jews are forbidden to practice נחוש, *divination* — the seeking of omens, or drawing auguries from certain events (see *Vayikra* 19:26). At first glance, it would appear that Eliezer was guilty of practicing divination in this verse, for he stated that if a maiden would come and act as he wished, this would be a sign that she was the proper wife for Yitzchak. Moreover, the Gemara in *Chullin* (95b) states that "any omen that is not similar in form to that stated by Eliezer is not considered divination." This Gemara also seems to imply that Eliezer's proclamation was forbidden divination. However, this conclusion is a difficult one, for Eliezer was a righteous man, and a true disciple of Avraham. Furthermore, there are Tannaim who maintain that even a non-Jew is forbidden to practice divination, and thus Eliezer certainly would not have done so.

The commentators offer several resolutions of this difficulty. *Tosafos* (to *Chullin* ibid.) explain that Eliezer was not guilty of divination because he did not rely upon the sign that he was given; rather, he ascertained whose family Rivkah came from before giving her the gifts (as the verse indeed states during the recounting of the story as told by Eliezer to Lavan and Besuel; see below, 24:47, and *Ramban* here). Only one who blindly follows omens is guilty of divination.

Sforno notes further that one who practices divination will not mention the Name of Hashem, as Eliezer did (*it is she whom You will have designated*). He understands Eliezer's request as a *prayer*, in which he beseeched Hashem to provide him with some way to recognize Yitzchak's designated wife. Because such a request does not indicate any reliance on anything other than Hashem, it is not forbidden. [According to *Sforno*, the Gemara in *Chullin* means only that one who requests a sign *of the sort* that Eliezer did (but not as a prayer, and without mentioning Hashem) would indeed be guilty of divination.]

A third approach is that of *Ran* (*Chullin* ibid.), who maintains that Eliezer's behavior was not forbidden (even though its *formulation,* taken out of context, *would* be divination), for Eliezer was not asking for a sign. Rather, Eliezer, who sought for Yitzchak a wife who had Jewish compassion and displayed selfless generosity, devised this test to identify the correct girl. Thus, far from being a magical device, Eliezer's test would provide him with information upon which he could logically base his decision.

THURSDAY
PARASHAS CHAYEI SARAH

MISHNAH OF THE DAY: SHABBOS 6:2

The Mishnah lists those items which a man may not wear outside on the Sabbath:

לֹא יֵצֵא הָאִישׁ בְּסַנְדָּל הַמְסוּמָּר — *A man may not go outside* on the Sabbath *with a hobnailed sandal;*[1] וְלֹא בְיָחִיד — *nor* may he go out *with a single* sandal of any sort,[2] בִּזְמַן שֶׁאֵין בְּרַגְלוֹ מַכָּה — *when there is no wound on his foot;*[3] וְלֹא בִתְפִילִין — *nor* may he go out *with*

---- NOTES ----

1. These were clogs studded with nails (the nails served to fasten the soles to the uppers, and they protruded through to the undersides of the soles). The hobnailed sandals were prohibited because of an unfortunate incident that took place during a time of persecution. A group of fugitives were hiding in a cave when they heard a noise of someone walking atop the cave. Suspecting that this was an enemy attack, they started pushing one another in panic, and many of them were killed by the nails of their fellows' shoes. More were killed in panic than were killed by the foes (Gemara 60a). Lest the memory of this calamity bring sadness to people on the Sabbath, the Sages decreed that no hobnailed sandals be worn on the Sabbath or on holidays, both occasions of gathering when no work may be done (*Rav* from Gemara 60a). [Although the Mishnah states only that one may not go outside while wearing these sandals, the Sages extended the decree to prohibit one from wearing them altogether on the Sabbath (*Ran*).]

2. *Rav* and *Rashi* cite two possible explanations for this prohibition: (a) The Sages were concerned that people would suspect a person wearing a single sandal of carrying its mate underneath his clothing (cited in the name of *Yerushalmi*). (b) The Sages were concerned that people would make fun of him, and he would take off the single sandal and carry it (cited in the name of *Rashi's* teachers).

3. If there is a wound on one foot, he may go out wearing just the shoe on the other foot, since people will realize that he cannot wear a shoe on the wounded foot, and that he therefore left the other shoe at home. Moreover, they will not jeer at him for going with only one shoe (*Ran; Rashi* to 61a).

פרשת חיי שרה

THURSDAY

PARASHAS CHAYEI SARAH

בִּזְמַן — tefillin;[4] וְלֹא בְקָמִיעַ — nor with an amulet[5] שֶׁאֵינוֹ מִן הַמּוּמְחֶה — when it is not from an expert;[6] וְלֹא בְקַסְדָּא — nor with a coat of armor;[7] וְלֹא בְשִׁרְיוֹן — nor with a helmet, nor with shinguards.[8] וְלֹא בְמַגָּפַיִם — But if he went out from a private domain into a public domain wearing any of these articles, וְאִם יָצָא — אֵינוֹ חַיָּב חַטָּאת — he is not liable to a chatas offering.[9]

───────── NOTES ─────────

4. Since the Sabbath is not a time for putting on *tefillin*, they are considered neither a garment nor an ornament. Hence, one may not go out while wearing them (see *Tos. Yom Tov* from Gemara 61a).

5. An amulet is a piece of parchment upon which certain of God's Names or certain prayers are written. Alternatively, it may be composed of roots of herbs reputed to cure certain ailments. It is hung around the neck as either a curative or preventive measure (*Meiri*).

6. If the maker of the amulet did not show success with his handiwork at least three times, one may not wear it on the Sabbath. However, if he was successful with other of his amulets on at least three previous occasions (even though this particular amulet has not yet been known to be effective), it may be worn on the Sabbath. Since the maker of the amulet has been established as reliable, the new amulets he makes are also considered reliable, even though they are as yet untested. Since the wearer is secure in the efficacy of the amulet, it is considered an item of apparel for him, and he may wear it on the Sabbath. The amulet may not be worn on the Sabbath only when the reliability of the maker (and therefore the amulet) has not been established (*Rav* from Gemara 61a), for since the wearer does not rely on the therapeutic properties of the amulet, he may come to remove it and carry it in the street (*Meiri*).

7. A coat of armor is worn only in battle and never as ordinary dress. That being the case, if one were to wear a coat of armor, people would suspect him of going off to battle. This is forbidden on the Sabbath (except in cases of imminent danger). Therefore, according to the rule that a person is forbidden to act in a manner that will cause others to suspect him of engaging in prohibited activities, one is not permitted to wear armor on the Sabbath (*Ran*).

8. These articles are all battle attire, and therefore may not be worn on the Sabbath (*Rav*).

9. Since all the objects and articles of clothing mentioned in the Mishnah are worn on weekdays — not carried — by Torah law they have the status of garments, not burdens, and thus are prohibited only by Rabbinic decree. Hence, as is the case with any violation of a Rabbinic decree, a *chatas* offering is not brought (*Tos. Yom Tov* from *Ran*).

QUESTION OF THE DAY:

Why did Eliezer wait for a girl by the well, instead of entering the town?

For the answer, see page 55.

GEMS FROM THE GEMARA

פרשת חיי שרה

THURSDAY PARASHAS CHAYEI SARAH

The Gemara (60b) explains that just as the Rabbis forbade the wearing of hobnailed sandals on the Sabbath because there is a gathering of people at that time (and the tragic incident that occurred also involved a group of people who were gathered on the Sabbath), so too did they forbid the wearing of the hobnailed sandals on Yom Tov, when there is also a gathering of people.

The Gemara then asks: Why is it not forbidden to wear hobnailed sandals on public fast days, when there is also a gathering of people?

The Gemara answers that since the incident occurred on the Sabbath, a day when there is a gathering due to a prohibition against performing labor, therefore, the prohibition was applied only in the cases of the Sabbath and Yom Tov, days when there is a gathering due to a prohibition against performing labor. On a fast day, on the other hand, the gathering is one of people who are permitted to do work. Since the "gathering" on fast days is not similar to the "gathering" of the Sabbath and Yom Tov, the decree was not extended to include fast days.

The Gemara then notes that the inclusion of Yom Tov in the decree is defensible even according to R' Chanina the son of Akiva, who holds that Rabbinic decrees are applied only to *very* similar cases. [The Gemara in *Chagigah* (23a) relates that the Sages prohibited the transport of the waters or ashes of the *parah adumah* across a body of water. They promulgated this decree because of an incident that once occurred, where waters were transported across the Jordan River in a boat, and it was later discovered that an olive-size piece of a corpse had been lodged in the flooring of the boat, rendering the precious waters and ashes useless. The Gemara there cites a dispute as to the extent of this decree. The Sages maintain that the decree applies to any body of water, and to any mode of transportation (e.g., the waters may not be thrown over a bridge [see *Maharam*] or carried across a river by a swimmer). R' Chanina disagrees, and maintains that the Sages prohibited only transporting of these items over *the Jordan River by boat (Rashi)*.]

Although, according to the opinion of R' Chanina the son of Akiva, the Rabbis issued their decree only to forbid transport that is *very* similar to the transport that was used in the unfortunate incident that transpired, still, in our case he would concur that Yom Tov should be included in the decree. For while a limitation is defensible in the case of the Jordan, as it is clearly different from other rivers [as it is unique in its width or in its depth (*Rashi*)], it is not defensible in our case, as Yom Tov and the Sabbath are virtually alike.

A MUSSAR THOUGHT FOR THE DAY

פרשת חיי שרה

THURSDAY
PARASHAS CHAYEI SARAH

The prohibition against divination, found in *Vayikra* 19:26, is closely linked to the obligation to trust in Hashem. The *Sefer HaChinuch* (§249) writes that "divination is insanity and utter foolishness ... it is not proper for the holy nation that Hashem chose as His own to be swayed by such lies. Furthermore, such practices can cause a person to be turned away from belief in Hashem and His Torah, for he can come, through them, to the heretical belief that all matters that befall him are blind chance, rather than under the control of his Creator ... Hashem wishes to remove such thoughts from our hearts, and to impress upon us that all occurrences, good and bad alike, are His doing, and that the diviners and their omens have no effect at all. This is the meaning of the verse found in the prophecy of Bilam (*Bamidbar* 23:23): *For there is no divination in Yaakov, and no sorcery in Israel*" (cf. *Rashi* there).

Ohr HaChaim makes a similar observation with regard to the verse in *Devarim* (18:13) that exhorts us: *You shall be wholehearted (tamim) with Hashem, your God.* This verse tells us that although idolaters may have means by which they seek to foretell the future, we are enjoined to simply follow Hashem with perfect faith, without feeling a need to know what will happen (see *Rashi* ibid.). States the *Ohr HaChaim:* If one has wholesome faith in Hashem, all the soothsaying of magicians will be meaningless to him, because Hashem can reverse any evil tidings foretold against the Jews. The proof is from Avraham and Sarah, who, according to the stars, were unable to have children. Hashem, however, changed the message of the heavens (see *Bereishis* 15:5). Thus, the Jews have no need for divination or sorcery — all they require is wholehearted obedience to, and faith in, Hashem, Who controls all.

Having proper *bitachon,* trust in Hashem, however, is far from a simple matter. In the preface to his discussion of *bitachon,* R' Shlomo Wolbe notes in *Alei Shur* that there is no other desirable trait that is quite so misunderstood, nor is there another regarding which so many people delude themselves into thinking that they possess it. Many people mistakenly believe that they can attain the highest levels of faith with little or no preparation, and inquire casually about the various parameters of *bitachon* as if it is a simple thing to master. The truth, says R' Wolbe, is that one who has mastered *bitachon* asks no questions — for he has no questions. He does not even realize that he is practicing *bitachon,* for it is part of the very fiber of his being.

HALACHAH OF THE DAY

פרשת
חיי שרה

THURSDAY
PARASHAS
CHAYEI
SARAH

We have seen so far that one is permitted to remove "waste" from "food" in the following cases:
(1) When it is impossible to access the food without removing the waste, one may first remove the waste, as is the case with peeling fruits and vegetables;
(2) when the "waste" will be used later on in the same meal;
(3) by removing the waste from inside the mouth;
(4) by removing some of the food together with the waste;
(5) in cases of attached mixtures, one leaves the sliver of waste that contacts the food;
(6) in cases of large piled mixtures, one may remove the top items to reach the bottom ones.

We will now discuss actions that involve the separation of mixtures, but are not considered *sorting* at all.

One may rearrange a mixture in order to access the item that he desires. For example, if one has before him a bowl of salad in which the tomatoes are located at the bottom and are covered by the rest of the vegetables, he may toss the entire salad to bring the tomatoes to the top so that they may be removed. To *remove* the unwanted vegetables in order to reach the tomatoes would be forbidden — this would be a case of removing "waste," the unwanted items, to reach the "food," the tomatoes. However, by tossing and rearranging the entire salad, he gains access to the food without ever selecting the waste out of the mixture.

One is also permitted to scatter a mixture over a large area in order to separate the individual items that make up the mixture. For example: If one has a mixture of cutlery with which he desires to set the table, he may not sort this mixture until immediately before the meal. At that time, it would be permissible to sort the mixture by removing the desired items from the mix one at a time. However, if one desires to set the table well in advance of the meal, he may scatter the entire mixture of cutlery over the surface of the table, thereby breaking up the mixture and allowing each individual piece to stand on its own. Now there is no longer any question of *sorting,* and he need not wait to set the table until immediately before the meal.

A mixture of different-size samplings of the same item may be sorted by size, because, as we noted previously, the difference in size is not significant enough to mark the different samplings as different "types" of items. A mixture of different types of items may also

פרשת חיי שרה
THURSDAY
PARASHAS CHAYEI SARAH

be sorted according to size, as long as the different types of items are not thereby isolated one from the other. For example, a platter of sliced meats may be sorted into groups of different *size* slices, but they may not be sorted into piles of different types of meat.

A CLOSER LOOK AT THE SIDDUR

In the thirteenth blessing of the weekday *Shemoneh Esrei* (the blessing of *Al HaTzaddikim*), we find the following prayer:

וְתֵן שָׂכָר טוֹב לְכָל הַבּוֹטְחִים בְּשִׁמְךָ בֶּאֱמֶת, וְשִׂים חֶלְקֵנוּ עִמָּהֶם לְעוֹלָם, וְלֹא נֵבוֹשׁ כִּי בְךָ בָּטָחְנוּ. — *And give good reward to all those who trust in Your Name in truth, and place our lot with them always, and we will not be ashamed, for we trust in You.*

This prayer is difficult to understand. First, we know that it is not proper for one to perform Hashem's will in order to receive reward. Why, then, do we ask here for a reward for faith? Second, we ask that our lot be placed with that of those who trust in Hashem, which implies that we are not ourselves part of that group. But then we conclude the prayer by saying that we, too, trust in Hashem! If we ourselves practice trust in Hashem, then we should not need a separate request to include us in the group rewarded for their trust! Finally, what is the meaning of the cryptic statement, *and we will not be ashamed*?

Many different approaches to these difficulties are suggested by the commentators. *Chasam Sofer* (*Derashos* §31) explains that those "who trust in Hashem's Name in truth" are the very righteous, who desire most of all that all of the Jews will come to recognize Hashem and His control of the world. Their fondest wish is that all the world will realize Hashem's majesty. Thus, we pray that they be given their wish — and what is that? *That our lot be placed with them, so that we will not be ashamed, for we too* (will) *trust in You.* In other words, we pray that we, too, be elevated to the point where we can correctly comprehend, as the *tzaddikim* do even now, the providence of Hashem, and that we come to the correct level of *bitachon*. This will prevent us from suffering humiliation; for while one who puts his trust in others shows that he feels helpless on his own, one who trusts in Hashem is never ashamed to have done so, for no one can succeed without His help (see *Doveir Shalom*). And this will bring to fruition the "reward" that truly righteous men crave — the revelation of the ultimate redemption.

פרשת חיי שרה

THURSDAY

PARASHAS CHAYEI SARAH

R' Shlomo Kluger, in his *sefer Yedios Shlomo,* understands the matter somewhat differently. He notes that in the beginning of the prayer we speak of those who trust in Hashem *in truth,* while at the end we speak simply of those who have trust in Hashem. He offers the following parable:

Suppose a powerful ruler came to a small town, and stayed at the house of one of the town's wealthy men. Many of the townspeople would desire to catch a glimpse of the king, but this would be impossible — for the guards and servants would prevent common men from entering. Their only hope of entering would be when an important personage would come to seek an audience. The guards would open the gate to let the important person in, and a determined villager might be able to quickly push through the opening, and at least get a look at the king. But a villager who was not willing to push himself forward would have no chance at all to see the king.

Those who have faith in Hashem, writes *R' Shlomo Kluger,* can be divided into two categories. Some have such strong *bitachon* that they never attempt to accomplish things through their own efforts; they trust in Hashem completely. Others have a lesser level of *bitachon;* they attempt to do whatever they can, but when they see that they are unsuccessful in their efforts, they rely on Hashem to help them.

The first group are those "who trust in Hashem in truth," and it is for them that Hashem reserves his great reward. But it is *we* — those in the second group — who request that these righteous men be given the great reward they deserve, in the hope that once the "door" of Heavenly blessing is open, we, with our smaller level of *bitachon,* will be able to "squeeze through" and be redeemed as well, rather than be left behind, humiliated by our lack of faith.

In the *siddur Beis Tefillah* we find another insight with regard to this prayer. We ask that Hashem give us "good reward" (שָׂכָר טוֹב). The question may be asked: Is there such a thing as reward that is not good? What is the reason for this seeming redundancy? *Beis Tefillah* explains that the reward we request is that Hashem assist us in our service to Him, enabling us to do His will. This is the dearest wish of those who truly trust in Him — that they be successful in cleaving to Hashem as much as is humanly achievable. Such reward is truly "good reward," for it fulfills the very purpose of our existence. [For another explanation of the term "good reward," see *Siddur Yaavetz.*]

פרשת חיי שרה

A TORAH THOUGHT FOR THE DAY

FRIDAY
PARASHAS CHAYEI SARAH

וַיֹּאמַר עֶבֶד אַבְרָהָם אָנֹכִי
*And [Eliezer] said:
I am a servant of Avraham*
(*Bereishis* 24:34).

As soon as Eliezer entered the house of Besuel, food was placed before him. Yet, he refused to eat, and insisted that he be allowed to speak. And what was the first thing he said? "I am the servant of Avraham!" Why was it necessary for Eliezer to emphasize this point so prominently?

Many commentators explain that this declaration reveals Eliezer's great humility. He did not seek grandeur by representing himself as Avraham's agent or partner, nor did he claim that any of the wealth he was carrying belonged to him. Rather, he immediately identified himself as nothing more than a servant, who was bound to carry out his charge, even before partaking of refreshment (see *Radak* and *Alshich*).

The Gemara (*Bava Kamma* 92b) derives from Eliezer's behavior a basis for the popular aphorism: "Be the first to tell whatever is degrading about yourself." It is better to take the initiative in revealing one's shortcomings than to attempt to hide them and be exposed by others.

The *Zohar* notes that with his self-denigration, Eliezer actually brought honor to his master Avraham, for when Besuel and Lavan saw that such a distinguished personage was nothing more than a servant of Avraham, Avraham's stature was greatly increased in their eyes. Thus, Eliezer personified the faithful servant, as the verse states (*Malachi* 1:6): *A slave honors his master.* [This approach is supported by the fact that Eliezer followed his declaration by speaking of Avraham's riches and the fact that Hashem had blessed him.]

A different approach is taken by *Minchah Belulah,* who suggests that Besuel and Lavan might have included forbidden foods among the ones that they placed before Eliezer. In order that they not be offended by his refusal to eat, Eliezer explained that he was a servant of Avraham. As a member of Avraham's household, he was bound to observe the laws of the Torah, in accordance with Avraham's wishes; as a result he could eat only permissible foods.

MISHNAH OF THE DAY: SHABBOS 6:3

פרשת חיי שרה

FRIDAY
PARASHAS CHAYEI SARAH

The Mishnah lists those items with which a woman is Biblically forbidden to go out on the Sabbath: לֹא תֵצֵא אִשָּׁה בְּמַחַט הַנְּקוּבָה — *A woman may not go out* on the Sabbath *with a pierced needle* thrust into her garments;[1] וְלֹא בְּטַבַּעַת שֶׁיֵּשׁ עָלֶיהָ חוֹתָם — *nor while wearing a ring that bears a signet;*[2] וְלֹא בְּכוֹלְיָאר — *nor with a brooch,*[3] וְלֹא בִּצְלוֹחִית שֶׁל פַּלְיָיטוֹן — *nor with a spice bundle,*[4] — *nor with a perfume flask.*[5] וְאִם יָצְתָה — *And if she went out* from a private domain into a public domain wearing any of these items, חַיֶּבֶת חַטָּאת — *she is liable to a chatas offering;* דִּבְרֵי רַבִּי מֵאִיר — these are *the words of R' Meir.*[6] וַחֲכָמִים פּוֹטְרִין בְּכוֹבֶלֶת — *But the Sages exempt* her from a chatas if she goes out *with a spice bundle* וּבִצְלוֹחִית שֶׁל פַּלְיָיטוֹן — *or with a perfume flask.*[7]

NOTES

1. A needle that is pierced and has an eye is used for sewing, and therefore cannot be considered an ornament. It may not be worn outside on the Sabbath, even if it is thrust into the woman's clothing, for this is a common way of carrying such a needle (see *Rav; Tos. Yom Tov*).

2. Since it is not customary for women to wear such rings, they are not considered ornaments for a woman. Since the ring is neither a garment nor an ornament, it is deemed a burden (*Tiferes Yisrael*).

3. A snail-shaped brooch used to fasten a cloak (*Rashi;* cf. *Rav*). Since most women do not wear this item, it is considered a burden rather than an ornament (*Rav*).

4. A vial made of silver or gold, containing spices [balsam (*Rashi*)]. It is worn by women who suffer from bad body odor (*Rav;* see below, note 6).

5. A flask filled with balsam (*Rashi*) or musk (*Rav; Rambam;* see next note).

6. R' Meir considers all of these items as burdens rather than accessories (*Rashi*). Therefore, going out with them on the Sabbath is Biblically prohibited, and one who does go out is liable to a *chatas*. [The pierced needle and the signet ring are not ornamental; and the other items mentioned in the Mishnah are not considered ornaments in R' Meir's view, since the majority of women do not wear such items (see *Rashash*).]

7. The Sages consider these items to be ornaments. Hence, a woman who wears them when going out from a private domain into a public domain is not liable to a *chatas* offering. Nevertheless, the Rabbis forbade her to wear these items lest she go out with them into the public domain and remove them to show to her companions (*Rav* from *Gemara* 62a).

פרשת חיי שרה

GEMS FROM THE GEMARA

FRIDAY
PARASHAS CHAYEI SARAH

Our Mishnah considered the law of a "perfume flask." Such flasks usually contained fragrant balsam oil. The Gemara (62b) discusses balsam oil in a different context. The Gemara cites Rav Yehudah in the name of Shmuel, who said that the following verse [that speaks of those who regaled themselves with luxuries even as the prophets warned of the Temple's impending destruction], *And they anoint themselves with the finest of oils* (Amos 6:6), refers to anointing with balsam oil.

This interpretation is challenged by Rav Yosef, on the basis of a Baraisa (*Tosefta Sotah* 15:4) that lists practices that were banned because of the Temple's destruction. [The Rabbis banned certain joyful practices in order to ensure that the people realized the gravity of the tragedy that had befallen them (see *Sotah* 49a-b).] Included in the list of bans is R' Yehudah ben Bava's ban against the use of balsam. The Sages, however, did not agree with him and continued to permit the use of balsam oil.

Rav Yosef asks: If you say that the aforementioned verse refers to balsam, it is evident that balsam was used for purposes of pleasure. Why, then, did the Sages not agree with R' Yehudah ben Bava, who banned the use of balsam oil?

This argument is refuted by Abaye, who countered to Rav Yosef that according to his reasoning, all the activities listed in this verse should be forbidden. If so, a problem arises with another section of the same verse: *who drink out of bowls of wine*. R' Ami and R' Assi gave different interpretations of this phrase. One said it refers to *kenishkanin* — a tall glass vessel with two spouts (*Rashi*) out of which two people could drink simultaneously (*Rabbeinu Chananel*); while the other said it refers to a joyous practice in which revelers threw their cups to each other — a skillful trick in which they would juggle [the cups of wine] between one another (see *Rashi*). Asks Abaye: Shouldn't Rav Yosef forbid these activities as well, as they are included in the verse? But we know that this is not so, for when Rabbah bar Rav Huna visited the house of the Exilarch and found him drinking out of *kenishkanin,* Rabbah bar Rav Huna did not say anything to him at all by way of rebuke! Thus, we see that not everything listed in the verse was prohibited.

Abaye concludes: Rather, the criteria for prohibition were as follows: The Rabbis prohibited the use of everything that involves pleasure and also involves joy. But activities that involve only pleasure and do not involve joy, such as anointing oneself with balsam oil, were not subject to the Rabbinic prohibition.

A MUSSAR THOUGHT FOR THE DAY

פרשת
חיי שרה

FRIDAY
PARASHAS CHAYEI SARAH

Rav Eliezer Menachem Man Shach related the following story in praise of Rav Yechezkel Levenstein, the *mashgiach* of Mir and Kletzk:

When Rav Shach was a Rosh Mesivta in the Yeshivah of Kletzk, Rav Aharon Kotler was the Rosh Yeshivah and Rav Yechezkel was the *mashgiach*. Rav Shach was sent by Rav Aharon to Volozhin to find out if the yeshivah, which had fallen on hard times, would be allowed to use the empty building formerly used by the Volozhiner Yeshivah.

Rav Shach went, but the meeting was unsuccessful, and the idea was rejected outright. Rav Shach returned to Kletzk, and arrived right before Shabbos. He quickly dressed for Shabbos, and went to the house of the *mashgiach*, where the weekly lecture had already begun. As soon as Rav Shach entered, the *mashgiach* looked at him and said, "I am the servant of Avraham!" All the listeners were puzzled, until the *mashgiach* explained:

"Reb Leizer (as Rav Shach was then known) has just returned from performing a mission for the Rosh Yeshivah! Now, I will tell you what happened there in Volozhin. He went in and said, 'I have come to discuss the possibility of moving the Kletzker Yeshivah here.' They asked him, 'Are you the Rosh Yeshivah of Kletzk?' When he said that he was not, they asked, 'Well, are you the *mashgiach*?' When he again replied in the negative, they asked, 'So, who are you?' Reb Leizer then told them that he was a Rosh Mesivta of the yeshivah, who had been sent by the Rosh Yeshivah.

"Now, this was not the proper way to proceed," said the *mashgiach*. "We see that Eliezer the servant of Avraham introduced himself immediately to Rivkah's family by saying, 'I am the servant of Avraham!' This is how we must present ourselves. It is the greatest honor to say, 'I am a Rosh Mesivta who has been sent on a mission by my Rosh Yeshivah!' Such an introduction makes a more favorable impression." The *mashgiach* concluded by saying, "And now you can ask Reb Leizer if I described his meeting accurately!"

Rav Shach concluded: No one in the room was amazed more than I, for the *mashgiach* had indeed described precisely what had occurred in Volozhin! But this was not an example of *ruach hakodesh* (Divine Inspiration) on the part of the *mashgiach*. Rather, the knowledge came from his great Torah wisdom — for, as the Gemara says (*Bava Basra* 12a), a wise man is on an even higher level than a prophet. From his immense wisdom in analyzing the Torah, and his tremendous understanding of human nature, he was able to figure out exactly what had happened.

(from *Rav Shach on Chumash*)

HALACHAH OF THE DAY

FRIDAY
PARASHAS CHAYEI SARAH

As mentioned previously, the *melachah* of *sorting* pertains equally to liquids and solids. One is forbidden to strain a liquid on Shabbos in order to remove its impurities or unwanted matter. For example, if one has a bottle of wine that has developed sediment, he may not strain the wine in order to remove the sediment. However, there is an important caveat to this rule. A liquid that remains fully drinkable despite the presence of its impurities may be filtered in order to attain a more purified state. Since the impurities contained in the liquid do not impinge upon one's ability to drink it, they are considered to be a part of the liquid itself, and not foreign matter that may not be removed.

For this reason, in instances where tap water is fully drinkable, and one has installed a filter to remove perceived or very minor impurities such as chlorine and the like, such filtering is not in violation of the *melachah* of *sorting*.

However, it is important to note that for very finicky individuals, to whom even the presence of minor impurities renders the water undrinkable, even such filtering would be forbidden.

To summarize, the following acts of separation are not considered to be acts of *boreir*:

(1) turning over a mixture in order to rearrange its contents;
(2) scattering a mixture over a large area in order to break it down into its individual components;
(3) sorting a mixture of foods according to size;
(4) filtering minor impurities out of liquids.

In closing, we will mention some common occurrences of this *melachah*, and the proper method of handling them.

Particles of dirt or an insect found in a drink: The foreign matter may be removed together with some of the liquid. Since some of the mixture is also being removed, there is no act of *sorting*.

Spoiled grapes on a cluster: One must select the desirable grapes immediately prior to eating them.

Fat attached to meat: One may cut away the fat while leaving a thin layer of fat still attached to the meat; alternatively, one may cut away all the fat if he removes some of the meat together with the fat.

Fat in soup: It may be removed from the soup either by pouring it away or spooning it off together with some of the soup.

Oil in a can of tuna: One may squeeze the oil out of the tuna for immediate use. [However, the lid of the can may not be used to aid in the removal of the oil, as it improves the efficiency of the oil's removal.]

This concludes our discussion of the *melachah* of sorting.

פרשת חיי שרה

FRIDAY

PARASHAS CHAYEI SARAH

A CLOSER LOOK AT THE SIDDUR

In the prayer of *Elokai Netzor,* which we recite at the conclusion of the *Shemoneh Esrei,* we ask: וְלִמְקַלְלַי נַפְשִׁי תִדּוֹם, וְנַפְשִׁי כֶּעָפָר לַכֹּל תִּהְיֶה — *To those who would curse me, let my soul be silent; and let my soul be like earth to everyone.* R' Yechezkel Levenstein, the *mashgiach* of the Mirrer Yeshivah, noted that in this request we find two distinct levels of humility. Humility begins, he said, by being able to keep silent while another wishes to curse you. By refraining from responding in kind, a person breaks down his natural inclination toward arrogance. This is an attitude that is highly prized by Hashem, as the Gemara states (*Shabbos* 88b): Those who suffer insult but do not insult in return, and hear their disgrace but do not reply . . . regarding them the verse states (*Shoftim* 5:31): *But they who love Him shall be as the sun going forth in its power.*

The second level of humility, explains the *mashgiach,* is a more lofty one that is more difficult to reach. This is the aim of the prayer, *let my soul be like earth to everyone.* One who attains this height has reached the very pinnacle of humility [indeed, we find that Avraham said of himself, *I am but earth and ashes* (*Bereishis* 18:27)]. Such a person is not only characterized by his lack of response to those who would vilify him; he is of truly humble spirit, and rejoices in whatever Hashem designates as his lot, even if it entails suffering.

R' Chaim Vital notes that a lesson is to be learned from the comparison of the humble man to the earth. Just as a clod of earth is not useful, and it must be broken down and finely ground before it can be processed into a vessel, so it is with man. For a man to be a true servant of Hashem, he must be tested and refined, so that he can reach true heights.

QUESTION OF THE DAY:

What custom is derived from the feast served to Eliezer in the house of Besuel?

For the answer, see page 55.

פרשת חיי שרה

SHABBOS
PARASHAS CHAYEI SARAH

A TORAH THOUGHT FOR THE DAY

וַיִּקְבְּרוּ אֹתוֹ יִצְחָק וְיִשְׁמָעֵאל בָּנָיו אֶל־מְעָרַת הַמַּכְפֵּלָה אֶל־שְׂדֵה עֶפְרֹן בֶּן־צֹחַר הַחִתִּי אֲשֶׁר עַל־פְּנֵי מַמְרֵא

And his sons Yitzchak and Yishmael buried him in the Cave of Machpelah, in the field of Ephron the son of Tzochar the Chittite, which was near Mamre (Bereishis 25:9).

The Gemara (*Bava Basra* 16a) offers several interpretations of a verse that appears earlier in this *parashah* (*Bereishis* 24:1): *... and Hashem had blessed Avraham with everything.* One of the interpretations is that Avraham merited that his life ended without his seeing any wicked descendants, for his grandson Eisav did not rebel until after his death (see *Rashi* to *Bereishis* 25:30), and his son Yishmael repented of his sins while Avraham was yet alive. The Gemara proves this from the verse above, which speaks of Avraham's burial. Yishmael was the older of the two sons; seemingly, he should be mentioned first. Why does the Torah mention Yitzchak first? It must be, concludes the Gemara, that Yishmael accorded honor to Yitzchak by allowing him, as the more righteous son, to precede him; and Yishmael would not have done so unless he had repented of his sins.

The Gemara asks: But is it not possible that the Torah listed Yitzchak first because he was the greater of the two, but in actuality Yishmael did not allow Yitzchak to precede him? The Gemara replies that this possibility can be disproven by the fact that when the Torah tells of the burial of Yitzchak by *his* sons, Yaakov and Eisav, Eisav is listed first (see *Bereishis* 35:29) although Yaakov was greater. Thus, it must be that the Torah is telling us what actually occurred; and while Eisav, who was wicked, would not allow Yaakov to precede him, Yishmael, who had done *teshuvah,* accorded honor to Yitzchak.

However, another difficulty presents itself. Although it is clear from the verse that at the time of the burial Yishmael accorded honor to Yitzchak, how does that prove that he had already repented *during Avraham's lifetime*? Perhaps he repented only after Avraham had died!

Rabbeinu Bachya explains that for Yishmael to have agreed to give precedence to Yitzchak at such an important time, it must have been that he had already *been accustomed* to accord honor to Yitzchak; and this would be true only if he had already repented *before* Avraham's death. [Alternatively, it is possible that the Gemara means that it was in the merit of *Avraham* that Yishmael found the will to repent (so that Avraham would die without seeing any wicked offspring), and therefore the repentance *must* have occurred during Avraham's lifetime.]

MISHNAH OF THE DAY: SHABBOS 6:4

פרשת
חיי שרה

**SHABBOS
PARASHAS
CHAYEI
SARAH**

The Mishnah lists those items that a man is Biblically forbidden to wear outside on the Sabbath:
לֹא יֵצֵא הָאִישׁ לֹא בְסַיִיף וְלֹא בְקֶשֶׁת וְלֹא בִתְרִיס וְלֹא בְאַלָּה וְלֹא בְרוֹמַח — *A man may not go out* on the Sabbath *neither with a sword, nor with a bow, nor with a shield, nor with a buckler,* [1] *nor with a spear.* וְאִם יָצָא חַיָּיב חַטָּאת — *And if he went out* from a private domain into a public domain with one of these implements of war, *he is liable to a chatas offering.* [2]

A dispute concerning this ruling:
רַבִּי אֱלִיעֶזֶר אוֹמֵר תַּכְשִׁיטִין הֵן לוֹ — *R' Eliezer says: They are ornaments for him.* [3] וַחֲכָמִים אוֹמְרִים אֵינָן אֶלָּא לִגְנַאי — *But the Sages*[4] *say: They are nothing but a disgrace,* שֶׁנֶּאֱמַר ,,וְכִתְּתוּ חַרְבוֹתָם לְאִתִּים וַחֲנִיתוֹתֵיהֶם לְמַזְמֵרוֹת לֹא־יִשָּׂא גוֹי אֶל־גּוֹי חֶרֶב וְלֹא־יִלְמְדוּ עוֹד מִלְחָמָה — *as it is stated* (Yeshayah 2:4): *"They shall beat their swords into hoes, and their spears into pruning shears; nation shall not lift up a sword against nation, neither shall they learn war anymore."* [5]
בִּירִית טְהוֹרָה וְיוֹצְאִין בָּהּ בְּשַׁבָּת — *A garter is ritually pure,* [6] *and they*

--- NOTES ---

1. The translation follows *Rav* and *Rambam Commentary* (a "buckler" is a round wooden shield). Alternatively, an אַלָּה is a mace [a club with a spiked round ball attached to its tip] (*Rav; Rashi*).

2. Since these items are neither garments nor ornaments, they are considered a burden, and one who carries them from a private domain to a public domain has performed the forbidden labor of הוֹצָאָה, *transferring.*

3. R' Eliezer bases his contention on the words of the Psalmist 45:4: *Gird your sword upon your thigh, O mighty one — your majesty and your splendor.* This indicates that the sword is an object of splendor. Therefore, it is considered an ornament.

[The sword discussed here refers to a sword worn hanging from the belt (in a scabbard, for instance) or strapped to one's thigh (see *Magen Avraham* 301:10; *Eliyah Rabbah* 301:36). Even so, the Sages consider it a burden. The other weapons mentioned here, however, seem to be weapons that are carried in one's hand (*Tiferes Yisrael; Machtzis HaShekel* on *Magen Avraham* 301:27; cf. *Eliyah Rabbah* 301:36).]

4. These Sages do not represent a third view, but are identical with the Tanna Kamma (*Tos. Yom Tov*).

5. If these weapons also functioned as ornaments, they would not be consigned to oblivion in the future (*Rav; Rashi*).

6. A garter is a band worn around the leg to hold up a stocking (or around the arm to hold up a sleeve). Since it is not a garment in its own right, but is merely an article that serves another garment, — e.g., the stocking — a garter is not susceptible to *tumah*. This in analogous to rings that serve vessels, that also are not susceptible to *tumah* contamination (*Rav*).

SHABBOS

PARASHAS CHAYEI SARAH

בְּבָלִים טְמֵאִים *may go out with it on the Sabbath.* [7] וְאֵין יוֹצְאִין בָּהֶן בְּשַׁבָּת — *Leg chains*[8] *are susceptible to becoming ritually impure,*[9] *and they may not go out with them on the Sabbath.* [10]

──────────── NOTES ────────────

7. A woman is permitted to wear a garter when going outside because there is no danger that she will remove the garter to show a friend, for if she did so her leg would be exposed (*Rav; Rashi*).

8. There was a family in Jerusalem whose girls were accustomed to walking with long strides, thereby destroying the internal membranes that are the signs of virginity. They therefore hung golden chains connecting one garter to the other, thus forcing the girls to take smaller steps (*Rav* from Gemara 63b).

9. Since the chain is used to serve the body, in contrast to the garter, it is considered a garment, and therefore is susceptible to *tumah* contamination (*Rav; Rashi* 63b).

10. Since the chains were made of gold and can be removed without exposing the leg, we fear that a woman may remove them to show to her friend (*Rav*, from *Rashi* 63b).

GEMS FROM THE GEMARA

The Gemara (63a) cites a Baraisa that elaborates on the debate between R' Eliezer and the Sages, in which the Sages ask R' Eliezer: Inasmuch as these weapons are ornaments for a man, why will they be eliminated in the Messianic era? R' Eliezer replies: Because they will not be needed for war, as it is stated (*Yeshayah* 2:4): *Nation shall not lift up a sword against nation.*

The Gemara then asks: But even if the weapons are no longer needed for war, why are they not still worn as ornaments? Abaye answers that a useless weapon is similar to a lamp in broad daylight — i.e., just as a lamp in broad daylight is useless and therefore unattractive, similarly, when weapons will no longer be needed, they will lose their appeal as ornaments, and hence will be beaten into hoes and pruning shears (see *Yeshayah* ibid.).

The Gemara then notes that this Baraisa disagrees with the opinion of Shmuel, who maintains that the Messianic era does not usher in any change in the natural order, except that the subjugation of the Jews in the various exiles will cease. [Shmuel's source is the verse (*Deuteronomy* 15:1): *For the poor will not cease from the midst of the land,* which implies that in this world there will always be poverty and wealth — and the Messianic era is part of this world.]

On the other hand, the Baraisa supports the opinion of R' Chiya bar

Abba, who said that all the prophets [including Yeshayah, in the prophecy cited in the Mishnah predicting the end of warfare] prophesied only about the Messianic era, but regarding the World to Come it is said (*Yeshayah* 64:3): *No eye has seen, O God, except You, that which He will do for one who waits for Him.*

The Gemara then cites a different version of the Baraisa, in which R' Eliezer responds to the Sages that even in the Messianic era weapons will not be eliminated.

The Gemara comments that according to this second version of the Baraisa, R' Eliezer's opinion *is* consistent with the opinion of Shmuel, who maintains that the Messianic era will not usher in any change in the natural order, and hence weapons will still be needed; and it disagrees with the opinion of R' Chiya bar Abba, who holds that all the prophecies, including *Nation shall not lift up a sword against nation*, refer to the Messianic era.

פרשת
חיי שרה

SHABBOS

PARASHAS
CHAYEI
SARAH

A MUSSAR THOUGHT FOR THE DAY

Chovos HaLevavos, in Chapter Two of his *Shaar HaTeshuvah*, identifies three categories of penitents:

The first type of penitent is one who repents simply because he cannot find any opportunity to sin again. But when he does find such an opportunity, his Evil Inclination will again overpower his intellect, and he will not hold himself back from sinning. However, after he sins again, he will once more see the evil of his actions and repent of them.

Such a person repents with his mouth, but not in his heart; with his tongue, but not in his deeds. He is surely deserving of punishment for his actions, for he has not truly repented of his deeds at all . . .

A second penitent is one who repents in heart and body of the sins he has committed, and stands in opposition to his desires, continually warring with his urge to sin. Nevertheless, his soul constantly pulls him toward the path of sin, and he must always battle his desires. He attempts to control himself, but he is not always successful; sometimes he wins the battle with his *yetzer hara*, and sometimes he is conquered by it.

Such a person has not yet fully found his way to the path of repentance, and he still requires forgiveness. In order to accomplish complete *teshuvah*, he must separate from sin completely, as the verse states (*Yeshayah* 27:9): *Therefore, with this the sin of Yaakov will be forgiven . . . when he levels all of the stones of the (idolatrous) altars into shattered*

פרשת חיי שרה
PARASHAS CHAYEI SARAH — SHABBOS

pieces, so that the Asheirim and the altars of incense can never be returned.

The third penitent is the one who fulfills all of the conditions of repentance. His intellect conquers his desires, and he constantly examines his actions. He fears his Creator, and is ashamed of his lapses before Him. He is cognizant in his heart of the enormity of his sins, and he recognizes the greatness of the One against Whom he has rebelled. He is aware always that he has transgressed the word of Hashem, and keeps this in his mind always. He regrets the sins that he has committed, and asks forgiveness for them every day of his life.

This is the complete penitent, one whom the Creator will find worthy of salvation.

HALACHAH OF THE DAY

The next one of the thirty-nine forbidden labors of Shabbos is the melachah of טוֹחֵן, *grinding*. Grinding took place in the Mishkan either as part of the production of herbal dyes used for the dyeing of the various tapestries and vestments used in the Mishkan, or in the production of flour for the *lechem hapanim*.

The definition of *grinding* as it relates to forbidden activity on Shabbos is the breaking down of a substance into small particles. This *melachah* applies to both foods and non-food items. However, our discussions here will focus on the *melachah* of טוֹחֵן as it pertains to food and food preparation.

Although טוֹחֵן is literally defined as *"grinding,"* which implies the reduction of the ground item into powder, the forbidden *melachah* includes any activity that reduces a large item into very small pieces. Thus, shredding, grating, and chopping can all be prohibited under the umbrella of the *melachah* of *grinding*. Furthermore, even dicing or otherwise cutting a food into very small pieces is prohibited under this *melachah*.

The precise definition of what constitutes "very small pieces," however, is unclear. Therefore, one is obliged to refrain from cutting any food item into pieces generally considered by people to be "very small," even if those pieces are of a size that could in turn be reduced to even smaller pieces.

The prohibition against grinding forbids the use of any utensil to reduce an item to very small pieces. This includes not only implements designed especially for grinding, such as grinders or graters, but even utensils commonly used in ordinary food preparation, such as a knife or fork. We will see further along, however, that there is an important difference in halachah between the use of specialized utensils and common ones. Specialized grinding tools may not be used even when grinding foods that may be ground on Shabbos, as their use is *totally* forbidden.

פרשת
חיי שרה

SHABBOS
PARASHAS
CHAYEI
SARAH

The prohibition against grinding foods applies only to foods that are products of the earth, such as fruits, vegetables, and grains. Meat, poultry, eggs, fish and all other foods that are not produce of the earth, are not subject to the restrictions of this *melachah,* and they may therefore be chopped even into tiny particles on the Sabbath. However, even these foods which may be ground, may not be ground with specialized grinding implements. As noted above, the use of such implements is forbidden with all foods.

A CLOSER LOOK AT THE SIDDUR

Immediately before beginning the *Shemoneh Esrei* prayer during *Maariv* on Friday night, it is the custom in many Ashkenazic communities to recite the following verses found in *Shemos* (31:16-17): *And the Children of Israel shall observe the Sabbath, to make the Sabbath an eternal covenant for their generations. Between Me and the Children of Israel it is a sign forever; that in a six-day period* HASHEM *made the heavens and the earth, and on the seventh day He relaxed and He rested.*

Mention of this custom is found in early *siddurim* such as those of *Rav Amram Gaon* and *Rav Saadiah Gaon.* Abudraham writes that these verses are recited after the blessing that follows the *Shema,* which speaks of redemption, to underscore the fact that if the Jewish nation keeps the Sabbath properly, they will merit the ultimate redemption. *Tur* (*Orach Chaim* §267) also records the custom to recite these verses. *Mishnah Berurah* notes that the custom is also to recite verses appropriate to the three festivals, Rosh Hashanah, and Yom Kippur on each of those occasions at this point in the prayers. *Perishah* (ibid.) is at a loss to identify the source of this custom (as the aforementioned reasoning of *Abudraham* does not apply in those cases), but he posits that it became the custom to recite these verses to alert the congregation as to the contents of the *Shemoneh Esrei* to follow, much as the sexton in

פרשת חיי שרה
SHABBOS PARASHAS CHAYEI SARAH

some congregations would announce before the prayers on a Rosh Chodesh that *Yaaleh VeYavo* was to be said.

Other congregations (most notably those in Eretz Yisrael, and especially those that follow the customs of the *Gra*) omit all these verses, even on Friday nights. The rationale for this would seem to be that in their view, reciting verses of any kind at this point in the prayers would constitute a forbidden interruption between the prayers for redemption and the beginning of *Shemoneh Esrei*. [Indeed, it is for this reason that most congregations do not allow the sexton to announce the *Yaaleh VeYavo* prayer before *Shemoneh Esrei*, and instead simply have the sexton slap the lectern loudly, to alert everyone that an additional prayer is warranted.] Those who do say the verses maintain that these verse are connected either to the subject of redemption, as explained above, or that they are considered linked to the beginning of the Friday night *Shemoneh Esrei*.

Next week, we will examine the verses themselves more closely.

QUESTION OF THE DAY:

Why does the Torah mention again at Avraham's burial that he had purchased the land from Ephron?

For the answer, see page 55.

ANSWERS TO QUESTIONS OF THE DAY

Sunday:

Daas Zekeinim suggests that this refers to the two *parts* of Sarah's life — before Yitzchak's birth and afterward. He notes that the *gematria* of the word וַיִּהְיוּ in the verse is 37, the numbers of years Sarah lived after Yitzchak was born.

Monday:

Either because it was a double cave, with two chambers one above the other, or because it was destined to contain four couples who were buried there — Adam and Chavah, Avraham and Sarah, Yitzchak and Rivkah, and Yaakov and Leah (see *Rashi*, and *Eruvin* 53a with *Maharsha*).

Tuesday:

The Gemara (*Kiddushin* 2a) derives, from the common term of *kichah* (taking) found both in connection with Ephron and regarding acquiring a wife through *kiddushin*, that money or its equivalent can be used to effect *kiddushin* (generally, a ring is used).

Wednesday:

After Avraham and his family left Ur Kasdim (see above, 11:31), they settled in Charan. Nachor, who had lived there, was the oldest surviving kin of Avraham and thus the city came to be called the city of Nachor.

Thursday:

Chizkuni explains that he wished to ascertain the girl's own true character, and not to observe what she might do at home due to the watchful eyes of her parents and family.

Friday:

The Midrash states that this was the betrothal feast of Rivkah; and the *Netziv* (*Hercheiv Davar*) states that it took place at night, as Eliezer first arrived at the well in the evening (see v. 11). This is a source for the custom to make wedding feasts at night (see also *Kiddushin* 65b).

Shabbos:

Radak states that the Torah underscores Avraham's righteousness. Although Hashem had promised him the land but he nevertheless had to purchase it, he did not question Hashem's ways and his faith remained complete.

פרשת תולדות

Parashas Toldos

פרשת תולדות
A TORAH THOUGHT FOR THE DAY

SUNDAY
PARASHAS TOLDOS

וַיֶּעְתַּר יִצְחָק לַה' לְנֹכַח אִשְׁתּוֹ כִּי עֲקָרָה הִוא
וַיֵּעָתֶר לוֹ ה' וַתַּהַר רִבְקָה אִשְׁתּוֹ

And Yitzchak prayed to HASHEM opposite his wife, because she was barren; and HASHEM heard his prayers, and his wife Rivkah conceived (Bereishis 25:21).

Rashi, citing the Gemara in *Yevamos* (64a), explains that both Yitzchak and Rivkah prayed for children — he in one corner, and she in the opposite corner (according to the Gemara, this is the meaning of the verse's statement that Yitzchak prayed *opposite* his wife). Nevertheless, the verse continues by stating that Hashem hearkened to *Yitzchak's* prayer, and not that of Rivkah, for the verse states that Hashem heard *his* prayers, and not *their* prayers (*Mizrachi*). The Gemara explains that Yitzchak's prayers were heard over Rivkah's because there is no comparison between the prayers of a righteous person who is the child of a righteous person (in this case, Yitzchak, son of the righteous Avraham), and the prayers of a righteous person who is the child of a wicked person (here, Rivkah, daughter of the wicked Besuel).

One might wonder why this should be so. Seemingly, a person who was raised by a wicked person, and yet found the strength to break away from the evil ways of his home to become righteous, should be even *more* deserving of Divine blessing than one who is righteous because he follows in the ways of his fathers! Yet, the Gemara seems to tell us that this is not the case.

Maharsha (to *Yevamos* ibid.) writes that this rule (that the prayer of a *tzaddik* the son of a *tzaddik* is more effective) applies only when the prayer is for the *tzaddik* to have children. *Ben Yehoyada* explains that since there is a Talmudic dictum that "grandchildren are like children," children that are born represent a blessing for the grandfather as well. Thus, the merit of the grandfather is added to the merit of his son (or daughter) when he (or she) is praying for children. A righteous person who is the son of a wicked person, however, has only his own merits to speak for him when he prays for children. [Indeed, his lineage may actually impede his prayer, as it is possible that Hashem will be disinclined to grant grandchildren to the wicked grandfather.]

This question has halachic ramifications as well. There are some authorities who rule that it is preferable to appoint a *tzaddik* who is the son of a *tzaddik* as a *shliach tzibbur* [communal prayer leader], in line with the Gemara's statement that his prayers are more effective (see *Magen Avraham* to *Orach Chaim* 53:5, and *Mishnah Berurah* there §13). However,

Maharshal (*Responsa* §20) writes that the Gemara's principle applies only to someone who is praying for his own personal needs, since the merit of his ancestors will aid him in his requests. But if one is praying on behalf of the public, writes *Maharshal,* the opposite is true, for the prayers of one who broke from his parents' ways and became righteous are more readily accepted than the prayers of a *tzaddik* who simply continued in the ways of his predecessors.

פרשת תולדות

SUNDAY

PARASHAS TOLDOS

MISHNAH OF THE DAY: SHABBOS 6:5

The following Mishnah lists the items with which a woman is permitted to go out on the Sabbath:

יוֹצְאָה אִשָּׁה — **A woman may go out** on the Sabbath בְּחוּטֵי שֵׂעָר — **with** artificial braids made up of **strands of hair,**[1] בֵּין מִשֶּׁלָּהּ — **whether** the strands are **of her own** hair, בֵּין מִשֶּׁל חֲבֶירְתָּהּ — **whether** they are **of her friend's** hair,[2] בֵּין מִשֶּׁל בְּהֵמָה — or **whether** they are **of an animal's** hair;[3] וּבְטוֹטֶפֶת וּבְסַרְבִּיטִין בִּזְמַן שֶׁהֵן תְּפוּרִין — **with a frontlet**[4] **or with head bangles**[5] **when they are sewn** to her

———————— NOTES ————————

1. As we learned in Mishnah 1 of this chapter (see note 4 there), the reason why artificial braids made of materials other than hair may not be worn outside on the Sabbath is because they will prevent *mikveh* water from reaching the woman's natural hair. We are therefore concerned that a woman who goes to immerse on the Sabbath will remove them entirely, forget to retie them in her hair, and carry them home. It was to avoid such a desecration of the Sabbath that the Rabbis prohibited a woman to go out on the Sabbath with braids of other materials.

Strands of real hair, however, cannot be drawn tightly enough around a woman's own hair to keep water from penetrating. Therefore, they need not be removed during immersion in a *mikveh,* and hence we are not concerned that a woman might remove them and carry them (*Rav*).

2. The Mishnah here teaches that even if the strands of hair are from another woman's head, and therefore might be repulsive to her, we are nevertheless not concerned that that she will take them off and carry them in a public domain (*Rav* from Gemara 64b).

3. The Mishnah here teaches that even if the strands are of horsehair, which does not match her own hair, we are nevertheless not concerned that she will be ridiculed and come to take them off and carry them in a public domain (*Rav* from Gemara ibid.).

4. This is an ornament worn on the forehead, which stretches from ear to ear (see Mishnah 1, note 5).

5. Sometimes, attached to the frontlet were ribbons, which hung over the temples, reaching down to the cheeks. They were made either of gold, silver or colored cloth, depending upon the wearer's financial status (see Mishnah 1, note 6).

פרשת תולדות

SUNDAY

PARASHAS TOLDOS

hat;[6] בִּכְבוּל וּבִפֵּאָה נָכְרִית לֶחָצֵר — *with a forehead pad[7] or with a wig[8] into a courtyard;[9]* בְּמוֹךְ וּבְמוֹךְ שֶׁבְּאָזְנָהּ — *with a wad that is in her ear,[10]* שֶׁבְּסַנְדָּלָהּ — *or with a wad that is in her sandal,[11]* וּבְמוֹךְ שֶׁהִתְקִינָה לְנִדָּתָהּ — *or with a wad that she prepared for her menstruation;[12]* בְּפִלְפֵּל — *with a peppercorn,[13]* וּבְגַרְגַּל מֶלַח — *with a lump of salt,[14]* וְכָל דָּבָר שֶׁנִּיתָּן לְתוֹךְ פִּיהָ — or with *anything* else of this sort *that was*

——— NOTES ———

6. Since they are sewn to her hat, she cannot show these ornaments to others without removing her headcovering, and we are not concerned that a woman may come to remove her headcovering in a public domain (*Rav*).

7. A cloth pad, usually worn under the frontlet, that protected the forehead from irritation (see Mishnah 1, note 8).

8. A hairpiece made of human tresses and worn by women with thinning hair, to give the appearance of a full head of hair (*Rashi; Rav; Meiri*).

9. Although the forehead pad and the wig may not be worn when going out to the public domain, they may be worn when going into a courtyard.

While the items mentioned earlier in this Mishnah may be worn even when going out to a public domain (*Rashi; Ran*), that is because they are items that a woman would never take off in public. On the other hand, a woman might indeed remove the forehead pad to show to a friend (since it was also ornamental), and she might remove the wig if she feels it does not look right on her and therefore she might be ridiculed by those who see her.

Why, then, is it not forbidden to go out even to a courtyard wearing the forehead pad or the wig, just as it is forbidden to go out even to a courtyard with the other prohibited items listed in this chapter? It is because the Rabbis did not want to entirely forbid wearing ornaments, for fear a woman might become plain and unattractive in the eyes of her husband. They therefore permitted women to wear these two items in a courtyard (where, even if she were to come to carry these items, she would not be in violation of Torah law), as long as she did not wear them into the public domain.

10. Wool or cotton inserted in the ear to absorb any wax that might drip from the ear (*Rav; Rashi*).

11. Wool or cotton inserted into a sandal to prevent the sandal from irritating the sole of the foot (*Rav*).

12. A woman may go out with the wadding intended to absorb her menstrual flow, so that it not soil her clothing (*Rashi; Rav*). [To go out with wadding in one's ear or sandal is permissible only if it is fastened securely, lest it fall out and come to be carried. To go out with the wadding prepared to absorb the menstrual flow, however, is permissible even if it is not tied in place. Since it is repulsive, even if it were to fall out, she would surely not pick it up and carry it through the public domain (*Rav* from Gemara ibid.).]

13. A woman with bad breath may go out with a peppercorn in her mouth to combat the bad odor (*Rav; Rashi*).

14. The lump of salt is used to alleviate a toothache (*Rashi; Rav*).

פרשת תולדות

SUNDAY
PARASHAS TOLDOS

placed in her mouth,[15] וּבִלְבַד שֶׁלֹּא תִתֵּן לְכַתְּחִלָּה בְּשַׁבָּת — but only provided that she does not initially place it there on the Sabbath,[16] וְאִם נָפַל לֹא תַחֲזִיר — and provided that if it fell from her mouth, she does not return it there.[17]

A dispute:

רַבִּי שֵׁן תּוֹתֶבֶת שֶׁל זָהָב — A false tooth made of gold: מַתִּיר — Rabbi Yehudah HaNasi permits one to go out with it,[18] וַחֲכָמִים אוֹסְרִים — but the Sages forbid it.[19]

---— NOTES ---—

15. A woman may go out with any spice that she puts into her mouth, such as ginger or cinnamon (*Tiferes Yisrael* from Gemara 65a). [Since these items are serving a therapeutic function in her mouth, they do not legally constitute a burden, but are viewed as ornaments; therefore, they may be "worn" outside.]

16. While a woman may go out with anything placed in her mouth for medicinal purposes, she may not place the item in her mouth on the Sabbath, as a person who observes her doing so — not knowing of her need for a remedy — may assume that her true intention is to transport the item to another domain. The observer might therefore be led to believe that such a transfer is permissible, and might thereby come to violate the Sabbath (*Tosafos*).

17. For the same reason that she may not put this item in initially, she may not put it back if it falls out. This is true only if it fell on the ground. If she held it in her hand, however, she may put it back (*Tos. Yom Tov*).

18. Rabbi Yehudah HaNasi permits a woman to go out with a false tooth or a gold crown. Since her own tooth is disfigured, and she would not want to reveal her blemish, we are not concerned that she may come to remove the false tooth or the crown (*Rav*).

19. Since a gold tooth stands out among a woman's natural teeth, people may ridicule her, and she may come to remove it from her mouth and carry it (*Rav*).

GEMS FROM THE GEMARA

As we have seen, women may not wear ornaments in a public domain, or in any area that has no *eruv*. Yet, at least since the times of the *Geonim*, women have been known to wear jewelry even in the street on the Sabbath! Rabbis throughout the ages have searched for the justification for this practice.

Aruch HaShulchan (*Orach Chaim* 303:22; see also *Rama* there §18) suggests a justification based on the passage we examined above, in Gems from the Gemara to Mishnah 1. He compares all jewelry in our time to the tiara that during Talmudic times was worn only by distinguished women (Gemara 59a-b). As we saw there, according to Rav Ashi all agree that such a tiara may be worn outside on the Sabbath, since

SUNDAY

PARASHAS TOLDOS

distinguished women are not likely to remove their tiaras and show them to other women in the street.

In our times, posits the *Aruch HaShulchan*, all women fit into the category of distinguished women in regard to all their jewelry; it is not common for them to remove their jewelry in public to show it to other women. He adds that in the time of the Talmud, women frequently did not go out of the house all week. Consequently, they seldom met their friends. Moreover, they did not visit their friends in their homes even on the Sabbath. There was no women's gallery in the synagogue where they could display their finery. The only place they met their friends was on the street. There was, therefore, a great probability that they would remove their jewelry to show it to their friends while meeting in the street. In our times, however, women go out and visit their friends even during the week. Moreover, they see each other in the synagogue. There is, therefore, no danger that they will remove their jewelry in the street to show it to their friends. [For other resolutions to this difficulty, see *Tosafos* and *Ritva* to 64a.]

A MUSSAR THOUGHT FOR THE DAY

Rav Simchah Zissel Ziv of Kelm takes a different approach to the Gemara's statement that Yitzchak's prayer was accepted first because he was "a *tzaddik* the son of a *tzaddik*." He notes that Yitzchak was not simply a disciple of Avraham, following in his father's ways and doing as he did. [Indeed, that would be a description of Eliezer, Avraham's servant, who "drew from the Torah of his master and gave it to others to drink."] Rather, Yitzchak was much more. He was one of the *Avos* in his own right. Avraham was the pillar of *Chesed*, while Yitzchak was the originator of the approach of *Gevurah-Pachad* — serving Hashem with *strength* and *awe*. [Although a thorough discussion of these aspects of the *Avos* is beyond the scope of this work, the aspect of *Gevurah* is exemplified by a total negation of one's self to Hashem, grounded in the realization that Hashem is the source of all power (as exemplified by Yitzchak's role at the *Akeidah*); and the aspect of *Pachad* complements this, as it demands a constant awareness of how one's every deed, word or thought is scrutinized by Hashem and thus must be as perfect as possible (for further discussion, see *Reishis Chochmah*, *Totza'os Chaim* §185, and *Pri Tzaddik*, *Rosh Hashanah* §8).] He played an essential role in the formation of the Jewish nation, as these two

SUNDAY

PARASHAS TOLDOS

approaches ultimately were fused to form the attribute of Yaakov, that of *Tiferes-Emes* — *Splendor* and *Truth*; and these three modes of service form the tripod upon which Judaism rests eternally. In succeeding Avraham, but not becoming merely his carbon copy, Yitzchak demonstrated that he was not merely the heir of a Patriarch, but a Patriarch in his own right.

Rav Simchah Zissel explains the meaning of *Rashi's* statement that Yitzchak's prayer was accepted before Rivkah's because he was a *tzaddik* the son of a *tzaddik* (see *A Torah Thought for the Day*) using this approach. While Rivkah's status as a righteous woman daughter of a wicked man was beyond reproach, her difficult path was made a little easier by the knowledge that whatever she had seen in the houses of her forebears could be totally disregarded. She knew that her past could serve as nothing more than impetus for change. Yitzchak, however, became an *original tzaddik*, blazing a new path in the service of Hashem, *despite* the fact that he was the son of a *tzaddik*, whose way was a correct one. To become a Yitzchak rather than a second Avraham was truly an awesome feat. Yitzchak sought his *derech* independently, and found a unique method of serving Hashem in thought and deed — and it was this that gave his prayers their greater efficacy.

HALACHAH OF THE DAY

Today we will continue our discussion of the *melachah* of טוֹחֵן, grinding.

A food that has been previously ground and then reconstituted into a solid may be ground once again on the Sabbath. This rule is known as אֵין טוֹחֵן אַחַר טוֹחֵן, *there is no [prohibition against] regrinding something that was [previously] ground*. However, here too, as we learned previously with regard to items that do not grow from the ground, these items may not be ground using specialized grinding implements; only ordinary utensils may be used.

A manifestation of this rule would be the crumbling of a cookie into small crumbs, or the grinding of matzah into matzah meal. Since these items are made primarily from flour — something that has already been finely ground prior to being reformed into a solid substance — one is permitted to now regrind them on the Sabbath in accordance with the rule of אֵין טוֹחֵן אַחַר טוֹחֵן.

Another exception to the prohibition against *grinding* is grinding that

SUNDAY

PARASHAS TOLDOS

is performed in a highly irregular, awkward fashion. For example, one may chop fruits and vegetables into tiny pieces using the handle of a knife or fork. Since this is a highly abnormal method of grinding, the Sages allowed it to be done on Shabbos. [We must make note of the fact that this exemption stands in contrast to the general rule that actions Biblically forbidden on Shabbos are forbidden by Rabbinic law when performed in an irregular manner.]

Many *poskim* rule that the prohibition against grinding does not apply in cases where the food is being prepared for immediate consumption. According to this view, one may cut a fruit or vegetable into very small pieces using an ordinary utensil immediately before the serving of a meal. [The definition of "immediate" in this context is similar to the definition which we discussed earlier, with respect to the *melachah* of *sorting*.] Other *poskim*, however, disagree, and forbid grinding even for immediate use.

While it is proper to follow the stricter opinion in this matter, in cases of necessity, the lenient view may be followed. For example, one may cut a vegetable into tiny pieces for immediate consumption by a baby if other foods are not available. Once again, the grinding may be done only with ordinary utensils, not specialized instruments.

This concludes our discussion of the melachah of *grinding*.

A CLOSER LOOK AT THE SIDDUR

We begin the first blessing of every *Shemoneh Esrei* Prayer with the words, *Blessed are You, Hashem, our God and the God of our forefathers: the God of Avraham, the God of Yitzchak, and the God of Yaakov*. Many commentators have noted the repetitious nature of this phrasing. If Hashem is the God of our forefathers, then by definition He is the God of Avraham, Yitzchak and Yaakov? Why must this fact be stated twice?

This question is addressed by *Mechilta* (*Bo* 13:3), which states that we derive this method of address from the Torah. When Moshe was instructed by Hashem to go to the Jews in Egypt and tell them that he had been sent by Hashem to redeem them from bondage, Moshe asked (*Shemos* 3:13): *"When I come to the Children of Israel and say to them, 'The God of your forefathers has sent me to you' and they say to me, 'What is His Name?'* — *what shall I say to them?"* Hashem replied (ibid. v. 6): *"So shall you say to the Children of Israel: 'Hashem, the God of your forefathers, the God of Avraham, the God of Yitzchak, and the God of Yaakov has sent me to you.' "* We see, then, that this is how Hashem wished to be identified to the Jews, and therefore this is how we address Him in prayer.

SUNDAY
PARASHAS
TOLDOS

Rav Simchah Zissel of Kelm, in line with his teaching that each of the *Avos* approached the service of Hashem in his own unique way (see above, *A Mussar Thought for the Day*), explains that this is reflected here in the singling out of each of the *Avos* separately. We begin by simply addressing Hashem as *the God of our forefathers*. Then we note that he is *the God of Avraham*, the pillar of *Chesed; the God of Yitzchak*, the pillar of *Gevurah* and *Pachad;* and *the God of Yaakov*, the pillar of *Tiferes* and *Emes.*

R' Shimon Schwab also understands the *tefillah* as highlighting the different approaches of each of the *Avos*, but he focuses on how each one dealt with the aspect of the *kingship* of Hashem. Avraham spread the word of Hashem to the multitudes; he proclaimed Hashem as מֶלֶךְ הָעוֹלָם, *King of the Universe*. Yitzchak focused upon himself; thus, he proclaimed Hashem as King over each individual. And Yaakov, the father of the Twelve *Shevatim*, exemplifies the proclaiming of Hashem as the God of the Jewish people.

QUESTION OF THE DAY:

Why does the verse stress that Yaakov prayed opposite his wife?

For the answer, see page 112.

פרשת תולדות

MONDAY
PARASHAS TOLDOS

A TORAH THOUGHT FOR THE DAY

וַיִּתְרֹצְצוּ הַבָּנִים בְּקִרְבָּהּ וַתֹּאמֶר אִם־כֵּן
לָמָּה זֶּה אָנֹכִי וַתֵּלֶךְ לִדְרֹשׁ אֶת־ה׳

The children struggled within her;
and she said, "If so, why am I thus?"
And she went to inquire of HASHEM (Bereishis 25:22).

Rashi cites the Midrash that explains that whenever Rivkah would near the Torah academies of Shem and Ever, Yaakov would struggle to exit her womb; and when she would be passing by an idolatrous temple, Eisav would struggle to exit. *Kli Yakar* notes that Rivkah was unaware that she was carrying twins; she therefore was distressed by the prospect that her unborn child, while possessed of the extraordinary ability to sense the proximity of good and evil, seemed unable to choose between the two. It was this that caused her to seek advice of Hashem.

Divrei Yosef cites the Gemara in *Sotah* (12a) that states that righteous women were not included in the decree issued on Chavah that childbirth be accompanied with pain. He also cites the Gemara in *Yevamos* (64a) stating that the Matriarchs were barren because Hashem desired their prayers. He explains that Rivkah was confused and uncertain as to how to apply these teachings to her own situation. If she was considered righteous, and therefore she was barren because Hashem desired her prayers, then why was she suffering pain? And if she was not considered righteous, then why had Hashem caused her to be barren? [*Ibn Ezra* adds that Rivkah inquired of other women as to whether the pains she was experiencing were normal. When she was told that they were unusual, she exclaimed, "If so (that my pains are not commonplace ones), why am I thus?"]

The *Brisker Rav* (in *Chidushei HaGriz al HaTorah*) explains Rivkah's question differently. The Gemara in *Berachos* (10a) relates that Chizkiyahu did not marry because he had foreseen through Divine inspiration that his children would be evil. The prophet Yeshayahu rebuked Chizkiyahu for this decision, telling him: "Why do you concern yourself with the hidden workings of Hashem? You must do as you are commanded, and Hashem will do as He sees fit." From this exchange it can be seen that one who knows that his offspring will be wicked is nevertheless required to have children, due to the commandment to father children (*peru u'revu*). However, Rivkah reasoned that since she, as a woman, was not obligated in this mitzvah (see *Yevamos* 65b), she would not be so commanded. Hence, when it became apparent to her that her offspring would be wicked, she exclaimed, "If so, why am I thus?," as if to say, "Why did I pray to have children, if this will be the result?"

MISHNAH OF THE DAY: SHABBOS 6:6

פרשת תולדות

MONDAY
PARASHAS TOLDOS

The following Mishnah lists additional items with which a woman may go out on the Sabbath: יוֹצְאָה בְּסֶלַע שֶׁעַל הַצִּינִית — A woman *may go out* on the Sabbath *with a sela-coin that is* bound *upon a wound* on the sole of her foot.[1] הַבָּנוֹת קְטַנּוֹת יוֹצְאוֹת בְּחוּטִין — *The young girls may go out* on the Sabbath *with threads,* וַאֲפִילוּ בְּקֵיסָמִין — *and even with slivers* שֶׁבְּאָזְנֵיהֶם — *that are* passed through holes *in their ears.*[2] עַרְבִיּוֹת יוֹצְאוֹת רְעוּלוֹת — *Arabian women may go out* on the Sabbath *wrapped* in head-cloths,[3] וּמָדִיּוֹת פְּרוּפוֹת — *and Median women* with their cloaks *fastened* by stones or nuts.[4] וְכָל אָדָם — *And* this is actually true concerning *any person,*[5] אֶלָּא שֶׁדִּבְּרוּ חֲכָמִים בַּהֹוֶה — *however, the Sages spoke of the prevalent* custom.[6]

NOTES

1. As a remedy, embossed *sela*-coins would be bound to wounds — such as calluses or bunions (*Rif*) — that were on the soles of the feet (*Rav* from Gemara 65a).

2. It was customary for girls to pierce their ears when young, although they would not acquire earrings until they were more mature. To keep the holes in their ears from closing, they would insert threads or splinters in place of earrings (*Rav; Rashi*). Although these slivers were not ornamental, nevertheless, since they were worn all the time and never removed, there was no concern that a girl might come to remove and carry them in a public domain (*Rav; Rashi*). Moreover, since they were of minimal value, there was little concern that the girl might come to carry them, should they in fact fall out (*Tiferes Yisrael*).

3. Arabian women customarily appeared in public with their faces veiled, leaving only their eyes exposed. Hence, Jewish women living in Arabia, who would follow the local custom, were permitted to go out into the public domain on the Sabbath while wearing such veils (*Rav; Rashi*). The Mishnah here teaches that a cloth worn in this unusual manner was not treated as a burden, but as a garment; a woman was therefore permitted to go out in this fashion on the Sabbath (*Mishnah Berurah* 303:71).

4. It was the custom among women of Media [a Persian province] to wear cloaks that had short straps attached to one of their upper corners. A stone, nut or coin would be wrapped into the opposite upper corner. The cloak was then fastened by tying the strap around the stone [which functioned as a button of sorts]. Since this was the usual manner of dress in Media, the Jewish women of that land were permitted to wear such cloaks on the Sabbath and were not considered to be carrying the makeshift button (*Rav; Rashi*). [The makeshift button was not considered a burden, but a part of the cloak; it was therefore permissible to go outside wearing it.]

5. Not only are Arabian and Median Jewish women permitted to go out in these manners, but so too may anyone else, provided that such items are accepted in a locale as a normal manner of attire. Otherwise, they are viewed as a burden, and are prohibited outside on the Sabbath (*Ritva*).

6. [The Sages referred to Arabian and Median women only because it was the well-known custom of those women to wear these garments. Since these are legitimate garments, however, even those who usually do not wear them may do so on the Sabbath.]

פרשת תולדות

GEMS FROM THE GEMARA

MONDAY
PARASHAS TOLDOS

The Gemara (65a) questions why our Mishnah specifies that a woman may go out on the Sabbath with a *coin* bound upon the wound on the sole of her foot. Why specifically a coin? If it is because anything hard is beneficial for the wound [since it protects it from thorns and from nails on the road (*Rashi*)], then let her use any other hard material, such as an earthenware shard [which would have the added advantage of not being *muktzeh*] to shield the wound!? Why must she use a coin?

The Gemara then suggests that perhaps a coin is beneficial not because it is hard, but because its silver generates moisture [which promotes healing (*Rashi*)]. This explanation, however, is also deemed insufficient by the Gemara, which asks: If this is so, let her use a smooth silver slug to cover the wound! Why must she use specifically minted coinage?

Rather, suggests the Gemara, perhaps the coin is not beneficial because of its moisture, but because of the image that is embossed upon it. But if this is the case, the Gemara persists, let her use an etched disk of wood to cover the wound?! Why must she use a coin?

The Gemara concludes, in the name of Abaye, that we learn from our Mishnah that only an object combining all these three qualities (i.e., hardness, generates moisture, and has a raised form) is beneficial for this type of wound.

Moreover, since an object with only one or two of these qualities will not heal this wound, it would accordingly be considered a burden, and one would be forbidden to go out with it on the Sabbath. Hence, the Mishnah specifies the use of an embossed *sela*-coin for this wound.

A MUSSAR THOUGHT FOR THE DAY

From the Midrash that tells us of the behavior of Yaakov and Eisav while yet in their mother's womb, we can learn valuable lessons about the service of Hashem.

R' Yerucham Levovitz, the *mashgiach* of Mir, would note that the very facts described in this Midrash seem strange to us. How is it possible, we ask ourselves, that Yaakov should have been able to detect the presence of a *beis midrash* while still an embryo in his mother's womb? Baffled, we shrug this off as just another example of the exalted status of the *Avos*.

But in truth, R' Yerucham would say, this should not be the case. Such

פרשת תולדות
MONDAY
PARASHAS TOLDOS

lack of understanding comes only from the fact that we are so very distant from true perception of things spiritual. We know, for example, that in the physical world there is something called a compass. When one holds a compass in his hand, the needle points unwaveringly to the north, no matter how it is held. It cannot be confused or tricked; as long as it is given freedom to spin, it will unerringly point to the north. Why is this so? It is because there is a force within the compass that is attracted to the north, and will be drawn to it.

What we fail to realize, said R' Yerucham, is that the same is true of *kedushah* as well. Holiness attracts holiness; *kedushah* exerts an attraction that the true *tzaddik* will always feel. Thus, Yaakov, in his holiness even as an embryo, was inexorably drawn to the *kedushah* of the Torah. It is only our lack of perception that makes this phenomenon difficult to comprehend.

Oznaim LaTorah cites a variant text of the Midrash according to which whenever Rivkah would *stand* near the Torah academies, Yaakov would *wriggle* (מְפַרְכֵּס) about and try to exit the womb, and whenever she would *pass* the house of idolatry, Eisav would *run and wriggle* and attempt to exit. From the change in phrasing, *Oznaim LaTorah* derives that Rivkah, in her righteousness, would never linger near idolatrous places; she would merely sometimes *pass* them by. Eisav, realizing that his proximity to these places were fleeting, bestirred himself to *run and wriggle* whenever the opportunity presented itself. When it came to the Torah academies, on the other hand, Rivkah was in no hurry to avoid them, and she would often spend time *standing* in their proximity. Thus, there was no need for Yaakov to *run* and attempt to exit. From this we see that even a righteous person should spend as little time as possible in the proximity of evil. [See further in *A Closer Look at the Siddur*.]

HALACHAH OF THE DAY

Next in the list of thirty-nine forbidden labors of Shabbos, we find the melachah of מְרַקֵּד, *sifting*. This activity was a necessary step in the preparations for the *avodah* that took place in the Mishkan. The flour for the *lechem hapanim*, as well as the various herbs needed for the dyeing of tapestries, had to be sifted in order to remove their impurities prior to their being used.

The *melachah* of sifting may be defined as perfecting a mixture by removing its impurities through the use of specialized utensils designed for this purpose — for example, sifting flour through a sieve. This

פרשת תולדות

MONDAY

PARASHAS TOLDOS

melachah may be distinguished from the previously discussed labors of sorting and winnowing, which also involve separating out parts of mixtures, in that the *melachah* of sifting can be transgressed only through the use of a specialized instrument, whereas sorting may be transgressed by using one's hand, and winnowing is accomplished through the use of wind or other forms of air pressure.

The Biblical prohibition of sifting applies only to items that grow from the ground. Specifically, the desirable part of the mixture must be produce of the earth. The undesirable elements being removed from the mixture, on the other hand, may be comprised of anything at all. Sifting items that do not grow from the ground is forbidden as well, but by Rabbinic decree only.

This *melachah* applies to both edible and inedible items, to solids as well as liquids. [The details of how sifting applies to liquids will be explained further on.]

In order to transgress the Biblical prohibition of sifting, one must sift a mixture that is, at a minimum, equal in volume to a dried fig.

While the classic case of sifting involves the sifting of flour — a useful product — in order to remove from it bits of chaff or bran — a useless waste product — one may transgress this prohibition even through the removal of a useful item from a mixture. As is the case with the *melachah* of sorting, as long as one of the items in the mixture is not desired at the present time, it is seen as waste in relation to the other, desired, element of the mixture. To remove the undesired element through the use of a specialized tool is, therefore, a violation of the *melachah* of sifting.

Generally speaking, a collection of different-size items of a single type are not seen as a mixture, and sifting such a combination would therefore be permissible. However, if the difference in size changes the function of the different items, it is then forbidden to sift the mixture. For example, one may not sift matzah meal in order to remove large chunks of matzah from the meal.

QUESTION OF THE DAY:

To whom did Rivkah turn when she wished to discover the explanation for her unusual pains?

For the answer, see page 112.

A CLOSER LOOK AT THE SIDDUR

פרשת תולדות

MONDAY
PARASHAS TOLDOS

R' *Yissachar Dov of Belz* was once asked: We can readily understand why Eisav wanted to exit Rivkah's womb whenever she neared a house of idolatry; after all, there was no idolatry available in Rivkah's womb. But why did Yaakov wish to leave to study in the academy of Shem? The Gemara tells us (*Niddah* 30b) that while a child is in the womb, he is taught all of the Torah by angels. Why would Yaakov wish to leave this superior setting?

From here, R' Yissachar Dov replied, we can learn a great truth: So great is the danger of having a neighbor like Eisav, that it is worth forgoing the opportunity of learning with an angel to avoid it.

In our *Shacharis* prayers, after the morning blessings, we find two *tefillos* focused on protecting ourselves from the evil influence of wicked people. In the first, we ask Hashem: וְהַרְחִיקֵנוּ מֵאָדָם רָע וּמֵחָבֵר רָע, *Keep us far away from an evil person and from an evil companion*. And in the second we repeat, שֶׁתַּצִּילֵנִי הַיּוֹם וּבְכָל יוֹם . . . מֵאָדָם רָע . . . וּמֵחָבֵר רָע, *[May it be Your Will] that You save me, today and every day . . . from an evil person . . . and from an evil companion*. [These two prayers are almost identical; the principal difference between them is that the first is offered in the plural, as a communal prayer on behalf of all of Israel, while the second is a personal prayer, in which each person asks for specific protection, although he may not have the merit of the congregation to protect him.]

What is the difference between an אָדָם רָע, *evil person*, and a חָבֵר רָע, *evil companion*? R' Shimon Schwab explains that an אָדָם רָע is someone who has sunk to such a low level that he no longer deserves to be called אָדָם. He has become enmeshed in wickedness to the point where his *tzelem Elokim*, his *Godly image* that distinguishes him from all of Hashem's creations, has become lost. Such a person has no redeeming qualities, and certainly is to be avoided.

A חָבֵר רָע, however, has not lost his *tzelem Elokim*; in fact, he might actually seem to be an upstanding individual. But he is an *evil companion* in the sense that association with him is likely to lead to bad things rather then good ones. His *chibbur* — connection — with us is one that is bad, because he will reinforce the Evil Inclination that we already battle, instead of helping to drive it away. We pray that we be spared such associations as well.

[It is noteworthy that after requesting that we be saved from evil companions, we do not ask Hashem to provide us with *good companions* —

פרשת תולדות

MONDAY

PARASHAS TOLDOS

rather, we ask him to *attach us to our good inclination* (וְדַבְּקֵנוּ בְּיֵצֶר הַטּוֹב). It would seem that we possess sufficient good within ourselves to impel us to seek the right associates, if we would but hearken to it. And the job to seek good friends is ours alone, as the Mishnah exhorts in *Avos* (1:6): *Make for yourself a teacher, and acquire for yourself a companion.*]

A TORAH THOUGHT FOR THE DAY

פרשת תולדות

TUESDAY
PARASHAS TOLDOS

וַיִּזְרַע יִצְחָק בָּאָרֶץ הַהִוא
וַיִּמְצָא בַּשָּׁנָה הַהִוא מֵאָה שְׁעָרִים וַיְבָרְכֵהוּ ה׳

And Yitzchak sowed in that land,
and in that year he reaped a hundredfold;
thus had HASHEM blessed him (Bereishis 26:12).

Rashi, quoting the Midrash, explains that Yitzchak realized that he reaped one hundred times as much as the normal harvest should yield because he had estimated the crop prior to actually gathering the produce. Thus, he was able to compare that figure to the amount that he actually brought in when the crop was harvested.

The Midrash (*Bereishis Rabbah* 64:6) asks why Yitzchak would estimate his crops, when the Gemara (*Bava Metzia* 42a) tells us that blessing does not come to a person in an obvious way. [For example, a mound of produce whose size has already been determined will not miraculously increase, making it clear to all that a miracle occurred.] *Rabbeinu Bachya* (in his introduction to *Parashas Ki Sisa*) and *Sfas Emes* (to *Taanis* 8b) explain that the reason for this limitation in Hashem's blessing is because Hashem, as part of His overall desire to conceal Himself within the laws of nature, does not want to perform an overt miracle. It is only when the person does not realize that Hashem's direct hand is at work that he is able to merit Divine assistance. Taking this into account, asks the Midrash, why did Yitzchak estimate how much produce was expected to grow in his field? By estimating the yield of his harvest, Yitzchak seemingly *decreased* the chance that Hashem would bless the harvest!

In answer to this question, the Midrash states that Yitzchak's only motive in estimating his produce was in order to know how much *maaser* he would be required to give to the poor. *Chasam Sofer* explains that the reason Yitzchak estimated his crop instead of actually counting the produce after it was in his storehouses was because, acting beyond the letter of the law, he wished to tithe even grains exempt from *maaser*, such as produce that was eaten by his workers or animals prior to the stage where the grain would become obligated in *maaser* (for further discussion, see *A Taste of Lomdus*). Since counting his finished crop would not include these grains, Yitzchak estimated his yield, in order to tithe the entirety of his field.

Yefei To'ar (see also *Matnas Kehunah* to *Bamidbar Rabbah* 12:11) points out that the Midrash's explanation of Yitzchak's motive in estimating his

פרשת תולדות

TUESDAY

PARASHAS TOLDOS

field's production also explains how it was able to miraculously produce one hundred times beyond what was expected, despite the Gemara's statement that overt blessing will not come after something has already been counted. Estimating in order to fulfill the mitzvah of *maaser* is the one exception to this rule. The Gemara (*Taanis* 9a) notes that when the Torah (*Devarim* 14:22) commands one to give *maaser,* it uses the term עַשֵּׂר תְּעַשֵּׂר, *Tithe, you shall tithe.* The Gemara expounds this double usage to teach: עַשֵּׂר בִּשְׁבִיל שֶׁתִּתְעַשֵּׁר, *Tithe so that you will become wealthy!* Thus, the Torah specifically guarantees that a person who properly gives *maaser* will prosper. This guarantee overrides any other considerations, such as Hashem's general desire to conceal His direct hand by withholding overt blessing, which may limit a person's affluence. [See *A Mussar Thought for the Day* for further explanation of the connection between *maaser* and prosperity.] Understanding this, Yitzchak was not afraid to estimate his produce, for he realized that he would not lose by giving *maaser,* as was borne out by his ultimate, hundredfold, blessing.

MISHNAH OF THE DAY: SHABBOS 6:7

In the previous Mishnah we learned that women may go out on the Sabbath with their cloaks fastened over their shoulders with makeshift buttons. The following Mishnah considers various unconventional sorts of fasteners that may be used for this purpose:

פּוֹרֶפֶת עַל הָאֶבֶן — A woman *may fasten* her cloak *upon a stone,* וְעַל הָאֱגוֹז — *or upon a nut,* וְעַל הַמַּטְבֵּעַ — *or upon a coin* on the Sabbath,[1] וּבִלְבַד שֶׁלֹּא תִּפְרוֹף לְכַתְּחִלָּה בְּשַׁבָּת — *but only if she does not initially fasten* with it *on the Sabbath.*[2]

—— NOTES ——

1. A woman may fasten her cloak around her neck by looping the straps of her cloak around any of these makeshift buttons. As we saw in the previous Mishnah, since the use of such makeshift buttons was normal and common, they are not considered a burden, but rather a part of the cloak; it is thus permissible go outside on the Sabbath while wearing them.

2. This qualification applies only to the case in which a coin serves as a button. The other unconventional fasteners listed here may be fastened on the Sabbath itself, but a coin may not. A cloak with a coin must be fastened from before the onset of the Sabbath (*Rav* from Gemara 65b). [This difference emerges from the laws of *muktzeh* — items that are set apart from use on the Sabbath, and therefore may not be handled on the Sabbath. Although a stone is *muktzeh* as well, if it is designated before the

פרשת תולדות
TUESDAY
PARASHAS TOLDOS

--- NOTES ---
Sabbath for Sabbath use as a button, it is not *muktzeh* (*Rashi*). This is because a stone has no intrinsic use or value. Hence, once the stone is designated as a fastener, it *becomes,* for all intents and purposes, a button, and consequently is no longer *muktzeh,* and it may be fastened and unfastened on the Sabbath at will. A coin, on the other hand, possesses an intrinsic value and use. Hence, since its value as a coin exceeds its value as a button, it will likely revert to being used as a coin, even if it is currently designated for use as a button. Therefore, it continues to be treated as currency, and it remains *muktzeh* even if used as a button.]

GEMS FROM THE GEMARA

The Gemara (65b) presents Abaye's inquiry: May a woman in a private domain employ a subterfuge and fasten her cloak on a nut in order to take it out to her young son in a public domain on the Sabbath? The question is whether, since the woman's purpose is obviously to transport the nut to her son, this act gives the *appearance* of a violation of the prohibition against transporting objects from one domain to another on the Sabbath (see *Mishnah Berurah* 303:76), thus leading people to treat this prohibition lightly. Abaye is therefore unsure whether one is permitted to perform this action.

The Gemara notes that this inquiry is relevant both according to R' Meir and according to R' Yose (see Mishnah below, 16:4). Their dispute concerns the Rabbinic decree limiting the property one is permitted to carry into a courtyard in the event of a fire. Although it is generally permissible to carry into a courtyard, the Rabbis feared that if one were permitted to rescue all one's belongings, in the tumult and confusion of doing so he might come to extinguish the fire. They therefore limited rescue to certain items essential to one's existence over the Sabbath.

With regard to rescuing clothing, however, R' Meir holds that one may don *any* number of garments and wear them into a courtyard to save them from a fire. This is because the requirement that the clothing be worn, not carried, will help him to remember that it is the Sabbath, and thus will keep him from extinguishing the fire. R' Yose, on the other hand, forbids one to don more than a normal complement of clothing.

The Gemara elaborates: According to R' Meir, perhaps it is only in the case of a fire that a subterfuge is permitted, since, if we do not permit him to wear the clothing outside, he may come to extinguish the fire so as not to lose his belongings. Here (regarding taking a nut outside for a

פרשת תולדות

TUESDAY

PARASHAS TOLDOS

child), on the other hand, if we do not permit her to employ a subterfuge, she will not come to take it out illegally, since it is not of vital importance that the boy receive the nut.

On the other hand, perhaps, even according to R' Yose, who rules that in the event of a fire one may not employ the subterfuge of donning many articles of clothing, here it is permissible to employ the subterfuge to do so. For in the case of the fire, since donning many articles of clothing is a method commonly used to transport clothing, the extra garments are regarded as a burden. Therefore, they may not be worn into a public domain, lest one mistakenly construe permission to do so as general permission to transport items on the Sabbath. Here, on the other hand, tying things into one's clothing is not a common method of transporting articles, and the nut cannot be regarded as a burden. Hence, even R' Yose might agree that one is permitted to fasten one's cloak on a nut in order to take it out on the Sabbath.

The Gemara leaves the inquiry unresolved. For the halachic ruling, see *Orach Chaim* 303:23.

A MUSSAR THOUGHT FOR THE DAY

The Gemara (*Bava Basra* 10a) compares one who does not give *tzedakah* to an idol worshiper. R' Shlomo Wolbe (*HaMitzvos HaMishkolos,* Ch. 3) explains this comparison in the following manner. Most, if not all, misers, he says, do not simply *choose* not to part with their money; they are actually *unable* to part with it. Amassing and saving their wealth has become an obsession with them, and they can no longer conceive of giving away their hard-earned money.

This, of course, is at odds with the Torah concept of *tzedakah.* The root of the mitzvah of *tzedakah* is the understanding that Hashem may give wealth to a person so he will distribute it to others who are less fortunate, and not hoard it for his own use. Proper disposition of wealth — how, when, and for what it is to be used — is taught to us by halachah. But one who does not give *tzedakah* denies Hashem's role in the creation of his wealth. Thus, he is in a sense like an idol worshiper, who refuses to admit that Hashem is the ultimate authority in his life, and attributes powers to other entities instead. And just as the idolater is obsessively devoted to his deity, the miser becomes excessively attached to his money, and cannot be budged.

פרשת תולדות

TUESDAY

PARASHAS TOLDOS

On the other hand, when one *does* give *tzedakah* such as *maaser* properly, in addition to his fulfilling one of the Torah's mitzvos, the act helps transform the person's entire lifestyle into one that is more focused on serving Hashem.

R' Wolbe points out that *Rosh* as well, in his mussar classic *Orchos Chaim* (§29), reminds man: וְאַל תָּשִׂים זָהָב כִּסְלֶךָ כִּי זֹאת תְּחִילַת עֲבוֹדָה זָרָה וּפַזֵּר מָמוֹנְךָ כַּאֲשֶׁר הוּא רְצוֹנוֹ — *Do not make gold your infatuation, for that is the beginning of idol worship. Instead, distribute your money in accordance with Hashem's will.* Giving *tzedakah* serves as a powerful means of keeping a person focused on Hashem and His will.

R' Wolbe illustrates further how distributing one's money in accordance with Hashem's will helps a person in his service of Hashem. He explains that giving *tzedakah* clearly reminds a person that enjoying the world with all the items that money can buy is not the ultimate purpose of life. Freely distributing money to the poor or to Torah institutions shows that money — like everything in this world — is only a means, given to us to be used to serve Hashem.

Perhaps even more importantly, giving away money because the Torah instructed one to do so changes the value system that a person often mistakenly uses to examine the world. When contemplating what he is doing — paying money and getting nothing tangible in return — a giver will develop the sensitivity to realize that money is not the final arbiter of importance, and that the true assessment of how much something is worth often has little to do with its cost.

A third benefit of giving *tzedakah* is that it serves to strengthen our *emunah,* awareness of Hashem. Giving away money that could be used for so many things shows that, in a very real way, a person understands that it is not money or hard work that is bringing him prosperity, but Hashem's kindness.

If one gives *tzedakah* and takes these lessons to heart, they can ultimately change the way he will view his entire life. The *Chofetz Chaim,* in his work *Ahavas Chesed,* points out that it is for this reason that one who gives *maaser* is rewarded with wealth. A person whose only motivation is to better serve Hashem in any way possible will naturally be given the resources to allow him to carry out these goals.

QUESTION OF THE DAY:

Where else in the Torah do we find the Avos speaking of tithing produce?

For the answer, see page 112.

פרשת תולדות

HALACHAH OF THE DAY

TUESDAY
PARASHAS TOLDOS

The Biblical prohibition of *sifting* applies only to a substance that cannot be used prior to removing the undesirable elements. If, however, a substance contains some impurities but would be used by most people anyway, one is permitted to remove the impurities on the Sabbath. This is because — since the substance is usable as is — the impurities are not regarded as a separate element of the mixture, but rather as an integral part of the main substance. This being the case, there is no mixture present for one to be liable for *sifting*.

If the level of impurities is not high enough to render the item in question unusable, but is great enough so that most people would not find it satisfactory under normal circumstances, it is forbidden by Rabbinic decree to sift the mixture.

As mentioned previously, while the term "sifting" leads one to think primarily of solids, this *melachah* applies to liquids as well. Accordingly, one may not strain impurities from a liquid with an implement designed for this purpose. Once again, as with solids, the extent of the prohibition against straining liquids varies depending on the level of impurities present in the liquid.

A liquid whose impurities are so minimal that most people would drink it unstrained may be filtered on Shabbos even through the use of specialized straining implements. As we explained in our discussions of *sorting*, these impurities are not seen as separate elements mixed into the liquid, but rather as an integral part of the liquid, which may be removed. It is therefore permissible to use a water filter on Shabbos to filter tap water in order to remove minor impurities. Since the tap water is essentially drinkable as is, there is no prohibition against straining it with a filter.

As noted with respect to the *melachah* of *sorting*, the above rule applies to people with average sensitivities. Extremely finicky people, to whom the presence of any impurity is intolerable, may not filter even such almost-pure water on Shabbos.

If the level of impurities in the liquid is not high enough to cause it to be undrinkable, but it is high enough to prevent *most* people from drinking it under normal circumstances, one is forbidden by Rabbinic law to strain it with a filter or strainer. The *poskim* disagree as to whether it is permissible to filter liquids of this quality through a makeshift filter, such as a piece of fabric or an article of clothing. Some *poskim* hold that this may be done provided that the filtering is also done in an unusual manner. However, other *poskim* maintain that even this is forbidden. It is preferable to follow the more stringent opinion in this matter.

If the level of impurities present in the liquid is so high as to render the liquid undrinkable, one is then Biblically forbidden to filter the liquid under all circumstances.

פרשת
תולדות

**TUESDAY
PARASHAS
TOLDOS**

A CLOSER LOOK AT THE SIDDUR

Perhaps not surprisingly, the obligation of *maaser,* or mention of any *tzedakah* that a person gives, is hardly found in the *siddur. Tefillah,* when we speak directly to Hashem by concentrating on our praises of Him and our needs and desires, is not the place to describe interpersonal obligations or boast about how well we fulfill them. However, included in many *siddurim* are instructions and the appropriate blessings for separating *terumah* and *maaser* from fruits grown in Eretz Yisrael, as well as for *hafrashas challah,* the separation of a piece of dough when baking bread. The Torah directs that *terumah* and *challah* be given to a Kohen, and *maaser* to a Levi. Since it is required that these holy gifts be eaten while one is in a state of ritual purity, Kohanim and Leviim are precluded from receiving them nowadays; therefore, when the appropriate amount is separated as required, since it cannot be eaten it is disposed of in a respectful manner instead.

Maharal (*Be'er HaGolah* 2:7) explains that separating a prescribed portion of a person's produce — 10 percent in the case of *maaser,* 2½ percent for *terumah,* and a *kezayis*-size piece for *challah* — serves more than just helping to sustain the Kohen or Levi who receives it; rather, the deeper purpose of these gifts is to show appreciation to Hashem for the food that He has given us. Separating part of a person's produce shows that the farmer or baker, although he greatly appreciates the value of these items that he has worked so hard to cultivate and desires very much to enjoy his newly acquired wealth, also understands where the money really comes from. Wishing to show this appreciation, he gives some of it back, as it were, to Hashem. *Maharal* points out that the true purpose of agricultural charities is for one to show gratitude for the rest of the crop, and this perspective is evident from the law stating that a person who renders his entire field *terumah* or *maaser* does not accomplish anything. The Torah prescribes that only *part* of a person's crops be given away in fulfillment of these mitzvos. Hashem, of course, does not need this person's money — He has no more use for the entire field than He has for the small percentage that He directed one to give — and He is certainly able to provide for the Kohen and Levi without assistance. Rather, the purpose of the priestly gifts is for the landowner to give back to Hashem from what he has received from Him. Donating the whole field

פרשת תולדות

TUESDAY

PARASHAS TOLDOS

to the Kohen and being left with nothing, however, does not show that a person appreciates what Hashem has given him; on the contrary, by keeping none of it for himself and his own personal use, this person is showing that he does not wish to receive Hashem's gifts at all.

[*Maharal* also offers another reason why the priestly gifts of *terumah, maaser* and *challah* specifically enjoin a person to give only part of his produce: A person who gives his entire crop to the Kohen or Levi does not show an appreciation for the fact that Hashem's emissaries deserve the best, or even the dignity of receiving a chosen portion. The small percent that a person is mandated to give is supposed to be from the best part of the crop. Even if this is not the case, and an ordinary part is given, the very act of selecting a portion to use as a priestly gift is itself respectful. Neither of these objectives are fulfilled, however, when the entire field is given.]

A TASTE OF LOMDUS

As we learned above (see *A Torah Thought for the Day*), *Rashi* (*Bereishis* 26:12) tells us that Yitzchak estimated how much the land would normally yield, and it produced one hundred times as much. *Rashi* states further that this estimation was performed in order to calculate how much *maaser* Yitzchak would need to take from the crop.

Rambam (*Hilchos Melachim* 9:1) observes that many of the people mentioned in the earlier *parshiyos* of the Torah, such as Adam, Noach, and the *Avos*, instituted the performance of some of the Torah's mitzvos even before the Torah was given. *Rambam* understands the above verse in the way *Rashi* and the Midrash explain it, and therefore lists *maaser*, tithes of produce, as one of the mitzvos introduced by Yitzchak.

The Gemara (*Bava Metzia* 88b) explains that the Torah commands us to separate *maaser* only from produce that we grow ourselves. *Chazal* derive this ruling from a verse in *Devarim* (14:22): עַשֵּׂר תְּעַשֵּׂר אֵת כָּל־תְּבוּאַת זַרְעֶךָ, *You shall tithe the entire crop of **your** planting*. Rabbinic law, however, extends the obligation of *maaser* to food that one purchases as well. *Rabbeinu Tam* (cited in *Tosafos* to *Bava Metzia* 88a) explains that if a farmer sells his crops before tithing them and then buys them back, they are still considered זַרְעֶךָ, ***your** planting*, and would thus be subject to the *maaser* obligation on a Biblical level.

Minchas Chinuch (395:8) asks the following question: If the customer in this transaction tithed the produce to fulfill his *Rabbinic* obligation, would the farmer have to separate *maaser* a second time, after buying back his crops, in order to fulfill the *Biblical* commandment? *Zichron Shmuel* (*Michtavim* §2) points out that nothing in the *Shulchan Aruch* or in any other classic halachic text even suggests such a ruling. From the halachic literature, it seems clear that a farmer who buys back his crops after the original purchaser tithed them would *not* need to separate *maaser* again. But how can this be true? How can carrying out a mitzvah on a *Rabbinic* level absolve a person from his *Biblical* obligation?

Minchas Chinuch, answering his own question, explains that even though the Torah did not include purchased fruits in the *commandment* to take *maaser* from זַרְעֶךָ, *your* planting, nevertheless, they are not precluded from the *possibility* of being tithed. Since these crops may potentially be resold to the farmer, possibly obligating them in *maaser* in the future, they are already included within the guidelines of produce that is allowed to be tithed. Although the crop can in no way be viewed as currently subject to a Biblical *maaser* obligation, the possibility that a Biblical *maaser* obligation will exist in the future allows this obligation to be fulfilled, albeit voluntarily, through tithing even now. Thus, when the customer separates the Rabbinic *maaser*, this effectively fulfills the farmer's Biblical mitzvah, exempting the farmer if and when he buys back his produce in the future.

Minchas Chinuch cites *Pnei Yehoshua* (*Beitzah* 13a) and *Rash* (*Terumos* 1:6) to demonstrate that this legal concept — that one can separate voluntary *maaser* now to exempt himself retroactively when the fruit becomes subject to a Biblical *maaser* obligation — applies to a number of different *maaser* situations. For example, one needs to take *maaser* only from processed produce that has reached the stage of כַּדָּגָן מִן־הַגֹּרֶן, *like grain from the threshing floor* (*Bamidbar* 18:27). [This stage is identified as מֵרוּחַ, smoothing, which occurs when the pile of harvested grain is smoothed down.] Nonetheless, a farmer who tithes his crops while they are still in the field does not have to tithe them a second time when he takes them from the threshing floor. The fact that the commandment to take *maaser* will possibly apply to this produce in the future means that the farmer can take *maaser* now, and thereby have already fulfilled his obligation when it becomes activated at a later date. Even though the mitzvah has not yet taken effect, the future possibility of a *maaser* obligation makes the *maaser* removed from these crops legitimate, to the extent that one may eat the remaining fruit, even after the pile of grain is smoothed down, without taking any new *maaser*.

פרשת תולדות

A TORAH THOUGHT FOR THE DAY

WEDNESDAY
PARASHAS TOLDOS

הַקֹּל קוֹל יַעֲקֹב וְהַיָּדַיִם יְדֵי עֵשָׂו
*The voice is the voice of Yaakov,
but the hands are the hands of Eisav (Bereishis 27:22).*

The simple meaning of this verse is that it describes Yitzchak's reaction when he felt the animal skins that were covering Yaakov's arms, having grown suspicious of the refined speech that was used by Yaakov (see v. 20 — *because* HASHEM *your God so arranged it for me*), which was out of character for Eisav. The hairy animal skins convinced Yitzchak that he was indeed speaking to Eisav, and thus he commented, "Although the speech is that of Yaakov, the hands are those of Eisav."

[*Sforno* notes that there really is a great distinction in feel between animal skins and hairy human arms; he suggests that either the skins were specially prepared, or Yitzchak's sense of touch had deteriorated with age.]

Sfas Emes sees in this verse Yitzchak's description of the respective attributes of his two sons. Spirituality is represented by קוֹל, *voice*, for voice is man's means of articulating the wisdom of Torah and the words of prayer. Material ascendancy, however, is exemplified by יָדַיִם, *hands*, for it is the labor of one's hands that brings forth sustenance from the world.

Many commentators explain that it was Yitzchak's original intent for Eisav to be the master of the physical world, while Yaakov would devote himself completely to the spiritual, with Eisav's consent and support. However, Hashem knew that Eisav would not uphold his end of this bargain, and He arranged matters so that Yaakov would receive the physical blessings as well. But even after Yaakov received the blessings, Eisav was still granted superiority during times when Yaakov was undeserving.

This too, says *Sfas Emes,* is hinted at in our verse. Yaakov's *only* power lies in his spirituality, his voice; he does not possess the power of the hands. Yaakov can use his Torah and prayer to dominate Eisav and attain dominion over even the material world — through spiritual means. Indeed, the Midrash states that when Yaakov's voice is stilled (the word הַקֹּל in the verse is spelled deficiently, without the *vav,* so it can be read as הַקַּל, which means *when it grows weak*), Eisav's hands gain in strength, and Yaakov is subservient to his mightier brother. But when Yaakov's voice is strong, no hands are necessary. When Yaakov orders his life around the realization that it is Hashem Who controls all, he is truly invincible.

[In stating above that Yitzchak's suspicions were aroused by *the refined speech* used by Yaakov, we are following the view of *Rashi*. This answers the obvious question that would otherwise be asked: If Yaakov had gone to such lengths to disguise himself, why did he not disguise his voice as well? See, however, *Ramban,* who states (in v. 12) that Yaakov and Eisav had similar voices, and it was only the combination of factors — Yaakov's speedy return, his use of Hashem's Name, *and the slightly different voice* — that prompted Yitzchak to check Yitzchak's arms. For a different approach, see *A Mussar Thought for the Day.*]

MISHNAH OF THE DAY: SHABBOS 6:8

The following Mishnah considers several laws that concern prosthetic devices:

הַקִּיטֵּעַ יוֹצֵא בְּקַב שֶׁלּוֹ — *An amputee may go out* on the Sabbath *with his wooden foot;* דִּבְרֵי רַבִּי מֵאִיר — *these are the words of R' Meir.* [1] וְרַבִּי יוֹסֵי אוֹסֵר — *But R' Yose prohibits* an amputee from going out with his wooden foot.[2] וְאִם יֵשׁ לוֹ בֵּית קִבּוּל כְּתִיתִין טָמֵא — *And if* the wooden foot *possesses a receptacle for rags, it is susceptible to* contamination with *tumah.* [3]

——————————— NOTES ———————————

1. R' Meir here refers to an artificial foot constructed from wood, into which the amputee's stump fits. According to R' Meir, even if the amputee does not use this wooden foot for support, he may still go out with it on the Sabbath, since it is considered his shoe (*Rav; Rashi*).

2. R' Yose holds that only shoes made of leather are considered normal footwear. A shoe made of wood is not a typical shoe, and is therefore classified not as a garment, but as a burden, whose transport is prohibited on the Sabbath. Accordingly, an amputee's wooden foot is considered a burden, and he may not go out with it on the Sabbath. Moreover, even if an amputee wears this foot to conceal his infirmity, it is not considered an ornament, since the general public would not utilize this item for ornamental wear (*Rav; Rashi; Tos. Yom Tov*).

3. If the cavity to which the amputee inserts his leg was cut large enough to provide space for a cushion of soft rags, the wooden foot is susceptible to contamination with *tumah* transmitted by contact. However, if the cavity is only large enough to contain the stump of the amputee's lower leg, but has no extra space for rags, the wooden foot will not become *tamei.* This is because wooden utensils do not acquire *tumah* through contact unless they can be classified as כְּלֵי קִבּוּל, *receptacles* that are made to convey items placed into them. Hence, a wooden foot that serves as a receptacle for rags is susceptible to *tumah.* On the other hand, a wooden foot that was not large enough for a lining of rags is not susceptible to *tumah.* Even though the amputee's stump is in the cavity, the cavity is not the stump's receptacle, as the wooden leg does not serve to convey the stump; on the contrary, the wooden foot is itself conveyed by the amputee's leg, to which it is attached (*Rav; Rashi; Ritva*).

WEDNESDAY
PARASHAS TOLDOS

Three laws concerning another type of amputee: סְמוֹכוֹת שֶׁלּוֹ — *The* leather *supports* for the lower legs of a double amputee טְמֵאִין מִדְרָס — *are susceptible to contamination with the* **tumah** *of* **midras**,[4] וְיוֹצְאִין בָּהֶן בַּשַּׁבָּת — *and one may go out with them on the Sabbath,*[5] וְנִכְנָסִין בָּהֶן בָּעֲזָרָה — *and one may enter the Temple Courtyard with them* on.[6]

Three laws concerning a third type of amputee: כִּסֵּא וְסָמוֹכוֹת שֶׁלּוֹ — *The chair and* the leg *supports of* one whose lower legs have atrophied טְמֵאִין מִדְרָס — *are susceptible to* contamination with the **tumah** *of* **midras**,[7] וְאֵין יוֹצְאִין בָּהֶן בְּשַׁבָּת — *and one may not go out with them on the Sabbath,*[8] וְאֵין נִכְנָסִין בָּהֶן

--- NOTES ---

4. A double amputee cannot walk with crutches, and therefore must propel himself while in a kneeling position, using his knees and lower legs. A person who is compelled to propel himself in this manner often fashions leather pads for himself to protect his shins and knees. Since these pads are made to support one's weight, they are susceptible to *tumas midras* (literally, *treading*), a *tumah* that is imparted to an object when one who is *tamei* as the result of a bodily emission [i.e., a *zav, zavah* or *niddah*] rests his or her weight upon it, whether by sitting, lying, standing or leaning (*Rav; Rashi*). [Not every object can become *tamei* in this manner — rather, it must be an object whose intended use is to support the weight of a human being. Since the pads of a double amputee are intended for support, they are susceptible to *tumas midras* (*Rav; Rashi*).]

5. Since this amputee cannot propel himself at all without these pads, they are treated as ornaments, not as burdens (*Rav; Rashi*).

6. It is forbidden to wear shoes on the Temple Mount, and certainly in the Temple Courtyard (see *Berachos* 9:5). Our Mishnah teaches that although the double amputee's pads function somewhat as shoes, they nevertheless may be worn into the Temple Courtyard. This is because footwear is not regarded as a shoe unless it is worn at the end of one's limb [i.e., upon one's foot, or at the end of an amputee's stump]. These pads, however, are affixed to both the amputee's shins and his knees, and run along the length of the amputee's legs. Therefore, they are not regarded as shoes, and may be worn into the Temple (*Rav; Rashi*).

7. A person whose lower leg muscles and tendons have atrophied cannot even walk on his knees and lower legs. A person who is handicapped in this manner generally propels himself by means of a low chair strapped onto him from behind. He holds short bench-like crutches in his hands, and, using these crutches, pushes himself up and forward, coming to rest again in a sitting position. Since in the action of pushing forward, his legs will briefly support his weight, his feet (or stumps) are protected in wooden or leather supports. Since the chair and the leg supports are used to support the handicapped person's weight, they are susceptible to *tumas midras* (*Rav; Rashi*).

8. Since the leg supports are not this person's primary means of locomotion, they often are not attached very well. There is therefore a good chance that they might fall off in the street and that he might come to carry them in a public domain; hence, they may not be worn on the Sabbath (*Rav; Rashi*).

בָּעֲזָרָה — **and one may not enter the Temple Courtyard with them.** [9]

The Mishnah now presents two laws concerning masks:

אַנְקַטְמִין טְהוֹרִין וְאֵין יוֹצְאִין בָּהֶן — **Masks are not susceptible to** contamination with **tumah, and one may not go out with them** on the Sabbath.[10]

WEDNESDAY
PARASHAS TOLDOS

---— NOTES ———

9. Since these leg supports are worn upon the feet (or at the tip of the stumps), they are regarded as shoes, and therefore may not be worn into the Temple (*Rav; Rashi*). [The chair, however, is obviously not considered a shoe.]

10. The Gemara (66b) offers three opinions regarding the translation of אַנְקַטְמִין. These three translations themselves are in turn subject to different definitions. Our translation is the one used by *Rav* and *Rashi* to the Mishnah, and it refers to masks used to frighten children. Such masks are not considered useful utensils, and hence are not susceptible to *tumah* (*Rav; Rashi*). [Moreover, since a mask is not an ornament, adornment or garment, it may not be borne outside in a public domain.]

GEMS FROM THE GEMARA

R' Akiva, in a Baraisa cited by the Gemara (66a), rules that a sandal made of straw that is worn by a seller of plaster (plaster sellers wore these straw sandals over their leather shoes to prevent the plaster from burning the shoes) has the legal status of a shoe. Hence, it is susceptible to contamination with the *tumah* of *midras,* it may be used for the *chalitzah* ceremony, and one may go out wearing it on the Sabbath. The Sages, however (also cited in the Baraisa), disagree. They maintain that since it is not common practice to use straw for footwear, a sandal made of straw is not legally considered a shoe. Therefore, a straw sandal is not susceptible to *tumas midras,* is not suitable for *chalitzah,* and is considered a burden and therefore may not be worn out on the Sabbath.

The Gemara notes that the Sages seem to contradict themselves, as a Mishnah in *Eduyos* (2:8) apparently states that the Sages *agree* with R' Akiva! To resolve this contradiction, Rav Huna suggests that "the Sages" mentioned in *Eduyos* are, in fact, R' Meir, who holds in our Mishnah that one may go out on the Sabbath with a wooden foot — i.e., that even a shoe made of material that is not commonly used for footwear is accorded legal status as a shoe. He therefore agrees with R' Akiva that although straw is not commonly used for footwear, nevertheless, a sandal made of straw is treated as a shoe.

WEDNESDAY

PARASHAS TOLDOS

On the other hand, "the Sages" in the Baraisa who disagree with R' Akiva are R' Yose, who holds in our Mishnah that one may *not* go out on the Sabbath with a wooden foot — i.e., that a shoe that is not crafted of leather is not accorded the legal status of a shoe. Likewise, a sandal made of straw is also not treated as a shoe.

[The Gemara subsequently asks: Since a plaster seller's sandal is not made for walking, but only to protect his shoe from being burned by the plaster, why is it not subject to the law stated in the Gemara (59a) that the *tumah* of *midras* is limited to objects whose function is to support the weight of a human being? Although the plaster seller certainly rests his weight upon this sandal, that is not the reason he wears it — he simply wishes to avoid ruining his shoes! Rav Acha bar Rav Ulla answers that the sandal is susceptible to the *tumah* of *midras* because even after finishing his work, the plaster seller often continues walking in the straw shoes until he reaches his home. They are therefore considered to possess the function of bearing weight, and are therefore susceptible to the *tumah* of *midras*.]

A MUSSAR THOUGHT FOR THE DAY

When Yaakov went to Yitzchak to receive the blessings he had purchased from Eisav, he disguised his arms so that if Yitzchak should attempt to feel him and ascertain if he was indeed Eisav (which actually occurred), he would be able to pass for his brother. Yet, Yaakov seemingly did nothing to change his speech or his speech patterns — and it is clear that this is what aroused Yitzchak's suspicions (see above, *A Torah Thought for the Day*). Many commentators ask: Why did Yaakov not make an attempt to mimic Eisav's way of speech, so that Yitzchak's suspicions would not be aroused?

The masters of *mussar* answer that Yaakov did not change his speech to mimic that of Eisav because *he was unable to do so.* When it came to changing his *outward* appearance, Yaakov could imitate Eisav successfully. But to twist that which would come forth from his mouth and to speak coarsely, even for a brief period of time, was beyond his ability.

Beis HaLevi and *Minchas Yehudah* take a completely different approach. They suggest that Eisav, suspecting that Yaakov might try to come and receive the blessings, had arranged with his father that when he would come to Yitzchak for the blessings, *he would speak in the manner of Yaakov.* In this way, Eisav sought to ensure that Yaakov would be unable to trick Yitzchak; for surely if Yaakov would come to impersonate Eisav, he would use Eisav's mannerisms! But the stratagem backfired. Yaakov realized that Eisav would employ such a strategy; thus, he came and did *not* imitate Eisav's voice, whereupon Yitzchak declared with satisfaction, "The voice is the voice of Yaakov!," and gave Yaakov the blessings. And when Yitzchak found out the truth, he declared to Eisav, "Your brother has come with his wisdom (see *Targum*), divined your strategy, and taken the blessings."

From this, too, we can learn a great lesson. One can plot and plan, make all sorts of calculations and analyses. On the surface, it would seem that such preparation is essential to the success of any endeavor. But this is not the case. The best-laid plans of man will succeed only if Hashem wishes it to be so. Thus, when one wishes to ensure that his plans meet with success, he has only to ascertain what it is that Hashem wills to happen — for that is what will ultimately ensue.

HALACHAH OF THE DAY

The prohibition against filtering liquids applies only where the purpose of the filtering is to perfect the liquid in preparation for its use. One is, however, permitted to filter any liquid while in the act of drinking it. For example, it is permissible to place a straining cloth over the mouth of a cup while one is drinking, in order to ensure that any impurities found in the liquid will remain in the cup and not enter the mouth. Similarly, one may drink from a cup whose mouthpiece has small holes that act as a strainer during the process of drinking.

The *melachah* of *sifting* does not apply to large solid objects that are in a liquid. Since these items are clearly visible and distinct in the water, they are not seen as being halachically "mixed" into the water. As there is no mixture present, it is not possible for one to be liable for sifting. An application of this rule would be a pitcher of iced tea containing slices of lemon. Since the slices of lemon are clearly distinct from the iced tea, one would be permitted to pour the iced tea through a pitcher with a slotted spout even though such a spout is intended for the purpose of "sifting" out any larger objects found in the liquid.

Another manifestation of this rule would be large fruits sitting in

פרשת תולדות

WEDNESDAY

PARASHAS TOLDOS

water. Since the fruits are clearly distinct from the liquid, it is permissible to pour the liquid through a strainer in order to separate the liquid from the fruits.

The prohibition against *sifting* does not apply in cases where both elements of the mixture will be discarded. For example, one may pour a mixture of solids and liquids down a sink drain even though the solids will be caught in the strainer of the drain. Since the entire mixture is being discarded, there is no selection taking place, and this is therefore not considered an act of *sifting*.

This concludes our discussion of the *melachah* of *sifting*.

A CLOSER LOOK AT THE SIDDUR

In *A Mussar Thought for the Day*, we noted that all of man's machinations and plans come to naught when they are at odds with the will of Hashem. In the prayer of *Yehi Chevod*, which is said during *Pesukei D'Zimrah*, we cite a verse from *Mishlei* (19:21) that expresses this thought succinctly: רַבּוֹת מַחֲשָׁבוֹת בְּלֶב־אִישׁ וַעֲצַת ה׳ הִיא תָקוּם, *Many are the thoughts in the heart of man, but the Will of Hashem, it will endure.*

Clearly, however, Shlomo HaMelech does not mean simply to teach us that when Hashem's Will and man's wishes are in conflict, Hashem's Will will triumph. That goes without saying. *Ralbag* (to *Mishlei* ibid.) finds a deeper meaning in the verse. No matter what attempts a person makes to avoid what Hashem has decreed for him, they will all be fruitless. In the end, it will be the very plans that he makes which will be the Divine workings to ensure that Hashem's Will is fulfilled. Thus, we find that Eisav arranged with Yitzchak that he would disguise his voice when coming to receive the blessings (see *A Mussar Thought for the Day*), and it was exactly this that allowed Yaakov to fool Yitzchak. [This interpretation is hinted at by the wording of the verse, which does not state simply *the Will of Hashem will endure*, but rather *"it" will endure*. That is, even the machinations of man to the contrary will be employed by Hashem to play a role in the outcome that He wishes to bring about.]

The Gemara in *Succah* (53a) tells us that Shlomo HaMelech experienced this himself. Once, he was told by the Angel of Death that two members of his court were marked for imminent death, but it was unable to kill them. Shlomo immediately dispatched the pair to the city

WEDNESDAY

PARASHAS TOLDOS

of Luz, which was a place where the Angel of Death had no power (see *Sotah* 46b). However, as they came close to the gates of the city of Luz, they died before entering the city. The very next day, Shlomo found the Angel of Death rejoicing. When he inquired as to why, he was told: "To the very place where I had power over them (at the gates outside Luz), you sent them for me!" Immediately, Shlomo declared: "A person's feet are his guarantors: To where he is summoned [by Heaven], there they will lead him."

Rabbeinu Bachya sees in this prayer a warning to man not to rely overmuch on his intellect or industry while planning his days. Many are the thoughts that a man will have regarding how to achieve his goals; but it is only the scheme that *God* intends that will actually prosper. *Sfas Emes* (*Vayeishev* 5643) notes further that this applies to the spiritual as well as the physical. Even the service of Hashem that a person attempts (such as Torah study) will not succeed solely as a result of man's efforts; he requires Divine Assistance (*siyata d'Shmaya*) to succeed. Thus, one must always pray to Hashem for success in every endeavor that he undertakes.

QUESTION OF THE DAY:

What was it about Yaakov's speech that aroused Yitzchak's suspicions?

For the answer, see page 112.

פרשת תולדות

THURSDAY

PARASHAS TOLDOS

A TORAH THOUGHT FOR THE DAY

וְיִתֶּן־לְךָ הָאֱלֹהִים מִטַּל הַשָּׁמַיִם
וּמִשְׁמַנֵּי הָאָרֶץ וְרֹב דָּגָן וְתִירֹשׁ

*And may God give you from the dew
of the heavens and the fat of the land,
and abundant grain and wine (Bereishis 27:28).*

Rashi comments: "May He give you and continue to give you." Many layers of meaning have been found in these words. On the simple level, *Rashi* is bothered by the fact that Yitzchak began his blessing with the word *"and,"* which implies that it is the *continuation* of something. *Rashi* therefore explains that it is to be understood as Yitzchak's blessing that the giving be *constant;* that is, may Hashem give, and give more, and more . . .

Others connect this comment of *Rashi* to his next comment on this verse, in which he states that Yitzchak used the Name of Elohim (which signifies the Attribute of Justice) in this blessing to intimate that Yaakov's descendants would receive the blessings only when they deserved them. [See *A Mussar Thought for the Day,* Friday.] *Devek Tov* explains that Yitzchak wished to reassure Yaakov that although events in history (such as the destruction of the *Beis HaMikdash*) would herald the cessation of the blessings, such interruptions would be only temporary; the blessings would resume. Furthermore, the blessing were not intended for fulfillment only in this world; they would ultimately be permanently realized in the World to Come. *Maharshal* states that Yitzchak wished to tell Yaakov that even if his descendants' sins would cause the blessings to cease, they would ultimately be deserving enough for the blessings to resume.

[Although these interpretations appear to explain Yitzchak's thoughts during the blessings as being directed at *Yaakov,* while the Torah states that Yitzchak thought he was speaking to *Eisav,* this does not pose a difficulty. We may explain that Yitzchak was directing his blessing to his *righteous* son, without realizing which son that was. Alternatively, it is possible that since the blessings were Divinely inspired, the levels of meaning within them were spoken by Yitzchak without his realizing their full import at the time; this became clear only in hindsight. These explanations are necessary to understand many of the commentators' comments in these passages.] For other meanings of *Rashi's* comment, see *A Mussar Thought for the Day.*

MISHNAH OF THE DAY: SHABBOS 6:9

פרשת תולדות

THURSDAY
PARASHAS TOLDOS

The following Mishnah lists two additional items with which one may go out on the Sabbath:

הַבָּנִים יוֹצְאִין בִּקְשָׁרִים — Young **boys may go out** on the Sabbath **with knots,**[1] וּבְנֵי מְלָכִים בְּזוּגִין — **and princes** may go out **with** ornamental golden **bells** woven into their garments.[2] וְכָל אָדָם — **And** this is actually true of **any person,** אֶלָּא שֶׁדִּבְּרוּ חֲכָמִים בַּהוֶֹה — however, **the Sages spoke of the prevailing** custom.[3]

--- NOTES ---

1. There was a custom that a man who was leaving his home, who knew that his son would miss him, would take his right shoelace and tie it to his son's left arm. As long as the lace was tied to the arm, it would serve to diminish the son's longings (*Rav* from *Gemara* 66b). [Due to its remedial effect, the shoelace has the status of a garment, not of a burden, and therefore it may be worn outside on the Sabbath.]

2. Princes may go out on the Sabbath with bells — whose clappers have been removed — attached to their clothes. If the clappers have not been removed, they may not be worn at all, since it is forbidden to jingle a bell on the Sabbath (*Tiferes Yisrael*). [Such bells were customarily worn as ornaments on the garments of princes.]

3. [Actually, commoners are also permitted to go out on the Sabbath adorned with such bells. Nonetheless, our Mishnah discusses this law in regard to princes, because it was only customary for the nobility, or for those who were wealthy, to do so.] Although anyone may wear bells outside on the Sabbath, the wearing of laces was permitted only for children who needed them (*Tos. Yom Tov*).

GEMS FROM THE GEMARA

In regard to our Mishnah and the next one, the Gemara (66b-67a) cites many remedies, some based on folk medicine or psychology, some based on mysticism or incantations, and some based on superstition. As we shall see in the next Mishnah, remedies that originated in superstitious practices are called *Ways of the Amorites*. The Gemara (67a) cites Abaye and Rava, who rule that any practice that is of evident therapeutic value is not forbidden by the prohibition against following in the ways of the Amorites, even if it is a practice that the Amorites follow. This is because Jews are forbidden only to engage in superstitious practices that idolaters perform blindly, without rhyme or reason, since only such practices indicate an endorsement of paganism. On the other hand, when a Jew engages in a practice that has evident therapeutic value, he

THURSDAY

PARASHAS TOLDOS

clearly is not endorsing paganism, but simply seeking a remedy for his ailment. He is therefore permitted to perform such acts (*Maharik* 88:1).

The Gemara infers from this ruling that an Amorite practice that is *not* of evident therapeutic value *is* forbidden because of the prohibition against following in the ways of the Amorites. The Gemara questions this implication from a Baraisa that teaches that the owner of an overly vital tree that sheds its fruit early, may dye it red and load its branches with rocks, both of which were Amorite practices.

The Gemara develops its question: Loading the branches with rocks is understandably not a superstitious remedy, as in doing so one naturally saps the tree's vitality, preventing its fruit from ripening prematurely. Surely, however, dyeing a tree red is not therapeutic. Yet, nonetheless, the Baraisa permits this practice! It would thus seem that one is permitted to engage in an Amorite practice even if it is of no evident therapeutic value!?

The Gemara responds that, in fact, the tree is dyed for the purpose of drawing the attention of the public, so that people will see the owner's misfortune and pray that he be shown mercy. A Baraisa notes the precedent for this practice, in the law that a leper is required to announce: "I am *tamei*, I am *tamei*" (see *Leviticus* 13:45). This verse teaches that one must inform the public of his misfortune, so that the public will beg for mercy upon him. Here as well, the function of the red dye is not to heal, but to attract attention to the tree's plight, so that others will pray that the health of the tree be restored.

In his explanation of Abaye and Rava's rulings, *Rashi* gives two examples of practices that have definite therapeutic value: the drinking of various potions and the bandaging of wounds with certain materials, since these acts are of evident value in healing. On the other hand, as the example of a practice without therapeutic value, which is therefore prohibited by Abaye and Rava, *Rashi* mentions incantations.

Rosh challenges *Rashi* on the basis of the Gemara here, which recommends many incantations as efficacious — some of which were even taught by Abaye himself! *Rosh* therefore suggests that *Rashi* refers only to incantations that are clearly not being used for healing purposes; these are not of evident therapeutic value, and are thus prohibited. The incantations mentioned in the Gemara, however, were well-known to be healing incantations; they are therefore permissible (see *Orach Chaim* 101:27 with *Beur HaGra;* see also *Rashi* to *Chullin* 77b (ד״ה אין בו משום רפואה).

Mishnah Berurah (101:105-106) adds that even incantations that are not widely known to possess therapeutic value are permissible, since an onlooker, knowing of the existence of healing incantations, will assume that these too are of this sort. Thus, the only sorts of incantations prohibited are those of which it is definitely known that they are *not* for the purpose of healing (see *Teshuvos Chavos Yair* §234).

A MUSSAR THOUGHT FOR THE DAY

Many commentators understand *Rashi's* comment that "Hashem will give and continue to give" (see *A Torah Thought for the Day*) as referring to the *method* that Hashem will use to provide Yaakov's descendants with their blessing: Instead of providing it all at once, He will provide it little by little.

One might ask: Why is this a blessing? Seemingly, it would be better to receive Hashem's largesse all at once, without waiting to receive it little by little!

The Maggid of Dubno answers this question by offering a famous parable. A king had two sons, one of whom was the apple of his eye, while the other was the bane of his existence. The first could do no wrong, while the second was a constant source of frustration and problems.

When the lads came of age, the king lost no time in handing a large amount of gold to his troublesome son, and sending him to a distant province for several years. He did not give any gold at all to his other son, but bade him simply to continue living in the palace as before.

The good son was troubled. "Why is it," he asked his father, "that my brother, who has always given you grief, is given wealth and riches, while I, who have always been a source of joy, receive nothing?"

The king replied, "Do not misunderstand! It is you whom I love more than anyone, and therefore I wish to keep you near me at all times. You have no need for your own gold; my treasury is at your disposal. But I wish to distance your brother from here as much as possible, so I sent him off with a great deal of gold. It is my fervent wish that he does not return too soon . . ."

So too is it with the blessings we receive from Hashem. If we receive too much good at one time, we forget from Whom the wealth emanates, and we can fail to thank Him for all that He has done for us. Yitzchak therefore blessed Yaakov with a blessing that would be bestowed in

THURSDAY

PARASHAS TOLDOS

small increments, so that his descendants would always remember the source of the blessing.

R' *Shmuel Rozovski* takes this idea further, and notes that the closeness to Hashem that results from His largesse to us is in itself *part and parcel* of the blessing. Thus, in truth Yitzchak blessed Yaakov with two things — material wealth, and the closeness to Hashem that would result from the constant flow of Divine blessing.

Ksav Sofer notes that another benefit of measured blessing is that while it ensures that the recipient will not be poor, it will not necessarily make him rich either. Wealth is a test that not everyone is equipped to withstand; indeed, the Mishnah in *Avos* (2:7) tells us that one who increases wealth, increases worries as well. Thus, Yitzchak blessed Yaakov with sufficiency, but not with wealth and its accompanying problems.

HALACHAH OF THE DAY

We will now turn our attention to the next forbidden labor, the melachah of לָשׁ, *kneading*. Kneading was a necessary step in the preparation of the dyes used for the colored fabrics found in the Mishkan. (One step in the production of certain dyes was the grinding of various herbs into a powder which was then mixed with water in order to form a paste.) Kneading was also necessary in the preparation of the *lechem hapanim* and the meal-offerings that were an important part of the service that took place in the Mishkan.

In the context of labor forbidden on Shabbos, *kneading* may be defined as the binding together of small particles by means of a bonding agent in order to form one mass. For example, the classic case of kneading involves the binding together of tiny grains of flour through the use of water — the bonding agent — in order to form a single uniform mass — dough.

The *melachah* of *kneading* applies to non-foods as well as foods. Just as one may not pour water into flour in order to form dough, one may not pour water into sand in order to produce mud. Our discussions will focus on *kneading* as it applies to foodstuffs.

This *melachah* is not limited to the act of kneading alone. Any action that will serve to combine a binding agent together with small particles resulting in a single thick mass is forbidden. Stirring, beating, and mixing are all actions that may be restricted by this *melachah*.

The final product formed through the combination of the binder and the particles need not be as thick as dough in order for its kneading to be forbidden. Even if the consistency of the resultant item is not quite as thick as dough, but is rather more fluid, similar to the consistency of a thick cake batter, such mixing, too, comes under the restriction of the forbidden labor of kneading.

THURSDAY
PARASHAS TOLDOS

A CLOSER LOOK AT THE SIDDUR

After the conclusion of the *Maariv* prayer on Motza'ei Shabbos, many have the custom to recite a special prayer. *Tur* (*Orach Chaim* §295) writes: "It is the custom to recite verses in the Torah that speak of blessings, such as the verse in *Devarim* (28:12): *May Hashem open for you His storehouse* etc., so that our handiwork during the following week be blessed. Although *Tur* mentions the verse in *Devarim,* our version of this prayer begins with the verses of Yitzchak's blessing to Yaakov, and indeed, the name of the prayer has become known as *VeYitein Lecha,* after the first words spoken by Yitzchak — *And may Hashem give you of the dew of the heavens* etc.

Sefer HaManhig (*Hilchos Shabbos* §75) writes that "it is an accepted custom among the Jews to recite the prayer of *VeYitein Lecha* on Motza'ei Shabbos, as well as other verse of blessing, so that the Jewish people shall be blessed in the coming week, for now and forever."

We begin the prayer of *VeYitein Lecha* by reciting a series of verses of blessing found in the Torah. First we recite verses from Yitzchak's initial blessings to Yaakov, followed by the verses of the second blessing that Yitzchak bestowed upon him as he left to Charan (*Bereishis* 28:3-4). From the blessings Yaakov gave to his children, we include those he gave to Yosef (ibid. 49:25-26), as the word *blessing* appears five times in those verses. Then we follow with other verses in the Torah that speak of the blessings of Eretz Yisrael (*Devarim* 7:13-15); the blessing that Yaakov gave to Ephraim and Menashe (*Bereishis* 48:16); Moshe's blessing of the Jewish nation as they stood at the end of forty years in the Wilderness (*Devarim* 1:10-11); the blessings that Moshe said would descend upon the Jews if they would heed the word of Hashem (ibid. 28:3-6); and assorted additional verses from *Devarim* (28:8,12;15:6) that describe blessings that will descend upon the Jews when they observe the mitzvos.

THURSDAY

PARASHAS TOLDOS

The prayer then continues with verses that speak of redemption (גְּאוּלָה), salvation (יְשׁוּעָה), knowledge of Hashem (דַּעַת ה׳), rescue (פִּדְיוֹם), reversal of troubles (הֲפוּךְ צָרָה), and peace (שָׁלוֹם); the prayer then concludes with a citation from the Gemara (*Megillah* 31a) that speaks of Hashem's humility and closeness to the Jewish nation, and a chapter of *Tehillim* (Ch. 128) which is expounded by the Gemara (*Berachos* 8a) as teaching that one who earns a living honestly is assured of Hashem's blessing both in this world and in the World to Come. Thus fortified, a person can turn to face the coming week with a renewed sense of purpose and Divine support.

In light of that which was learned earlier (see *A Mussar Thought for the Day*) — that Yitzchak blessed Yaakov by telling him that Hashem would deliberately issue His blessing in measured increments, so that He would always be close to the Jews — it is especially appropriate that this blessing opens the prayer of *VeYitein Lecha,* for it is Hashem's proximity that a Jew requires most of all to help him maintain, through the week that follows, the level of spirituality attained on the Sabbath.

QUESTION OF THE DAY:

At what time of the year did Yitzchak give the blessings to Yaakov?

For the answer, see page 113.

A TORAH THOUGHT FOR THE DAY

פָּרָשַׁת תּוֹלְדוֹת

FRIDAY
PARASHAS TOLDOS

וַיֹּאמֶר עֵשָׂו אֶל־אָבִיו הַבְרָכָה אַחַת הִוא־לְךָ אָבִי בָּרְכֵנִי
גַם־אָנִי אָבִי וַיִּשָּׂא עֵשָׂו קֹלוֹ וַיֵּבְךְּ.
וַיַּעַן יִצְחָק אָבִיו וַיֹּאמֶר אֵלָיו הִנֵּה מִשְׁמַנֵּי הָאָרֶץ
יִהְיֶה מוֹשָׁבֶךָ וּמִטַּל הַשָּׁמַיִם מֵעָל

*And Eisav said to his father, "Have you only one blessing,
my father? Bless me too, my father!"
And Eisav raised his voice and wept.
So Yitzchak his father answered him and said to him,
"Behold, from the fat of the land shall be your dwelling place,
and of the dew of the heavens from above"* (Bereishis 27:38-39).

The sequence of events as related here by the verse requires explanation. Eisav first asks if he can receive a blessing as well (v. 36), to which Yitzchak replies that he has already given everything away to Yaakov, and granted him mastery over Eisav (v. 37). Upon hearing these grim tidings, Eisav reiterates: "Have you only one blessing? Bless me too, my father!" — and bursts into tears. Seemingly, Yitzchak then relents, and blesses Eisav with the fat of the land — the very same blessing that he bestowed upon Yaakov earlier (v. 28)! If Yitzchak had given this blessing away, why did Eisav's tears enable Yitzchak to suddenly bestow it a second time?

Another matter that requires explanation is *Rashi's* identification (in v. 39) of "the fat of the land" as אִיטַלְיָא שֶׁל יָוָן, *Italia of Yavan,* which literally means *the Italy of Greece* (seemingly, a reference to Rome). From where does *Rashi* obtain this definition? Furthermore, *Rashi* leaves the identical term undefined when it is used (in v. 28) with reference to Yaakov.

In the name of *R' Chaim of Volozhin* it is said that each of these questions is answered by the other. Indeed, Yitzchak was faced with a dilemma when Eisav cried and begged him for a blessing — for all of the riches of the earth had already been promised to Yaakov! But, Italia of Yavan was an exception. The Gemara in *Sanhedrin* (21b) relates that when Shlomo HaMelech married the daughter of Pharaoh, the angel Gavriel descended from heaven and embedded a reed in the bottom of the sea. Silt settled around the reed, and eventually it grew to a sandbar that ultimately became the peninsula of Italy — and upon it was built the great city of Rome (see also *Rashi* to *Megillah* 6b).

In this context, explains *R' Chaim,* we can understand Yitzchak's blessing. Although Yaakov was blessed with ascendancy over Eisav, this was the case only when his children obeyed the Torah. When Eisav cried and

פרשת תולדות

FRIDAY

PARASHAS TOLDOS

begged for a blessing, Yitzchak replied that when Yaakov's children would falter, Eisav's descendants would have the power to throw off the yoke of servitude (see v. 40). Thus, Yitzchak *could only* have blessed Eisav with the land of Italia of Yavan — for it was the only land that *did not yet exist* when the "fat of the land" was given to Yaakov. In fact, it did not come into existence at all until Shlomo committed the misstep of marrying Pharaoh's daughter, thus triggering the fulfillment of Yitzchak's blessing to Eisav.

MISHNAH OF THE DAY: SHABBOS 6:10

The following Mishnah discusses the permissibility of going out on the Sabbath with items that were regarded by the general populace as effective remedies:

יוֹצְאִין בְּבֵיצַת הַחַרְגּוֹל — *We may go out* on the Sabbath *with a locust's egg,* [1] וּבְשֵׁן שׁוּעָל — *or with a fox's tooth,* [2] וּבְמַסְמֵר מִן הַצָּלוּב — *or with a nail from one who was hanged,* [3] מִשּׁוּם רְפוּאָה — *for the purpose of healing.* [4] דִּבְרֵי רַבִּי מֵאִיר — *These are the words of R' Meir.* וַחֲכָמִים אוֹסְרִין אַף בַּחוֹל — *But the Sages prohibit* the use of these items *even during the week,* מִשּׁוּם דַּרְכֵי הָאֱמוֹרִי — *because of* the prohibition against following in *the ways of the Amorites.* [5]

─────────────── NOTES ───────────────

1. A locust's egg was hung from an afflicted ear as a remedy for an earache (*Rav* from *Gemara* 67a). [A *chargol* is one of the four species of locust, listed in *Leviticus* 11:22, that may be eaten (see *Chullin* 65a-b).]

2. A person who had insomnia would wear a tooth of a dead fox; a person who was constantly sleepy would wear a tooth of a live fox (*Rav* from *Gemara* 67a).

3. A nail with which a corpse was fastened to the gallows was believed to be a remedy for a swelling on a wound (*Rav; Rashi*).

4. [This phrase refers back to the first word of this Mishnah — viz., *We may go out* with these articles for the purpose of healing; since these items were perceived as healing, they were not treated as burdens, but as ornaments; therefore, one may go out with them on the Sabbath.]

5. The Sages maintain that the use of these items as remedies stems from the superstitions of the Amorites who dwelt in the Holy Land prior to its conquest by Israel. All superstitions of the non-Jews (Amorites being only an example) are forbidden under the Scriptural prohibition (*Leviticus* 18:3): וּבְחֻקֹּתֵיהֶם לֹא תֵלֵכוּ, *and in their ways you shall not go* (*Rashi*). R' Meir, on the other hand, is of the opinion that anything found to be effective in healing — i.e., physicians attest to its efficacy — is not categorized as prohibited because of following the practices of the Amorites (*Rambam, Hil. Shabbos* 19:13).

GEMS FROM THE GEMARA

פרשת תולדות

FRIDAY
PARASHAS TOLDOS

Today we continue the discussion begun yesterday in *Gems from the Gemara* regarding practices forbidden as "ways of the Amorites."

There is actually a good deal of contention among the authorities concerning the nature of Amorite practices, and what Abaye and Rava meant to permit. *Meiri* writes that Amorite practices are only those that have neither natural *nor* supernatural [דֶּרֶךְ סְגוּלָה] basis (in contradistinction to incantations), but are believed to be therapeutic by the foolish masses, who perform them as adjuncts to their idolatry. *Meiri* adds that it may well be that various incantations recommended in our *sugya* are entirely ineffective. Nevertheless, the Rabbis permitted these practices because they are so obviously without merit that no one could possibly be led astray by performing them. Alternatively, these practices were permitted because since the masses believed in their efficacy, they were psychologically beneficial and worked as a placebo for those who were ill (see *Yoreh Deah* 179:6).

Similarly, *Rambam* (*Hil. Avodas Kochavim* 11:16 and *Moreh Nevuchim* 3:37) states that all conjurations, charms, incantations and the like are entirely without substance, and are given credence only by fools (cf. *Beur HaGra* to *Yoreh Deah* 179:13). According to *Rambam,* the only practices that are permitted are those that have been proven by scientific inquiry, or that can be explained according to the laws of nature. *Rambam* accordingly posits that in the period of the Gemara the various cures found here, such as the nail from the gallows, were believed to be effective according to natural law.

Rashba (*Responsa* 1:413), however, points out many apparent contradictions in *Rambam*'s ruling. He also shows that many of the cures that the Gemara assumes to be effective cannot be explained at all according to the laws of nature. He therefore permits any practice which is known to be effective, be it natural or supernatural, as long as it is performed with the recognition that all healing is in Hashem's hands. However, practices that have no therapeutic value, or evil practices that lead one away from Hashem, such as drinking blood in order to consort with demons, are indeed prohibited (see *Rashba* at great length).

Shiltei HaGiborim (to *Rif* pp. 20,21) writes that one is permitted to perform not only those practices that cure one of disease, but even those practices that are designed to prevent monetary loss — with the exception of certain practices that were meant to heal physical ailments

פרשת תולדות

FRIDAY

PARASHAS TOLDOS

of animals (cf. *Riaz,* cited there; see *Tosafos, Bava Metzia* 27b ד"ה כיס וארנקי with *Rashash* and *Maharatz Chayes*).

[*Maharil* (quoted in *Taamei HaMinhagim,* p. 561) maintains that nowadays one may not apply the remedies recommended by the Gemara, for since we are not expert in their applications, they will not prove efficacious in any event, and may lead, God forbid, to ridicule of the Torah and its teachers. However, he did permit one remedy that he states was proven effective even in his day — one that the Gemara (67a) presents as a remedy for a bone stuck in one's throat (for further discussion of *Maharil*'s position, see *Likkutei Maamarim* by R' *Tzadok HaKohen of Lublin,* p. 130).]

A MUSSAR THOUGHT FOR THE DAY

Although Yitzchak included mention of *the fat of the land* and *the dew of the heavens* in both his initial blessings to Yaakov and his subsequent blessing to Eisav, the blessings are not identical. Most notable is the fact that Hashem's Name was not used in the blessing to Eisav. *Rashi* (to v. 28) explains that this was because Yaakov's blessing was conditional upon his being deserving (for this reason, the verse uses the Name of Elohim, which signifies the Attribute of Justice), while Eisav's was not.

R' *Shamshon Raphael Hirsch* notes that with respect to Yaakov, Yitzchak stated that *Hashem will give you,* implying that Yaakov's blessings would be received under the special management and guidance of Hashem, while Eisav's blessings would come about in the normal course of nature's functioning.

It is also noteworthy that in the blessing to Eisav, the *fat of the land* is mentioned before *the dew of the heavens,* while in the blessing to Yaakov *the dew of the heavens* is mentioned first. *Mishlei HaTzaddikim* explains this with a parable. A matchmaker wished to speak of the benefits of a certain match to two prospective bridegrooms. The father of the girl in question was a learned Torah scholar and a successful wealthy businessman. One of the young men was a budding Torah scholar whose only interest was learning Torah, while the second was less interested in learning and more concerned with building his career. When the matchmaker offered the *shidduch* to the young scholar, he was sure to begin by telling him that the prospective father-in-law was himself a *talmid chacham,* and would appreciate the wishes of a son-in-law looking to continue his learning. To the second young man, however, he emphasized the father's business success, noting that such a *shidduch* would certainly be helpful in furthering the young man's business ambitions.

פרשת
תולדות

FRIDAY

PARASHAS TOLDOS

The Midrash notes that *the dew of the heavens* refers to Torah (which like the dew, never ceases). Thus, when Yitzchak blessed his righteous son, he mentioned first the blessing of Torah, and only then added that the fat of the land would be his as well. But when he blessed Eisav, realizing that Eisav truly did not value spirituality, he spoke first of the material aspects of the blessing.

HALACHAH OF THE DAY

The process of combining food particles and liquid to form a uniform mass may be seen as consisting of two independent steps. When liquid is added to dry particles of food, typically some of the particles will bond with the liquid even without the ingredients being manually kneaded. This bonding is the first step in the kneading process. The second step is the actual kneading act, which serves to fully blend the ingredients together.

Each one of the above described steps is in itself a forbidden act. Therefore, one may not pour liquid into food particles or add food particles to liquid on Shabbos, as this will begin the process of *kneading.* And even after the ingredients have been put together, there is an additional prohibition against stirring or otherwise manually combining them further.

For example, when preparing powdered baby cereal, the cereal begins to bind and form a paste as soon as liquid is added to the dry mix. However, in order to complete the preparation of the cereal, the mixture still needs to be stirred and thoroughly combined. Even though the mixture is not complete until it has been stirred together, each act is independently forbidden.

This holds true only when a liquid is being used as the binding agent. When a thick substance such as mayonnaise is used, the particles will not bind until they have been mixed. Therefore, in such cases only the actual kneading is forbidden under the prohibition against *kneading.*

As we mentioned above, it is not only mixtures with the density of dough that may not be kneaded on Shabbos. Even mixtures that are less

פרשת תולדות

FRIDAY

PARASHAS TOLDOS

thick, for example a cake batter, may not be combined on Shabbos. There is, though, a major difference between these two categories.

The halachah recognizes a mixture as being a "thick mixture" if it forms a mass that does not flow, or flows only very slowly when it is poured. Examples of such mixtures would be bread dough, egg or tuna salad, chopped liver, or a heavy baby cereal mixture. The kneading of these and other "thick mixtures" is forbidden under the *melachah* of *kneading* on a Biblical level.

By contrast, the halachah recognizes a mixture as being a "thin mixture" if it has enough body so that it is perceived as being one mass, yet it will flow when poured from one bowl to another. This category would include such items as applesauce or ketchup. Forming these and other "thin mixtures" is also forbidden under the prohibition against *kneading*; however, they are included only by Rabbinic decree.

A CLOSER LOOK AT THE SIDDUR

This week, we will begin to discuss the sixth of the Thirteen Fundamental Principles (י"ג עיקרים) enumerated by *Rambam*. The Sixth Principle states:

אֲנִי מַאֲמִין בֶּאֱמוּנָה שְׁלֵמָה שֶׁכָּל דִּבְרֵי נְבִיאִים אֱמֶת
I believe with perfect faith that all the words of the nevi'im (prophets) are true.

The concept that Hashem communicates directly with man (during those times in history when we are on the level to merit such communication) is central to our belief. *Rambam* speaks at length concerning prophecy in his *Hilchos Yesodei HaTorah*. Although a thorough discussion of prophecy is beyond the scope of this work, we will attempt to cover the major points that *Rambam* covers.

Rambam begins Chapter 7 of *Hilchos Yesodei HaTorah* by discussing what type of man one must become to attain prophecy: "It is one of the foundations of our faith to know that Hashem grants *nevuah* (prophecy) to man . . . *Nevuah* will not be granted to a person unless he is a wise man, great in intellect. He must be of powerful character, such that his Evil Inclination never succeeds in overpowering him; rather, he always masters his impulses. Also, he must possess an encompassing intellect that is extremely well-grounded.

"A person who is filled with these *middos* can then enter into the study

FRIDAY

PARASHAS TOLDOS

of the spiritual realms (*Pardes* — see *Chagigah* 14b and *Hil. Yesodei HaTorah* 4:13), and be successful in using his great wisdom to understand the ideas that he will learn. This will cause him to become more and more holy, separating him from the ways of the common people, who are mired in their daily darkness. He must always be on his guard, constantly vigilant to never allow himself license to think about mundane or trivial matters; rather, his mind must always be fixed toward Hashem, striving to comprehend Hashem's greatness.

"Such a person must use his intellect to understand the tremendous wisdom of Hashem that is present in every aspect of Creation . . . if he succeeds in this, then a Divine Spirit (*ruach hakodesh*) will descend upon him. During those times when the *ruach hakodesh* is upon him, his soul will become connected to the sphere of the angels . . . he will literally be as a new man, and he will realize that he has changed from what he was, more than by simply becoming wiser; he has actually reached a new level of holiness. And indeed, we find stated regarding the *nevuah* of Shaul HaMelech (*I Samuel* 10:6): *and you shall prophesy with them . . . and you shall be changed into another man.*"

Next week, we will discuss different levels and types of prophecy.

QUESTION OF THE DAY:
What item from Gan Eden played a role in the blessings given to Yaakov?

For the answer, see page 113.

פרשת תולדות / A TORAH THOUGHT FOR THE DAY

SHABBOS
PARASHAS TOLDOS

וַיִּשְׁלַח יִצְחָק אֶת־יַעֲקֹב וַיֵּלֶךְ פַּדֶּנָה אֲרָם
אֶל־לָבָן בֶּן־בְּתוּאֵל הָאֲרַמִּי אֲחִי רִבְקָה אֵם יַעֲקֹב וְעֵשָׂו

*And Yitzchak sent Yaakov away,
and he went to Paddan Aram, to Lavan the son of
Besuel the Aramean, brother of Rivkah,
the mother of Yaakov and Eisav (Bereishis 28:5).*

Rashi professes himself at a loss to explain what the Torah means to teach us by repeating here the fact that Rivkah was the mother of Yaakov and Eisav. *Ramban* suggests that the Torah wishes to underscore that Yitzchak and Rivkah did *not* tell Eisav to seek a wife from Charan, although he too was their son, for they had settled upon Yaakov as the heir of Avraham and Yitzchak. *Tur* explains that it was as the mother of *both* Yaakov and Eisav that Rivkah wanted the two separated, to avoid bloodshed.

In truth, looking at the subsequent verses reveals other difficulties with this passage. The Torah states (vs. 6-8): *When Eisav saw that Yitzchak had blessed Yaakov and sent him to Paddan Aram to take a wife, for when he blessed [Yaakov] he commanded him saying, "Do not take a wife from the daughters of Canaan," and Yaakov obeyed and went to Paddan Aram — then Eisav saw that the daughters of Canaan were evil in the eyes of his father.* These verses present two difficulties. First, why does the Torah have to emphasize that Yitzchak told this to Yaakov *at the time of the blessings*? It could simply have stated that Eisav saw that Yaakov had been sent, and deduced that the daughters of Canaan were unacceptable. Furthermore, Eisav should have known already that his wives were unacceptable to Yitzchak, as the Torah tells us that his wives caused Yitzchak and Rivkah pain (see ibid. 26:35); and we know that Eisav fulfilled the mitzvah of honoring his father in an exemplary manner. If he did not heed his father before, what new information caused him to do so now?

Perhaps we may explain that while Eisav knew all along that his father wished his wives to come from Charan, he assumed that this was due to his father's mistaken impression that he (Eisav) was a righteous man. Eisav reasoned: "My father thinks that since he married a woman from Charan and had righteous children, I should do the same. But I, who know that this is not the case, have no need to marry a woman from Charan!"

This reasoning held true until the blessings were given to Yaakov, when it became clear to Yitzchak that his wife Rivkah had not borne two righteous children, but rather was *the mother of Yaakov and Eisav* — one righteous man and one wicked man. At this point, Eisav assumed, Yitzchak would not insist that Yaakov go to Charan to seek a wife. But this was not the case! Eisav saw, to his surprise, that even *after blessing Yaakov*, Yitzchak still insisted that Yaakov seek a wife in Charan! This proved conclusively to Eisav that Yitzchak did not approve of the daughters of Canaan as wives under any circumstances — and accordingly, he too followed this path, and took the daughter of Yishmael as a wife.

פרשת תולדות

SHABBOS

PARASHAS TOLDOS

MISHNAH OF THE DAY: SHABBOS 7:1

To better understand the following Mishnah, let us review some basic concepts:

(1) מֵזִיד — *willful desecration*: A person who *deliberately* performs one of the acts prohibited by the Torah as *melachos* (forbidden labors) on the Sabbath is liable to the death penalty. Even if the death penalty cannot be or is not imposed, the violator is still subject to the Divine punishment known as כָּרֵת, excision (see *Sanhedrin* 7:8).

(2) שׁוֹגֵג — *inadvertent violation*: A person who *inadvertently* performs one of the acts prohibited by the Torah as a *melachah* on the Sabbath is liable to bring a קָרְבַּן חַטָּאת, *sin-offering,* to the Beis HaMikdash in Jerusalem. Such inadvertent violation may occur if one forgot or was unaware:

(a) that such a thing as the Sabbath exists; or
(b) that a specific act is forbidden on the Sabbath; or
(c) that a specific day was the Sabbath.

The following Mishnah considers cases of multiple inadvertent violations of the Sabbath, and specifies the rules for determining how many *chataos* (sin-offerings) one is liable to offer in each case.

כְּלָל גָּדוֹל אָמְרוּ בַשַּׁבָּת — The Rabbis *stated a major rule concerning the Sabbath:*[1] כָּל הַשּׁוֹכֵחַ עִיקַר שַׁבָּת — *Anyone who forgets the essence of the Sabbath,*[2] וְעָשָׂה מְלָאכוֹת הַרְבֵּה בְּשַׁבָּתוֹת הַרְבֵּה — *and as a result*

--- NOTES ---

1. The special importance accorded this rule is a reflection of its topic, not of the rule itself. Because of the stringency of the laws of the Sabbath, the Tanna uses the expression כְּלָל גָּדוֹל, *a major rule,* rather than the usual זֶה הַכְּלָל, *this is the rule,* as if to say: This is *a rule of a major law* (*Tiferes Yisrael* from Gemara 68a).

2. A person who once knew about the mitzvah of observing the Sabbath subsequently forgot about the mitzvah in its entirety. Our Mishnah teaches that he is held responsible for his forgetting. Hence, while his violations were not willful, they were avoidable,

PARASHAS TOLDOS

SHABBOS

performed many melachos[3] on many Sabbaths,[4] אֵינוֹ חַיָּיב אֶלָּא חַטָּאת אַחַת — is liable to but one chatas that atones for all the melachos that he performed.[5] הַיּוֹדֵעַ עִיקַּר שַׁבָּת — One who knows the essence of the Sabbath,[6] וְעָשָׂה מְלָאכוֹת הַרְבֵּה בְּשַׁבָּתוֹת הַרְבֵּה — but inadvertently performed many melachos on many Sabbaths,[7] חַיָּיב עַל כָּל שַׁבָּת וְשַׁבָּת — is liable to a separate chatas for each and every Sabbath that he desecrated.[8] הַיּוֹדֵעַ שֶׁהוּא שַׁבָּת, וְעָשָׂה מְלָאכוֹת הַרְבֵּה בְּשַׁבָּתוֹת הַרְבֵּה — One who knows that it is the Sabbath, but inadvertently performed many melachos on

---— NOTES ---—

and they therefore require atonement (Rav from Gemara 68b; cf. Rambam, Hil. Shegagos 7:2). [Accordingly, a person who never knew of the existence of the mitzvah of observing the Sabbath — viz., a person who was captured by non-Jews in his childhood and grew up among them, or who converted to Judaism while living entirely among non-Jews — is not obligated to bring any chatas (sin-offering) at all. Since he never knew of the mitzvah of Sabbath observance, the violations he committed are regarded as unavoidable (אוֹנֶס), and therefore require no atonement.]

3. The next Mishnah lists all the categories of labor that are forbidden on the Sabbath.

4. The person forgot, or was unaware, that the Torah contains the laws of the Sabbath, detailing the various types of melachos that are prohibited on the Sabbath. He therefore repeatedly performed melachos over the course of many Sabbaths (Rav; Rashi).

5. Since all of this person's violations stemmed from his forgetting only one fact — the very existence of the Sabbath — he is obligated to bring but one chatas for all his violations (Rav).

6. In this case, the person knows that the Torah contains the mitzvah of Sabbath observance, and that various melachos are prohibited (Rav; Rashi).

7. Losing track of the calendar, he performed melachos on the Sabbath, thinking it was a weekday. He then repeated this mistake on subsequent Sabbaths without ever realizing his violation during the intervening weekdays (Rav; Rashi).

8. This ruling is based on the assumption that a person cannot go through an entire week, from Sabbath to Sabbath, without ever discovering, at least momentarily, what day of the week it really is. Although he has no recollection of having become aware of the day of the week, we attribute this forgetfulness to a failure to appreciate the significance of this realization; and we further assume that in turn, with the passage of a few more days, even the very realization of the error faded from his memory. Hence, the Mishnah treats the desecration of each separate Sabbath as a separate lapse. He is therefore obligated to bring a separate chatas for each Sabbath on which he performed melachos (Rav; Rashi; cf. Tosafos). On the other hand, even though he performed numerous melachos on each Sabbath, he is liable only to one chatas per Sabbath. This is because the number of chataos a person is liable to bring is determined by the number of matters that he forgot. In this case, since he knew that melachos are prohibited on the Sabbath and his forgetfulness was of the fact that the day is the Sabbath, he must bring as many chataos as the number of Sabbaths he desecrated (Rav; Rashi).

PARSHAS TOLDOS

SHABBOS

many Sabbaths,[9] חַיָּב עַל כָּל אַב מְלָאכָה וּמְלָאכָה — *is liable to one offering for every primary melachah that he performed.*[10] הָעוֹשֶׂה מְלָאכוֹת הַרְבֵּה מֵעֵין מְלָאכָה אַחַת — *One who performs many melachos of one category of melachah*[11] אֵינוֹ חַיָּב אֶלָּא חַטָּאת אַחַת — *is liable to only one chatas.*[12]

—————— NOTES ——————

9. In this case, the person knows of the mitzvah of Sabbath observance, and he also knows that the day of the week is the Sabbath; but he forgot, or was unaware, that certain types of labor are forbidden. Hence, he inadvertently performs several *melachos* over the course of several Sabbaths (*Rav*).

10. [The types of labor that are prohibited on the Sabbath are classified as either אָבוֹת, *primary labors* (lit., *fathers;* singular, *av*), or תּוֹלָדוֹת, *secondary labors* (lit., *descendants;* singular, *toladah*). *Avos* are the thirty-nine types of labor that were necessary for the construction of the Mishkan, the Tabernacle that was built in the Wilderness after the Exodus. These will be elaborated upon in Mishnah 2. *Tolados* are types of labor that are similar to respective *avos*. In our Mishnah, however, the term *av* is used in the sense of the category that it represents rather than the specific activity that it is (*Rashi*).]

The ruling in this case is that a person is obligated to bring a separate *chatas* for each of the thirty-nine types of forbidden labor that he performed. While he may have violated one particular category numerous times over the course of several Sabbaths, he is nevertheless obligated to bring only one *chatas* per category as his atonement.

This ruling is based on the principle that we learned above — viz., that the number of *chataos* a person is liable to bring is determined by the number of matters that he forgot. In this case, since he knew each week the fact that the day was the Sabbath, his forgetfulness was of the fact that each of the *melachos* that he performed was prohibited on the Sabbath. He therefore brings as many *chataos* as the number of *melachos* he performed (*Rav; Rashi*).

11. In this case, a person performed both an *av* and its *toladah,* or two *tolados* of one *av*, without becoming aware of his error in the interim (*Rav; Rashi*).

12. This ruling is a derivative of the previous ruling. As we have seen, a person who repeatedly performs a specific *melachah* during one period of forgetfulness is liable to only one *chatas*. Since all the *tolados* of a specific *av* are considered part of the prohibition of that category of *melachah,* therefore one is liable to only one *chatas* for all the *melachos* he performed in that one category of *melachah* (*Rashi*).

QUESTION OF THE DAY:

A chassan and kallah fast on the day of their chasunah. Where is this alluded to in our parashah?

For the answer, see page 113.

פרשת
תולדות

SHABBOS

PARASHAS
TOLDOS

GEMS FROM THE GEMARA

Our Mishnah considers cases involving a person who forgot what day was Sabbath. In conjunction with this discussion, the Gemara (69b) explains what one must do if he realizes that he has lost track of the days of the week, and he is in an uninhabited region where he cannot possibly determine what day it is. Rav Huna rules that a person who is traveling or lost in a desert, who does not know which day is the Sabbath, should count six days from the day he realizes his unawareness [including that day (*Bach, Orach Chaim* 344)] and then observe one day as the Sabbath. On the other hand, Chiya bar Rav rules that he first observes one day as the Sabbath and then counts six days as weekdays. [Here, he cannot observe the day he realized his predicament as the Sabbath, because he might have already performed *melachah* that day. He therefore observes the *following* day.]

The Gemara explains the dispute: Rav Huna holds that the person should count in a manner similar to the creation of the world — i.e., just as the Sabbath followed the six days of Creation, so too does he observe the Sabbath after counting six weekdays. Chiya bar Rav, however, holds that the person should count like Adam, the first man — i.e., just as Adam was created on Friday and the very next day was the Sabbath, so too this person observes the next day as the Sabbath. [The Gemara subsequently refutes Chiya bar Rav.]

The Gemara then cites Rava, who rules that on every day of the six he may work only enough for his sustenance, i.e., enough to stay alive, except for the day which he counts as the Sabbath. [Since any given day may in fact be the Sabbath, he cannot risk desecrating it by working. He may thus perform on any given day only as much work as he needs to stay alive. On the day which he actually observes as the Sabbath, however, he may not do *any* work.]

The Gemara objects: And on that seventh day should he die? The Gemara answers: He works the day before enough to supply sustenance for two days.

But the Gemara asks: Perhaps the day before was actually the Sabbath. How then is he allowed to work twice as much on that day?

The Gemara concedes: Rather, every day he works enough for his sustenance, even that day which he is observing as the Sabbath.

But, if so, asks the Gemara: How will that day be recognizable as the Sabbath? The Gemara replies: By his recital of the *Kiddush* at the beginning of that day and the *Havdalah* at the end. By performing these

פרשת
תולדות

SHABBOS
PARASHAS TOLDOS

services as a reminder of the Sabbath, he treats this one day differently than the other six. [Ordinarily, it would be prohibited to recite these blessings when there is a doubt if they are required, because it is forbidden to recite a blessing in vain. Nevertheless, the Rabbis here ruled that a person lost in a desert should recite these blessings, so as to reinforce his memory of the Sabbath (*Shaar HaTziyun* 344:2; see *Pri Megadim, Mishbetzos Zahav* 344:1, and *Yad David* for a discussion about whether the person should pray the weekday service or the Sabbath service on that day).]

A MUSSAR THOUGHT FOR THE DAY

In *A Torah Thought for the Day,* we noted that it was only through the blessings that it became clear that Yitzchak had one righteous son and one wicked son. *R' Yaakov Kamenetsky,* in his *Emes L'Yaakov,* takes this idea one step further. He asks: Why was it necessary for Hashem to require that the blessings be taken by Yaakov through deceit? [Indeed, Ramban writes (25:34) that one of the causes of Yitzchak's blindness was to enable Yaakov to receive the blessings undetected.] Why did Yitzchak have to be fooled?

R' Yaakov explains that just as Avraham was faced with the ultimate test of the *Akeidah,* where Hashem commanded him to go against all of his teachings of *chesed* and commit an act that seemed to be unbearably cruel, Yaakov needed to face such a test as well. Hashem wished to see if Yaakov could go against those principles that were the fiber of his being, when Hashem's will was that he do so. As we have discussed, Yaakov's special attribute was *Emes - Truth.* His entire nature was one of truth — lying to him was anathema, the equivalent of idol worship or murder.

To test Yaakov, Hashem arranged matters so that he would be forced to employ deceit — but it would be clear, through the prophetic words of Rivkah, that this was Hashem's will. The verse clearly shows Yaakov's extreme reluctance to deceive his father. He stated (27:12): *Perhaps my father will feel me and I shall appear as a liar,* using the word אוּלַי, which is usually used to mean *hopefully.* Yaakov's inner nature longed to be discovered, as deceit was torture to him. Even when posing as Eisav, he could not bring himself to imitate Eisav completely. Yet, he passed the test — his personal *Akeidah* — and received the blessings.

R' Yaakov notes that this leads us to an interesting question. Where do

פרשת תולדות
SHABBOS

PARASHAS TOLDOS

we find that *Yitzchak* faced such a soul-challenging test? [The *Akeidah* would not qualify as Yitzchak's ultimate *nisayon*, as his attributes — *Gevurah* and *Pachad* — would actually make it *easier* for him to offer himself as an *olah* to Hashem.] He suggests that Yitzchak's test is to come in the future, based on the Gemara in *Shabbos* (89b). The Gemara relates that in the future that is to come, Hashem will come to the *Avos*, asking them to defend the Jewish nation, who had sinned. Avraham and Yaakov will offer no defense, stating that the nation deserves to be destroyed for having profaned His holy Name. Only Yitzchak will rise to the fore, and offer to act as the guarantor of the Jews.

Explains R' Yaakov: The essence of Yitzchak — strict justice — surely will cry out against begging for leniency, especially in a place where Avraham, the pillar of *chesed*, could find no grounds for mercy. But, seeing that it is Hashem's will that he defend the Jewish people, Yitzchak will overcome his nature and be their champion.

HALACHAH OF THE DAY

As we explained yesterday, there are two types of mixtures forbidden under the *melachah* of *kneading*. The formation of a "thick mixture" is forbidden on a Biblical level, while the formation of a "thin mixture" is forbidden by Rabbinic decree.

The mixing of solid particles with an abundance of liquid so that the resulting combination is watery, having no body or thickness at all, is not considered kneading and is permitted. Thus preparing baby formula, chocolate milk, or iced tea from a powdered mix is permissible on the Sabbath, and does not fall under this prohibition.

It is nevertheless important when mixing such items to take care to mix the powder with a large amount of liquid at once. Mixing the powder gradually with small amounts of liquid will initially result in the formation of a paste, and is prohibited.

As a general rule, a *melachah* that is forbidden on Shabbos may not be performed even if it is being done with a שִׁינּוּי (*shinui*), in an *unusual manner*. The only difference between performing the *melachah* in its usual manner and performing it through an unusual method is that in the first case the act is forbidden on a Biblical level, whereas when it is done in an unusual fashion, it is forbidden by Rabbinic decree.

The *melachah* of *kneading* is an exception to this rule. If one performs the act of kneading with a modification that the halachah recognizes as being an unusual manner, it is permissible. It is important, however, to note that one's personal concept of what is considered "unusual" may not necessarily be considered unusual by Torah law. The acceptable forms of *shinui* are defined by halachah.

פרשת תולדות
SHABBOS
PARASHAS TOLDOS

The halachah prescribes different *shinuim*, "modifications," to be used for the different steps in the kneading process. Additionally, there are also different requirements as far as the extent of *shinui* necessary, depending on whether the mixture involved is a "thick mixture" or a "thin" one. Since the kneading of the "thick mixture" is Biblically prohibited, the *shinui* required to allow such kneading to be done is more extensive. It must be a modification which the halachah considers to be a complete, or drastic, change in the kneading process. By contrast, when kneading a thin mixture, it suffices to employ a more minor modification in order for the kneading to be allowed.

Beginning tomorrow, we will first outline the details of the modifications prescribed by halachah, and then discuss their utility, depending on the type of mixture being formed.

A CLOSER LOOK AT THE SIDDUR

As we learned last week, it is the custom in most congregations to include the prayer of *"V'Shomru"* (comprising the verses of *Shemos* 31:16-17) before beginning the *Maariv Shemoneh Esrei* on Friday night. Today we will examine the verses themselves more closely.

Shemos 31:16 states: וְשָׁמְרוּ בְנֵי־יִשְׂרָאֵל אֶת־הַשַּׁבָּת לַעֲשׂוֹת אֶת־הַשַּׁבָּת לְדֹרֹתָם בְּרִית עוֹלָם, *And the Bnei Yisrael shall observe the Sabbath, to make the Sabbath for all their generations, an everlasting covenant*. *Nesiv Binah* (by *R' Yissachar Jacobson*) cites several ways to understand the statement that the Bnei Yisrael are to "make the Sabbath." *Mechilta* cites a teaching that interprets the verse as explaining what is *accomplished* by one who observes the Sabbath: "R' Elazar ben Parta said: Anyone who observes the Sabbath is regarded as if he himself made the Sabbath." This concept is explained by *Torah Temimah* (*Shemos* ibid.) in the following manner. Most mitzvah items are inherently recognizable as such even when the mitzvah is not being performed. For example, an *esrog* is recognizable as one of the Four Species, and a *shofar* is obviously the object used to sound the *tekios* on Rosh Hashanah. The Sabbath, however, is different. There is no inherent physical difference between the Sabbath and any other day of the week. What makes the Sabbath day different from the other days of the

פרשת תולדות
SHABBOS
PARASHAS TOLDOS

week is the fact that we observe the Sabbath, and *make* it into the special spiritual time that it is. Thus, one who observes the Sabbath truly *makes* it.

Rabbeinu Bachya understands the phrase as an exhortation to the Bnei Yisrael. In addition to observing the Sabbath, they are enjoined to *make* the Sabbath — that is, to *prepare* properly for the Sabbath, so that it will be celebrated with the honor that it is due. [Other examples of this usage of the verb עשה can be found in *Bereishis* 18:7,8.] This requirement is mentioned by the Gemara in *Beitzah* (16a): מֵחַד שַׁבָּיךְ לְשַׁבְּתָיךְ, *From the first of your [week, prepare] for your Sabbath*. And this is echoed in the words of the prophet Yeshayah (58:13): *And you shall call* (וְקָרָאתָ) *the Sabbath a delight*. The word וְקָרָאתָ can also be understood to mean *and you shall invite;* thus, the sense of the verse is that one must prepare for the Sabbath as he would for an honored guest.

A third interpretation is offered by *Sforno*, who understands the verse to be referring to the World to Come, the time that is "completely Sabbath." If one properly observes the Sabbath in this world, he *makes* the Sabbath by bringing the final Redemption closer. [For yet another interpretation, see *Ohr HaChaim*.]

ANSWERS TO QUESTIONS OF THE DAY

Sunday:
The *Midrash* explains that each one prayed *with respect to the other;* Yaakov prayed that he be granted children *from Rivkah*, and Rivkah prayed that she merit to bear *Yaakov's* children.

Monday:
Rashi (25:22) states that she went to the academy of Shem, who as a prophet could seek Hashem's Word on her behalf. [See *Gur Aryeh* and *Tur*, who explain why she did not approach Avraham or Yitzchak.]

Tuesday:
Avraham gave a tithe to Malki-tzedek (*Bereishis* 14:20); and Yaakov pledged to tithe to Hashem if Hashem would protect him in Lavan's house and return him to his father's house in peace (ibid. 20:20-22).

Wednesday:
Yaakov spoke respectfully to his father, asking him to *rise up, please* (27:19); also, he invoked the Name of Hashem, giving Him credit for a successful hunt (ibid. v. 20).

Thursday:

Rashi (27:10), citing *Pirkei D'Rabbi Eliezer*, states that Rivkah prepared *two* goats for Yaakov to bring before Yitzchak because it was Pesach; one goat was for the delicious meal, while the other was for the *pesach*-offering.

Friday:

Rashi (27:27) cites a Midrash stating that the smell of Gan Eden entered along with Yaakov when he came before Yitzchak. *Targum Yonasan* states that Eisav's special clothes, which Rivkah gave to Yaakov to wear, had originally belonged to Adam HaRishon, and they were later owned by Nimrod, from whom Eisav stole them. See *Sifsei Chachamim*, who states that these clothes were possibly the source of the heavenly aroma.

Shabbos:

At the end of the *parashah*, the Torah relates that Eisav married Machalas, the daughter of Yishmael. *Rashi* (to 36:3) states that her name was really Basmas, but she is called Machalas to allude to the fact that one receives *mechilah*, forgiveness, on the day of marriage. Thus, the day of marriage provides *mechilah* for a new couple, as does Yom Kippur. It is for this reason that a *chassan* and *kallah* customarily fast on the day of their wedding.

פרשת ויצא
Parashas Vayeitzei

A TORAH THOUGHT FOR THE DAY

פָּרָשַׁת וַיֵּצֵא

SUNDAY
PARASHAS VAYEITZEI

וַיִּפְגַּע בַּמָּקוֹם וַיָּלֶן שָׁם
*And [Yaakov] encountered the place,
and he spent the night there (Bereishis 28:11).*

Rashi explains that the verse speaks of *the place* (using the definite article) because it refers to an already known place — Har HaMoriah, the future site of the Temple. And the word וַיִּפְגַּע, *and he encountered,* is expounded by the Gemara (*Berachos* 26b) to mean "and he prayed," from which the Gemara adduces that Yaakov Avinu established the prayer of עַרְבִית (*Maariv,* the evening prayer). *Rashi* further explains that the verse uses the word וַיִּפְגַּע rather than the more common וַיִּתְפַּלֵּל, *and he prayed,* to teach us the additional lesson that קָפְצָה לוֹ הָאָרֶץ, *the earth miraculously shrank for him.* Yaakov thus immediately "encountered" Har HaMoriah. The Gemara in *Chullin* (91b) explains further that Yaakov traveled as far as Charan; when he arrived there, he became upset upon realizing that he had not stopped at Har HaMoriah to pray, as Avraham and Yitzchak had. Immediately, he went back to Beth-el, and Hashem miraculously shrunk the earth and transported Har HaMoriah there. (Cf. *Ramban,* who understands the Gemara to mean that Yaakov was miraculously transported directly back to Har HaMoriah.)

R' Yaakov Kamenetsky notes that the sequence of events as recorded in the Gemara is alluded to not only by the word וַיִּפְגַּע, but also by the word בַּמָּקוֹם. He explains that we sometimes find the word מָקוֹם used as a reference to Hashem. However, this usage is generally reserved for a more informal mention of Hashem, as opposed to the standard Names that are used in blessings and prayer. Thus, in the *Haggadah Shel Pesach,* we find the phrase בָּרוּךְ הַמָּקוֹם בָּרוּךְ הוּא, *Blessed is the Omnipresent, Blessed is He!,* because it is essentially the recital of a story, rather than a formal prayer. Also, in the house of a mourner, we recite the formula: הַמָּקוֹם יְנַחֵם אֶתְכֶם בְּתוֹךְ שְׁאָר אֲבֵלֵי צִיּוֹן וִירוּשָׁלַיִם, *May the Omnipresent console you among the other mourners of Zion and Jerusalem,* because the setting may be inappropriate for usage of Hashem's Name. [For another example, see the Baraisa cited in *Berachos* 40b, where R' Meir teaches that if one happened to see bread and decided to eat it, and he recited: בָּרוּךְ הַמָּקוֹם שֶׁבְּרָאָהּ, *Blessed is the Omnipresent Who created it,* he has fulfilled his obligation to recite a blessing, and may eat. In this case, R' Yaakov explains, since the person had not initially intended to eat, he used the more informal term, הַמָּקוֹם; nevertheless, the blessing is valid.]

Along these lines, R' Yaakov explains that Yaakov Avinu was unprepared for prayer to Hashem, for he thought that he needed to return from Charan to Har HaMoriah; he did not realize that the earth had shrunk and that he was already there. [This is borne out by his statement on the following morning (v. 16): *Surely HASHEM is present in this place, and I did not know.*] Thus, the prayer alluded to in the verse was of a more informal nature, as indicated by the use of the word מָקוֹם. For the same reason, the word וַיִּפְגַּע, *and he encountered,* is more appropriate than the more formal וַיִּתְפַּלֵּל.

פרשת ויצא
SUNDAY
PARASHAS VAYEITZEI

MISHNAH OF THE DAY: SHABBOS 7:2 (I)

The types of labor (*melachah*) that are prohibited on the Sabbath are classified as either *avos*, "primary labors" (lit., *fathers;* singular, *av*), or *tolados*, "secondary labors" (lit., *descendants;* singular, *toladah*). *Avos* are the thirty-nine types of labor that were necessary for the construction of the Mishkan, the Tabernacle that was built in the desert after the Exodus from Egypt. *Tolados* are types of labor that are similar in method or purpose to *avos*. Our Mishnah lists the thirty-nine *avos melachos*:

אֲבוֹת מְלָאכוֹת אַרְבָּעִים חָסֵר אַחַת — *The primary labors are forty minus one* in number.[1]

The Mishnah first enumerates eleven labors necessary for the baking of bread:[2]

───────── NOTES ─────────

1. The Mishnah prefaces the list of *melachos* with their total so as to teach us the maximum number of *chatas*-offerings to which an inadvertent violator can become liable. [This will be discussed further in Tuesday's *Gems from the Gemara*.] It is because of this focus on the person performing the *melachah* that the Mishnah, in its list, relates to the person — viz., הַזּוֹרֵעַ, literally, *the one who sows,* and not to his activity — viz., זְרִיעָה, *sowing (Tos. Yom Tov* from Gemara 73a). [For discussion of why the Mishnah states "forty minus one" rather than simply "thirty-nine," see *Tos. Yom Tov* and *Mayim Chaim*; see also *Shem MiShmuel* vol. 1, p. 85.]

2. As we mentioned above, *avos* are activities that were performed in the construction of the Mishkan. The dyes required for the Mishkan's curtains and skins were prepared in the same way that food is cooked. However, our Mishnah relates these *melachos* in terms of the bread-baking process. The Mishnah follows this order, even though bread was not baked in the construction of the Mishkan, because baking bread is more common than cooking dyes (*Tos. Yom Tov* from *Ran*; alternatively, these *melachos* were used in the preparation of the *lechem hapanim*, the Showbread that was placed on the *Shulchan* [Table] inside the Mishkan).

The Mishnah begins its list of the *avos* with the bread-producing *melachos* because eating is the most essential human need. The Mishnah then mentions the thirteen

פרשת ויצא

SUNDAY

PARASHAS VAYEITZEI

הַזּוֹרֵעַ — *One who plants* seeds in the ground; וְהַחוֹרֵשׁ — *and one who plows;*[3] וְהַקּוֹצֵר — *and one who harvests;* וְהַמְעַמֵּר — *and one who gathers together* the harvested grain to a single place. הַדָּשׁ — *One who threshes;* וְהַזּוֹרֶה — *and one who winnows.*[4] הַבּוֹרֵר — *One who selects* refuse from the grain, by hand or by a sieve. הַטּוֹחֵן — *One who grinds* the grain into flour; וְהַמְרַקֵּד — *and one who sifts* the flour through a sieve;[5] וְהַלָּשׁ — *and one who kneads* the flour with water to make a dough וְהָאוֹפֶה — *and one who bakes* the dough into bread.[6]

Our elucidation of this Mishnah will continue tomorrow.

---— NOTES ---—

melachos required for the manufacture of clothing, which is the second most-basic need. A group of *melachos* required for writing follows, representing the need for communication. The Mishnah then concludes with various *melachos* that have a more explicit Scriptural source than the others (*Pnei Yehoshua*).

3. Although normally plowing prepares the ground and thus precedes planting, our Mishnah reverses the order of these two *melachos,* listing planting before plowing. This teaches us that in places where the earth is hard and requires replowing after the sowing, one is also liable for this second plowing (*Rav* from Gemara 73b).

4. After the threshing has detached the kernels from their husks, the mixture is cast into the air with a pitchfork. The wind blows away the chaff, leaving behind the heavier kernels (see *Rav; Tiferes Yisrael*).

5. Three of the preceding *melachos* — viz., winnowing, selecting and sifting — are closely related. All have one purpose — separating food from waste. They might have justifiably been considered one *av,* since their purpose is similar. Nevertheless, since all three were performed separately in the construction of the Mishkan, the Tanna considers them as separate *avos* (Gemara 74a). Moreover, each of these *melachos* is a distinct step in the process: Winnowing separates the straw from the grain; selecting separates the pebbles from the grain after it has been winnowed; and sifting is done after the grain has been ground to flour (*Rashi* 75b). Since all three labors are performed at different points in the process of preparing the grain (or, during the construction of the Mishkan, preparing the dye plants), they are counted as three distinct *avos* (*Rav*).

6. No baking was involved in the construction of the Mishkan. Rather, cooking was involved in the preparation of the dyes. However, the Mishnah chose to list baking, rather than cooking, because the bread-making process serves as a better framework [evidently for mnemonic purposes] for these *melachos* (*Rav* from Gemara 74b). [Both baking and cooking are considered *avos.*]

QUESTION OF THE DAY:
How long did it take Yaakov to get from his father's home to the well in Charan?

For the answer, see page 176.

GEMS FROM THE GEMARA

פרשת
ויצא

SUNDAY
PARASHAS
VAYEITZEI

The Gemara (74b), elaborating on the *melachah* of baking, cites Rav Acha bar Rav Avira, who said that a person who throws a moist peg into an oven so that the heat of the oven will dry it out and harden it, is liable to a *chatas* (sin-offering) for violating the prohibition against cooking.

The Gemara asks: Isn't this obvious?! After all, there should be no difference between cooking herbs (such as were used in building the Mishkan) and cooking other items (see 106a).

The Gemara answers that since the person only needs to harden the peg, you might have thought that he is not liable for cooking. [The Gemara assumes in its question that the *melachah* of cooking is defined by softening a hard object through fire. In the case under discussion, though, the person is apparently attempting only to strengthen the peg, not to soften it.] Rav Acha bar Rav Avira therefore informs us that [the peg] first softens and only then hardens — i.e., the wood first softens from the heat, and only afterwards, when the water evaporates, does the wood harden. Since the initial softening of the wood is needed to strengthen it, the person is liable for that act of cooking (*Rashi;* see also *Tosafos;* cf. *Rambam, Hil. Shabbos* 9:6).

In another case concerning cooking, Rabbah bar Rav Huna said that someone who heats pitch and thereby liquefies it is liable because he has performed the *melachah* of cooking.

Here too, the Gemara asks: Isn't this obvious?! The Gemara answers: Since the substance subsequently hardens (i.e., the effect of his cooking is only temporary) you might have thought that he is not liable for cooking. Rabbah bar Rav Huna therefore informs us that the person is nevertheless liable (see, however, *Eglei Tal,* אופה 6:9:6, who posits that both this and the previous case are *tolados* of baking, not *avos*).

The Gemara, in the name of Rava, then depicts a case involving multiple violations: Someone who makes an earthenware barrel on the Sabbath will be liable to seven *chataos* because he has performed seven *melachos* during the process of making the barrel. These are: (1) *grinding* clods of earth into fine particles; (2) *selecting* out the large pebbles; (3) *sifting* the dirt in a sieve; (4) *kneading* the dirt with water; (5) *smoothing* the mud when forming the structure of the barrel (see the next part of our Mishnah); (6) *kindling* the fire in the oven (see the next part of our Mishnah); and, (7) *baking* the barrel in the oven to harden it (*Rashi*).

פרשת ויצא — A MUSSAR THOUGHT FOR THE DAY

SUNDAY
PARASHAS VAYEITZEI

The Midrash at the beginning of *Parashas Vayeitzei*, in discussing the prayer of Yaakov, cites the famous prayer of Dovid HaMelech in *Tehillim* (121:1-2): *I raise my eyes to the mountains — from whence will come my help (ezri)? My help will come from Hashem, the Creator of heaven and earth.* The Midrash explains that when Yaakov left to Charan, Yitzchak sent him without any riches, so Eisav would not be tempted to pursue him. [According to other Midrashic sources, he was pursued by Elifaz, the son of Eisav, who had been commanded by Eisav to hunt Yaakov down and kill him. When Elifaz confronted Yaakov, Yaakov convinced him to take all of his valuables and depart, using the logic that a poor man is the equivalent of a dead person.] Yaakov, concerned as to how he would be able to attract a potential mate in his destitute state, asked: From where will my *eizer* [the word *eizer* is used in reference to a wife, as we find that Chavah was called the *eizer* of Adam HaRishon (*Bereishis* 2:18)] come? And immediately Yaakov answered his own question: Shall I then place my hope in flesh and blood? I have nothing to fear, for *My help will come from Hashem, the Creator of heaven and earth.*

The בִּטָּחוֹן, *trust in Hashem*, that Yaakov exhibited by declaring "My help will come from Hashem" is a cornerstone of our belief system. However, we must understand how to reconcile the requirement of *bitachon* with the issue of הִשְׁתַּדְּלוּת, the *effort* that one must expend to attain his physical needs. If all of one's success or failure is preordained, why does he have to engage in worldly activities at all?

Mesillas Yesharim, in *Middas Chassidus* (Ch. 21), states that one's efforts, in fact, play no role in one's success or failure; they are merely a necessary onus placed on mankind as a result of Adam's sin (see *Bereishis* 3:19). Accordingly, he states, one should minimize his engagement in worldy affairs as much as possible, and with minimal effort one will be blessed with all his needs.

Although many masters of *mussar* concur with this general approach, they note that this outlook is expected of one of truly elevated status. For the majority of people, it is sufficient that they be aware that ultimately, their welfare depends on Hashem alone, and that they should therefore not devote all their time to trying to better their circumstances (see *Tenuas HaMussar* 4:242).

[Obviously, these concepts are complex and require much more thorough study. We will revisit them, and provide other insights from many other luminaries, in the course of our continuing studies.]

HALACHAH OF THE DAY

פרשת ויצא

SUNDAY
PARASHAS VAYEITZEI

We have already explained that the kneading process consists of two independent steps, each of which is forbidden. These are the initial combination of the dry and liquid ingredients that initiates the binding process, and the stirring or actual kneading that acts to completely combine the ingredients into one mass. The *shinui* necessary to make kneading permissible on the Sabbath is different for each step in the process. These two *shinuim* are known in halachah as a שִׁנּוּי בַּסֵּדֶר, *a modification in the order [of the combining]*, and a שִׁנּוּי בַּלִישָׁה, *a modification in the [method of] kneading*.

The first *shinui*, a *modification in the order [of the combining],* is appropriate when dealing with the problem of the initial combination of the dry and liquid ingredients. By reversing the order in which the ingredients forming the mixture are typically combined, a sufficient *shinui* has been introduced so that the combining becomes permissible. It is, however, important to note that this modification is, according to many *poskim*, valid only for the formation of "thin" mixtures which are prohibited only by Rabbinic decree; it therefore renders only the creation of such mixtures permissible. According to these *poskim*, the formation of a "thick" mixture is forbidden even when this *shinui* is used. This will be discussed in greater detail further on.

When employing the *shinui* of modifying the order, one must obviously begin by taking note of the typical way the mixture in question is formed. For a mixture in which the common practice is to first add the solid particles followed by the liquid binding agent, one must reverse the order by placing the liquid into the bowl first, followed by the solid substance. If the solid is commonly added to the liquid, one must first place the solid in the bowl before adding the liquid. [If one is unsure of the common practice in a specific case, it is sufficient to reverse the instructions given on the item's packaging, as it can be assumed that this reflects common practice.]

In a case where there is no clear common practice at all, one should first place the solid substance into the bowl, followed by the liquid. However, this is a leniency that should be followed only in cases of great need, such as when preparing food for an ill person or a young child where one forgot to combine the necessary ingredients before Shabbos.

As we mentioned previously, when the binding agent being used is a thick substance such as mayonnaise, no combining takes place without the ingredients being stirred. In such cases there is no need to modify the order when first combining the ingredients.

פרשת ויצא

A CLOSER LOOK AT THE SIDDUR

SUNDAY
PARASHAS VAYEITZEI

The *Pesukei D'Zimrah* prayers that are recited on the Sabbath are somewhat more expansive than those recited during the weekdays. *Nusach Sefard* adds four of the fifteen chapters of *Tehillim* that begin with the words שִׁיר הַמַּעֲלוֹת, *A song of ascents.* One of them is the chapter we mentioned in *A Torah Thought for the Day,* Chapter 121. The message of this psalm is clear, powerful and fundamental to Jewish thinking. All salvation comes only from Hashem, Who guards us from faltering or misfortune, and Whose protection is constant and everlasting. Let us analyze the opening verses of this psalm a bit more closely.

The first point of interest is that it opens with the words שִׁיר לַמַּעֲלוֹת, *A song "to" ascents.* It is the only one of the fifteen psalms (120-134) that begins in this manner; the others all begin with שִׁיר הַמַּעֲלוֹת, *A song "of" ascents.* A brief explanation is in order. These fifteen psalms correspond to fifteen steps (מַעֲלוֹת) in the *Beis HaMikdash,* upon which the Leviim stood and recited these psalms on certain occasions. *Rashi* states that when the Leviim began their ascent, this was the first psalm they recited, despite the fact that it is the *second* psalm recorded in *Tehillim.*

Rabbi Shamshon Raphael Hirsch states that this phrasing is used to convey the thought that this psalm is a song meant to lead one to the paths of elevation. It is a song that expresses ideas from which we can obtain the strength and trust to be uplifted in all times and circumstances.

Many commentators understand the phrase *I raise my eyes to the mountains* as a concrete description of a people in dire straits, who cast their eyes upon the mountains to see if someone is coming to their aid (or, alternatively, they send scouts to the tops of mountains to see if help is at hand). *Sforno,* however, renders the phrase "to the mountains" symbolically, as referring to world leaders. His understanding of the phrase is that during the Diaspora, we will sometimes look to the kings of the world during our persecution, to see who would help us flee and be saved. However, in the end it becomes clear to us that our help is only from Hashem.

The Midrash also interprets the word "mountains" symbolically, stating that the word should be understood as אֶל הַהוֹרִים, *to the parents,* rather than אֶל הֶהָרִים, *to the mountains. Eitz Yosef* explains that this exposition is meant to teach us the importance of the teachers of Torah, those who can show us the way in proper performance of mitzvos.

Although our salvation is from Hashem, it is indeed proper to be guided by our leaders.

**SUNDAY
PARASHAS VAYEITZEI**

The question — from whence will come our help? — is answered in the next verse: It will come from Hashem, the Creator of heaven and earth. *Malbim* offers a homiletic understanding of this phrase. He explains that the verse is teaching us that *hashgachah pratis* — the Divine Providence that Hashem constantly exhibits for His people — comes from both "heaven" and "earth." "Earth" signifies the natural world and the natural order by which Hashem governs the world's everyday affairs, whereas "heaven" connotes supernatural or miraculous events. The phrase "Creator of heaven and earth" thus conveys the message that the עֵזֶר, *help,* that one seeks comes only from Hashem, whether the vehicle of that help is through the natural "earth" aspect of Hashem, or the miraculous "heaven" aspect of Hashem.

פרשת ויצא — A TORAH THOUGHT FOR THE DAY

MONDAY
PARASHAS VAYEITZEI

וַיִּדַּר יַעֲקֹב נֶדֶר לֵאמֹר אִם־יִהְיֶה אֱלֹהִים עִמָּדִי וּשְׁמָרַנִי . . .
וְנָתַן־לִי . . . וְשַׁבְתִּי בְשָׁלוֹם אֶל־בֵּית אָבִי וְהָיָה ה׳ לִי לֵאלֹהִים

Then Yaakov took a vow, saying, "If God will be with me,
will guard me . . . and give me . . .
and I will return in peace to my father's home,
and HASHEM *will be a God to me"* (Bereishis 28:20,21).

Rashi interprets this verse as a conditional vow, in which Yaakov says: "If You will indeed keep all of the promises (of safety and well-being described in verses 13-15) then I will worship You." Many commentators find this troubling, for it implies that Yaakov was doubting Hashem's promises. How can such a thing be said of Yaakov Avinu?

There are several approaches to resolve this difficulty, with many minor variations. *Ramban* explains that Yaakov did not make this condition as a result of lack of faith or trust in Hashem; rather, his uncertainty was ignited by the fear that שֶׁמָּא יִגְרֹם הַחֵטְא, perhaps his sins would cause him to be unworthy of Hashem's providential care.

Although *Sforno* and *Kli Yakar* agree with *Rashi's* and *Ramban's* explanations, they maintain that the particulars of the vow — such as "You will guard me," and "You will give me to eat" — do not refer to the need for protection and sustenance themselves, but to their usefulness in helping Yaakov to resist any temptation or influence that could cause him to sin. Thus, Yaakov was not stating that he would serve Hashem only if he were taken care of, but rather noting that his service of Hashem would be enhanced by Hashem's support and protection.

Ramban also offers a second solution (which is discussed also by *Daas Zekeinim* and *Ohr HaChaim),* asserting that Yaakov did not make a conditional vow, but a promise. This is based on translating the word אִם (which normally means *if*) in this verse as *when* [as found in the verse (*Bamidbar* 36:4): וְאִם־יִהְיֶה הַיֹּבֵל לִבְנֵי יִשְׂרָאֵל, which is translated, *And* ***when*** *the Jubilee will arrive for the Children of Israel*]. According to this interpretation, the meaning of Yaakov's statement is, "When it comes to pass that You were with me and guarded me . . . and I will have returned safely to my home, then I will pass the place chosen to be the House of God, and worship Him there."

Ramban explains the phrase *And I will return in peace* in v. 21 as being the final condition of the vow, and the phrase *And Hashem will be a God to me* as the beginning of the obligation Yaakov took upon himself to fulfill; this, although both phrases appear in the same verse. *Rashi, Rashbam* and others, however, explain that the entire verse is a condition for Hashem to fulfill, though they differ as to what Yaakov requested with the words *And Hashem will be a God to me. Rashi* explains that Yaakov requested that Hashem's Name be forever conferred upon him and his descendants, i.e., that no flaw be found among his offspring that would cause the relationship to be severed.

פרשת ויצא

MONDAY

PARASHAS VAYEITZEI

Abarbanel offers a different solution to the question of Yaakov's seeming lack of trust in Hashem's promises. He explains that Yaakov was unsure whether the dream he experienced was a *nevuah,* a direct prophecy received from Hashem, in which case the fulfillment of Hashem's promises were guaranteed; or simply a vision brought on by the holiness of the place, in which case those assurances were not necessarily guaranteed to come true. And since in verses 13-15 Yaakov was given assurances relating both to his personal welfare and to that of his children, he established a test to determine which of the above options was correct. To paraphrase *Abarbanel's* understanding of the verses, Yaakov said: "If Hashem is with me and watches over me, fulfilling all my needs . . . and returns me safely to my father's house, showing that my sins did not cause any damage, then I can be confident that my vision was truly a *nevuah,* and then I can be confident that the promises relating to my offspring will also come to pass."

MISHNAH OF THE DAY: SHABBOS 7:2 (II)

The Mishnah next enumerates thirteen labors involved in the preparation of wool:

הַגּוֹזֵז אֶת הַצֶּמֶר — **One who shears wool;**[1] הַמְלַבְּנוֹ — **one who bleaches it,** for example, by washing it;[2] וְהַמְנַפְּצוֹ — **and one who disentangles it;**[3] וְהַצּוֹבְעוֹ — **and one who dyes it;** וְהַטּוֹוֶה — **and one who spins** it into thread; וְהַמֵּיסֵךְ — **and one who mounts the**

---------- NOTES ----------

1. The following thirteen *melachos* are those that were performed in the preparation of wool, which was subsequently dyed with *techeiles,* that was to be used for the curtains of the Mishkan (*Rav; Rashi*).

2. I.e., by washing the wool in a river (*Rav; Rashi* and *Ran* according to some editions). [It is unclear why these authorities specified that the washing took place "in a river," unless that was the usual place to wash wool or clothing (*Magen Avos*). Other editions of *Rashi* and *Ran* read, "washing it with *natron* (a type of detergent).*"*]

3. Disentangling prepares the wool for spinning, and typically is accomplished by either beating the wool with a stick or by combing it with a comb (*Rav*).

PARASHAS VAYEITZEI

MONDAY

וְהָעוֹשֶׂה שְׁתֵּי בָתֵּי נִירִין — *and one who makes* warp;[4] *two heddles;*[5] וְהָאוֹרֵג שְׁנֵי חוּטִין — *and one who weaves two threads;*[6] וְהַפּוֹצֵעַ שְׁנֵי חוּטִין — *and one who removes two threads.*[7] הַקּוֹשֵׁר — *One who ties* a knot; וְהַמַּתִּיר — *and one who unties* a knot;[8]

──────── NOTES ────────

4. This *melachah,* along with the three *melachos* that follow, comprise the weaving process. A brief introduction of this process is in order. A weaving loom is fundamentally a frame upon which two rollers are mounted: one at the far end (called the warp beam) away from the weaver, and one at the near end (called the cloth beam). The warp thread is wound around the warp beam and stretched to the cloth beam, upon which the woven fabric will eventually be rolled. The weaving process consists of setting up the warp threads on the loom and introducing the weft threads between them to produce a woven fabric. The process of stretching the warp threads on the loom is the *melachah* of mounting the warp (see *Maaseh Oreg* p. 19 ff. and *Meleches Arigah* p. 19 ff. for further details of this *melachah*).

5. Between the two beams and perpendicular to them are two frames (called harnesses) through which the warp threads must pass. Each of these harnesses has numerous vertical threads or wires mounted upon it. Each set of adjacent threads on the harness is knotted in two places to form a loop (or eye) at the center. This arrangement of threads and a loop is called a heddle. [Heddles may also be made by tying a ring between two lengths of thread. Modern hand looms often use a metal strip pierced at its center.] Every other warp thread (for example, each odd-numbered thread) passes through the eye of a heddle of the front harness, and then between two heddles on the second harness. The even-numbered warp threads each pass between two heddles on the first harness, and through the eye of a heddle in the second harness. Placing two threads through the heddle eyes constitutes the *av* of setting two heddles (*Rav; Rashi;* cf. *Rambam's Commentary to the Mishnah, Tos. Rid*).

6. The weaver raises each of the two harnesses alternately (this is called shedding). First, he raises the front harness. In doing so. he raises all the odd-numbered warp threads (which pass through the rings of the heddles in that harness), and forms a "shed" between the two sets of warp threads. The weft thread is passed through this shed from right to left (this is called picking). He then raises the even-numbered warp threads by lowering the first harness and raising the other, and passes the weft back through from left to right. Inserting the weft thread twice through the warp [right to left and left to right] constitutes the *av* of weaving (*Tiferes Yisrael*).

7. I.e., either removing two threads of the woof from the warp or vice versa, in order to re-weave the fabric (*Rav*). [Were the threads not removed for the purpose of re-weaving, their removal would be treated as a destructive act [מְקַלְקֵל], which is not considered a מְלֶאכֶת מַחֲשֶׁבֶת, *purposeful labor,* and therefore not Biblically prohibited. Removing threads from a fabric constitutes purposeful labor only if the intention is to aid in the weaving of the fabric after the threads have been removed.]

8. Those who would hunt the *chilazon* — the sea-creature whose blood was used for the *techeiles-* dye for the curtains of the Mishkan — would both tie and untie their nets, since it was sometimes necessary to remove ropes from one net and attach them to another. Thus we find both tying and untying in the process of the construction of the Mishkan (*Rav* from *Gemara* 74b).

פרשת ויצא

MONDAY — PARASHAS VAYEITZEI

וְהַתּוֹפֵר שְׁתֵּי תְפִירוֹת — *and one who sews two stitches.*[9] הַקּוֹרֵעַ עַל מְנָת לִתְפּוֹר שְׁתֵּי תְפִירוֹת — *One who rips in order to sew two stitches.*[10]

We will conclude the elucidation of this Mishnah tomorrow.

---— NOTES ——

9. The curtains of the Mishnah were sewn together (*Rav, Rashi*). The Mishnah here teaches that a minimum of two passes of the needle [one in and one out] are required for one to be liable for sewing. [This in-and-out motion actually results in only a single stitch. We have nevertheless translated שְׁתֵּי תְפִירוֹת loosely as two "stitches" because there is no equivalent word in English for a single pass of the needle.]

10. When small holes bored by moths were found in the curtains of the Mishkan, the adjacent fabric would be torn in order to elongate the hole, thus enabling the tailor to make a neat repair (*Rav; Rashi* from Gemara 75a). [Here, as above, had the tearing been simply destructive, it would be treated as a destructive act, which is not considered a מְלֶאכֶת מַחֲשֶׁבֶת, *purposeful labor,* and therefore not Biblically prohibited.]

GEMS FROM THE GEMARA

In *Gems from the Gemara* to the first part of our Mishnah, we saw a case of multiple violations. The Gemara (74b) goes on to cite Abaye, who discusses the case of a person who makes a large round reed basket on the Sabbath. In this case, he will be liable to eleven *chataos*, since he has performed eleven *melachos* while making the basket.

The eleven *melachos* are: (1) and (2) uprooting the reeds that he will use — this act is a violation of both the prohibition against *harvesting* and the prohibition against *planting* (if this act will promote the growth of the remaining plant — see 73b); (3) *gathering* the reeds together; (4) *selecting* the good ones; (5) *smoothing* them; (6) slicing them very thinly (which falls into the category of *grinding*); (7) *cutting* them to a specific size; (8) *setting up the warp* on which the basket will be woven; (9) looping two reeds around the warp reeds, thus locking them into position (which falls into the category of *making heddles*); (10) *weaving* the basket; and, (11) cutting the protruding reeds after weaving to even them out (which falls into the category of *striking with a hammer*).

Abaye adds that if he sews the basket's mouth (i.e., he adds a border around its opening), then he will be liable to thirteen *chataos*. This is because he has performed the additional two labors of: (1) *sewing* on the border; and then (2) *tying* the threads.

[*Rashi* writes that in neither of these cases, nor in the case we cited previously (making a barrel) is there liability for building, since that

MONDAY

PARASHAS VAYEITZEI

melachah does not apply to the crafting of utensils (see 122b). *Tosafos* and *Ritva* disagree, arguing that this is the case only when parts are attached to preexisting utensils; however, when a new utensil is created, there is liability for building (see *Pnei Yehoshua*).

[Furthermore, writes *Rashi*, the basket-weaver incurs no liability for *skinning* when he peels the reeds, because that *melachah* is applicable only to the hides of animals (see *Rosh Yosef*).]

A MUSSAR THOUGHT FOR THE DAY

The Mishnah in *Avos* (6:4) states: "This is the way of the Torah: Eat bread with salt, drink water in measured amounts, sleep on the ground, live a life of deprivation, but toil in the Torah. If you do this, you are praiseworthy and it is well with you." According to *Rashi*, this Mishnah is not advocating a life of poverty and deprivation as the key to the successful pursuit of Torah. Rather, it is an admonition to a poor person, that he must not allow his poverty to hamper his pursuit of Torah; the Tanna assures him that he will eventually merit to learn Torah in a state of wealth.

Midrash Shmuel, however, understands differently. He explains that the Tanna is addressing a wealthy person, who has the financial capability to indulge in worldly pleasures, and warning him not to acclimate himself to having every comfort, for such a lifestyle is not conducive to the study of Torah. Furthermore, keeping up such a lifestyle requires a great deal of time, and pursuit of material wealth will hinder his Torah study.

In his commentary to Yaakov Avinu's vow (see *A Torah Thought for the Day*), *Kli Yakar* notes that the phrase, *If you will give me bread to eat and clothes to wear* is seemingly redundant. Why else would anyone want bread if not to eat it, or clothes if not to wear them? *Kli Yakar* explains that the language used by the verse is meant to deliver the message that luxuries, those things that are beyond one's basic necessities, "awaken the eyes of their owners, and restrain a person from a proper path." Yaakov wished nothing more than enough bread to eat, and enough clothing to cover himself.

[It would appear from *Kli Yakar's* analysis that while wishing for delicacies to gratify the palate, or wanting the most fashionable and flattering clothing, is inadvisable, it is quite acceptable to wish for basic food needed for sustenance and for clothing needed for wearing.]

פרשת ויצא
MONDAY
PARASHAS VAYEITZEI

Rabbeinu Bachya also interprets this phrase to mean that one should pray only for his necessities and not for מוֹתָרוֹת, *extras,* which will only bring him great confusion and anxiety. Both he and *Kli Yakar* cite the following verse as proof to their position: רֵאשׁ וָעֹשֶׁר אַל־תִּתֶּן־לִי הַטְרִיפֵנִי לֶחֶם חֻקִּי, *Give me neither poverty nor wealth, but allot me my daily bread* (*Mishlei* 30:8). *Rabbeinu Bachya* explains that both poverty and wealth are undesirable, and can lead one away from the Torah. A poor person must resort to flattery or begging, and a rich person may come to be boastful and arrogant. Therefore Shlomo HaMelech asked only for his daily bread, and no more. *Rabbeinu Bachya* notes further that a person must realize that God has promised and provided sustenance for all of Creation; pursuit of luxuries is an invention of the Evil Inclination, and the Torah finds such pursuit repulsive.

As a concluding note, one should heed the warning of *Chovos HaLevavos* (*Shaar Avodas Elokim* Ch. 4) regarding this matter. He says that one who minimizes his consumption of permissible things voluntarily in order to tame his own desires and elevate his spiritual level is to be commended. However, if this behavior emanates from miserliness (i.e., the desire to accumulate more wealth) or to gain a reputation as an ascetic (one not needing worldly pleasures), and is carried to extremes, it is undesirable and ugly, for such a person has (unnecessarily) departed from the "middle road" and has robbed his body of the sustenance it requires.

HALACHAH OF THE DAY

The second step in the kneading process is the act of manually mixing the combination of ingredients in order to form a single uniform mass. The *shinui*, or modification, appropriate to this step is the second one mentioned above, the שִׁינּוּי בַּלִּישָׁה, *a modification in [the method of] kneading.* In order for this step in the process to be undertaken in a permissible manner, the actual mixing of the ingredients must be done in an irregular way. There are a number of modifications approved by the *poskim* as meeting the criteria for being irregular; we will discuss three methods which seem to have the most practical value.

(1) One acceptable modification is to move the mixing utensil through the mixture in a crisscross fashion, changing direction with each stroke, as opposed to the more typical method of stirring in a continuous

פרשת ויצא

MONDAY

PARASHAS VAYEITZEI

circular motion. When using this method, it is preferable that the utensil be lifted out of the mixture with each change of direction.

(2) It is also permissible to stir a mixture with one's bare hands or finger. However, one may not wear a glove while doing so.

(3) It is permissible to stir a mixture with the handle of a spoon or fork, or with either the handle or blade of a knife. [This modification, however, is not valid for thick mixtures.]

Let us now place the permit granted when employing the aforementioned modifications in the context of creating mixtures of differing densities:

One is permitted to knead a mixture on Shabbos in a halachically approved irregular fashion. The ramifications of this leniency are different depending on the consistency of the mixture. When forming a loose mixture, one must first add the ingredients together in the reverse of the typical fashion, and then mix the ingredients using one of the three irregular methods described above. When adding the ingredients together, one must take care to add all of the liquid at once, so as not to form a paste, which is forbidden.

As mentioned above, the rules for thick mixtures are more stringent, since the preparation of a thick mixture involves a prohibition on the Biblical level. Accordingly, it is the opinion of many *poskim* that the שִׁינוּי בַּסֵּדֶר, *the modification in the order of the ingredients,* used to allow the first step in the kneading process is not valid for the preparation of thick mixtures. According to these *poskim,* a thick mixture may be formed on the Sabbath only in two ways: (1) Either one may initially combine the ingredients (without mixing them together) before the onset of Shabbos, thus avoiding the problem of the initial combining, and then use one of the three approved modifications in the mixing method to mix them on the Sabbath; or alternately, (2) one may form the mixture without the use of a liquid, but rather with a thick coagulated substance such as mayonnaise, which is not subject to the restriction against the first step of the kneading process.

QUESTION OF THE DAY:

Where else in the Torah do we find the word אִם *used to mean "when" rather than "if"?*

For the answer, see page 176.

A CLOSER LOOK AT THE SIDDUR

פרשת ויצא

MONDAY
PARASHAS VAYEITZEI

We find vows discussed in the *siddur* with regard to one day of the calendar year — Erev Rosh Hashanah, when it is the custom of many to perform *hataras nedarim*, "annulment of vows" (see further below). In discussing the desirability of making *nedarim*, the Gemara (*Chullin* 2a) concludes that it is preferable not to make vows at all, rather than to make vows even if one keeps them. *Rashi* there explains that one who regularly makes vows will certainly come to transgress the prohibition of *he shall not desecrate his word* (*Bamidbar* 30:3). Though the Gemara may appear to be simply giving good advice, *Tur* cites the Gemara in *Nedarim* (22a) in which Shmuel adduces that even one who keeps a vow is called a wicked person, and the Gemara in *Nedarim* (77b) in which Rav Dimi calls one who vows a sinner. Furthermore, even one who fulfills his vows invites extra Divine scrutiny of his overall behavior, as R' Yannai said to those who make vows: "If you were aware that your ledger [in Heaven] would be opened and your activities examined (in reaction to having shown excessive confidence in your ability to make and keep vows) would you have made your vow?"

Therefore, concludes the *Tur*, one should not even make an oath to give charity unless he has the money at hand and will immediately give it. Only in cases where a person feels that he is exceedingly lax in performing a mitzvah or avoiding a prohibition and needs the impetus of a vow to strengthen his resolve should he resort to vows. *Rambam*, who agrees with this exemption, states that nevertheless, one should not become accustomed to using vows as a crutch to reinforce positive behavior, and should voluntarily (without vows) avoid things that are problematic for his proper behavior (*Hilchos Nedarim* 9:24).

Tosafos (*Chullin* 2b) question the principle of avoiding vows from our *parashah*, which states explicitly that Yaakov Avinu made a vow and which apparently condones this behavior. They answer that it is permissible to make vows בְּעֵת צָרָה, during trying (dangerous) or difficult times (see *Torah Temimah* on this verse (28:20) for *Rashba's* solution to the question, and for a discussion of whether under these circumstances a vow is only permissible or even desirable).

Although the source for the retroactive annulment of vows is described in the Mishnah (*Chagigah* 10a) as פּוֹרְחִין בָּאֲוִיר, *flying in the air* (i.e., the Biblical source is unclear), the procedure is nevertheless unquestionably accepted as halachically valid, and promoted by the *poskim* as a mitzvah. Thus, in light of the severity of making vows and

פרשת ויצא

MONDAY

PARASHAS VAYEITZEI

the danger of not keeping them, it has become a virtually universal custom to annul one's vows on Erev Rosh Hashanah before a tribunal of three of one's peers. [If one did not do so on Erev Rosh Hashanah, he may do so until Yom Kippur.]

Although technically one should always specify before the tribunal the vow that he wishes to annul, the text of *hataras nedarim* features a disclaimer (or request) stating that in light of the many vows, in many forms, that one has made during the course of the year, he be exempted from specifying the vows. Nevertheless, if one remembers actual vows, he should reveal them to at least one member of the court. Furthermore, the annulment does not affect vows that one made which relate to others, unless they consent (*Otzar HaTefillos*).

A second part of the *hataras nedarim* text is the declaration (after the court's formal annulment) that any oaths or promises which one will make in the future are to be considered null and void from the outset, and not have the legal status or force of a vow. This works, however, only when the person forgot his declaration at the time he makes the new vow. If he makes a vow in the future despite remembering his declaration, it has the full power of a vow, and he must keep it [unless he annuls it anew] (*Yoreh Deah* 211:2).

A TORAH THOUGHT FOR THE DAY

פרשת ויצא

TUESDAY
PARASHAS VAYEITZEI

וַיַּרְא וְהִנֵּה בְאֵר בַּשָּׂדֶה וְהִנֵּה־שָׁם שְׁלֹשָׁה עֶדְרֵי־צֹאן רֹבְצִים עָלֶיהָ כִּי מִן־הַבְּאֵר הַהִוא יַשְׁקוּ הָעֲדָרִים וְהָאֶבֶן גְּדֹלָה עַל־פִּי הַבְּאֵר. וְנֶאֶסְפוּ־שָׁמָּה כָל־הָעֲדָרִים וְגָלֲלוּ אֶת־הָאֶבֶן מֵעַל פִּי הַבְּאֵר . . . וְהֵשִׁיבוּ אֶת־הָאֶבֶן עַל־פִּי הַבְּאֵר לִמְקֹמָהּ

And [Yaakov] looked, and behold — a well in the field!
And behold! Three flocks of sheep lay there beside it,
for from that well they would water the flocks.
And the stone over the mouth of the well was large . . .
when all the flocks would be assembled there,
they would roll the stone from the mouth of the well . . .
then they would put back the stone over the mouth of the well,
in its place (Bereishis 29:2,3).

Ramban explains that the detailed description of all that Yaakov experienced in meeting Rachel at the well, which is seemingly superfluous, is meant to teach us the lesson that קֹוֵי ה' יַחֲלִיפוּ כֹחַ, *those who hope in Hashem will have renewed strength* (*Isaiah* 40:31). Although Yaakov was tired from his journey and his many years of study without proper rest, he was still able to roll away the large stone from atop the well, unaided, while the shepherds gathered there could not budge it.

Ramban also notes that these details can be interpreted as pertaining to the future of Klal Yisrael, Yaakov's children; many commentators discuss the lessons to be gleaned from the various details.

One of the prevalent themes in the interpretation of this story is that it portends regarding the Jews' exiles. *Chasam Sofer* says that the length of the exile between the First Temple and the Second, represented by Sarah and Rivkah respectively, was relatively brief, a mere seventy years. This is indicated in the episode of Rivkah at the well, where she simply placed her buckets in the well and was able to easily retrieve the water. But the exile between the Second Temple and the Third Temple, which is represented by Rachel, will be difficult and protracted. There is a great stone, symbolic of our sins, which prevents the exile from coming to an end, until Yaakov himself will come and remove it, like one removing a cork from a bottle (see *Rashi* to 29:10).

Malbim, too, relates the symbolism of this story to future exiles. He explains that the well in the field and the three flocks signify the three exiles of Mitzrayim, Bavel and Edom, during which the Jews survived only by "drinking from the well," that is, though the Divine protection and sustenance of Hashem. But the great stone of the Evil Inclination and the resulting iniquities covered the mouth of the well, not allowing

פרשת ויצא

TUESDAY

PARASHAS VAYEITZEI

the waters of redemption to be drawn. Redemption would not come unless "all the flocks would be assembled there"; that is, until the Jews came together in unity and love. This unity would allow them to roll the stone away (albeit with some difficulty, to which *Malbim* finds allusion in the double *lamed* in the word וְגָלֲלוּ), and open the source of their bounty and salvation once more. Ultimately, Yaakov, in whose merit the Third Temple will be built, will come and bring about the final redemption, in which the stone will be rolled away with relative ease (as indicated by the single *lamed* found in the words וַיָּגֶל אֶת־הָאֶבֶן, *he rolled the stone [easily]*).

Malbim expands his association of unity to redemption, and lack of unity to exile, by citing the story of the elders of Bei Atuna (see *Bechoros* 8b), who asked R' Yehoshua how they could move their well, which was out in the fields, into the city. He told them that they could do so by constructing a rope made of straw and using it to pull the well in. Homiletically, says *Malbim*, the well signifies the source of goodness and benevolence. When the Jews occupy Eretz Yisrael, the well is considered to be located in the city. When the Jews are in exile, however, it is out in the fields. The elders asked how the well could be returned to its proper place in Zion, where it could shower its goodness unencumbered with the yoke of exile. R' Yehoshua replied that the main cause of the exile was שִׂנְאַת חִנָּם, *unwarranted hatred*, and fragmentation of Jewish society, in which people (or groups) are viewed and treated as straw — insignificant and unfavorable. Unless society comes together and fashions a rope of unity that includes all of the "straw," the exile would continue.

MISHNAH OF THE DAY: SHABBOS 7:2 (III)

The Mishnah now mentions labors required for the preparation of hides, and two labors involving writing:[1]

הַצָּד צְבִי — *One who traps a deer*; הַשּׁוֹחֲטוֹ — *one who slaughters it* or kills it by any other means; וְהַמַּפְשִׁיטוֹ — *and one who skins it.* הַמּוֹלְחוֹ — *One who salts it*;[2] וְהַמְעַבֵּד אֶת עוֹרוֹ — *and one who tans*

— NOTES —

1. In the construction of the Mishkan, the *melachos* of this category were performed on the *tachash* animal (see *Exodus* 26:14), from whose hide a covering for the Mishkan was made (*Rashi*; cf. *Shoshanim LeDavid, Yad David*). The *melachos* required for the preparation of hides begin the Mishnah's group of *melachos* needed for writing, because hides were processed into parchment for scrolls.

2. Salting the hide is the first step in tanning (*Rashi* 75b).

its hide; [3] וְהַמּוֹחֲקוֹ — *and one who smoothes it;* [4] וְהַמְחַתְּכוֹ — *and one who cuts it.* [5] הַכּוֹתֵב שְׁתֵּי אוֹתִיּוֹת — *One who writes two letters;* [6] וְהַמּוֹחֵק עַל מְנָת לִכְתּוֹב שְׁתֵּי אוֹתִיּוֹת — *and one who erases in order to write two letters.* [7]

The final six labors:

הַבּוֹנֶה — *One who builds;* וְהַסּוֹתֵר — *and one who demolishes.* [8] הַמְכַבֶּה — *One who extinguishes;* וְהַמַּבְעִיר — *and one who kindles.* [9] הַמַּכֶּה בְּפַטִּישׁ — *One who strikes with a hammer.* [10] הַמּוֹצִיא מֵרְשׁוּת לִרְשׁוּת — *One who takes out from domain to domain.*

The Mishnah concludes:

הֲרֵי אֵלּוּ אֲבוֹת מְלָאכוֹת אַרְבָּעִים חָסֵר אַחַת — *These are the primary labors — forty minus one.* [11]

——— NOTES ———

3. The Gemara objects to the separate listing of salting and tanning, on the grounds that salting is the beginning of the tanning process; hence, the two are actually one *melachah*. The Gemara therefore deletes one of these two *melachos* and inserts שִׂרְטוּט, *tracing lines,* in its place. [Before leather is cut, lines are traced into the skin to indicate the desired design. In the Mishkan this was done before cutting the hides of rams and *techashim* for the Mishkan coverings (*Rav* from Gemara 75b).]

4. I.e., he scrapes the hair off the hide (*Rav; Rashi*).

5. I.e., he trims and cuts the hide into a specific size, for straps or shoes (*Rav; Rashi*).

6. The wall boards of the Mishkan were inscribed with letters, to facilitate matching them each time the Mishkan was erected. Hence, writing even two letters suffices to constitute a violation of the *av* (*Rav; Rashi* from Gemara 103a-b).

7. I.e., he erased in order to write two letters in that place. If the Mishkan's builders erred in writing letters on the boards, they would erase them in order to write the proper ones (*Rav; Rashi*).

[As above, if the erasure was not intended to prepare for writing again, it would be treated as a destructive act, which is not considered a מְלֶאכֶת מַחֲשֶׁבֶת, *purposeful labor,* and therefore not Biblically prohibited.]

8. [Here, as above, if the demolition is simply destructive, it would not be Biblically prohibited (*Tos. Yom Tov*).]

9. Both extinguishing and kindling were involved in stoking the fire used for cooking the dyes (*Rav; Rashi*). [The purpose of extinguishing in the construction of the Mishkan was to make charcoal (since otherwise, extinguishing is not a constructive act). This was done because wood that has become charcoal ignites faster and burns better than "raw" wood.]

10. Although the concept of finality is not inherent in the name given to this *av,* the Gemara (75b) understands it as the finishing touch at the completion of a job — viz., the hammer blow which the craftsman delivers to the anvil after finishing a job, flattening its surface so as to leave himself a smooth surface for the next job (*Rav; Rashi*).

11. The repetition of the number of *melachos* (thirty-nine) at the end of the Mishnah is to preclude the opinion of R' Yehudah, who counts as *avos* two more labors that the Sages deem *toladas*. The Mishnah therefore repeats: *these are the primary [categories of] labors, forty minus one,* to emphasize that there are no others (*Tos. Yom Tov*).

פרשת ויצא

GEMS FROM THE GEMARA

TUESDAY
PARASHAS VAYEITZEI

In note 1 to the Mishnah, we learned that the Mishnah states that there are thirty-nine *melachos* (even though they are each enumerated separately, and there would seem to be no need for a number) to teach that the maximum number of *chataos* (sin-offerings) to which a person can be liable for transgressions on a single Sabbath, no matter how many violations he commits, is thirty-nine. The Gemara (70b) notes that it would seem to be impossible to be liable to thirty-nine *chataos,* for the following reason: One is liable to a *chatas* only if he is unaware that the act he commits is forbidden. Now, if he is unaware of *any* of the thirty-nine *melachos,* then he is completely unaware of the prohibition against performing *melachah* on the Sabbath. And we learned in the first Mishnah of this chapter that one who is unaware of the basic prohibition of the Sabbath brings only *one chatas* for each Sabbath, regardless of how many *melachos* he performed! It would seem, therefore, that the maximum number of *chataos* to which one can be liable would be thirty-eight, not thirty-nine.

The Gemara provides two solutions to this problem. One, offered by R' Yochanan, is that we are dealing with a person who *was* aware of the prohibition against performing *melachah,* but he was unaware of its severity. That is, he did not know that the prohibition bears the penalty of *kares* (Divinely imposed premature death) for willful transgression (when not performed in the presence of witnesses and therefore not subject to punishment by the court). According to this approach, committing the violation while unaware of its severity can be considered an inadvertent violation with respect to a *chatas,* although it was committed with the knowledge that it was forbidden.

The second approach follows the opinion of R' Akiva. He is of the opinion that there is a Biblical prohibition against traveling a distance of more than one *mil* (2000 *amos,* which in contemporary measures equals between approximately three-fifths and four-fifths of a mile, depending on the various opinions) from one's place of residence on the Sabbath. [According to the sages who dispute R' Akiva, this is only a Rabbinic prohibition.] According to R' Akiva's view, it is possible for a person to have been aware of the prohibition against labor on the Sabbath, but to mistakenly believe that it applied only to the prohibition to travel beyond a *mil.* In this way, it is possible for a person to be totally unaware of all of the thirty-nine categories of *melachah,* and yet be aware of the basic existence of the Sabbath — and, if he inadvertently violates all thirty-nine *melachos* on a single Sabbath, he will be liable to thirty-nine *chataos.*

A MUSSAR THOUGHT FOR THE DAY

פרשת ויצא

TUESDAY
PARASHAS VAYEITZEI

The Midrash says that R' Chama offered six interpretations of the verses describing Yaakov's experience at the well. Most of them involve highly elevated and exalted Jewish symbols such as Zion, the *Avos*, the Sanhedrin, and *Ruach HaKodesh*. One of them, however, is very down-to-earth. *A well in the field* — this is a synagogue; *three flocks of sheep* — these are the three who are called [to the Torah on Monday and Thursday]; *from that well they would water the flocks* — for there they heard the Torah read. *And the stone was large* — this is the Evil Inclination; *when all the flocks would be assembled* — this is the congregation; *they would roll the stone* — for they would hear the Torah which kept the Evil Inclination at bay; *and they would put back the stone* — from the time they left (the synagogue), the Evil Inclination returned to its place.

The symbol of the stone as the Evil Inclination is derived from the verse: *I will remove the heart of stone from your flesh and give you a heart of flesh* (*Yechezkel* 36:26). *Malbim* explains that stone is difficult to penetrate, and a heart of stone is incapable of absorbing *mussar,* whereas flesh is porous, and can easily accept the teachings of fear and love of Hashem.

And through what vehicle does this transformation take place? The Gemara in *Kiddushin* (30b) says that Hashem created the Evil Inclination, and He created Torah as its antidote. If one engages in Torah one will not succumb to its overtures. In a follow-up to this statement, the Gemara cites a Baraisa that says: "If this מְנֻוָּבָל, *disgusting one* (the Evil Inclination), engages you, pull him into the study hall; if he is like a stone he will dissolve, and if he is like iron he will shatter."

Quoting this Gemara, the *Mesillas Yesharim* states (Ch. 5) that it is obvious that if the Creator created this antidote to the Evil Inclination, it is impossible for one to be cured of its disease without the cure of Torah. Moreover, one who thinks that he can, is mistaken, and will in the end die of his sins. *Mesillas Yesharim* likens this person to one who has a fatal disease that has been diagnosed, and for which there is a prescribed medication. If the person fails to take the proper medication, and instead takes another medication, it will not be surprising if he dies.

R' Elchanan Wasserman points out that when a person does not engage in Torah study, his weaponry in fighting the Evil Inclination is lost, and therefore so is the battle. If he falters by committing other sins, however, even if they are severe, there is a possibility that Torah study will ignite the spark of repentance within him. This is, R' Elchanan

פרשת ויצא

TUESDAY

PARASHAS VAYEITZEI

continues, why the Chofetz Chaim used to say, "The Evil Inclination does not mind if a Jew fasts, cries and prays all day long, as long as he does not study Torah."

This concept explains why the "big stone" of the Midrash tries to block the entrance of the Jews into the synagogue, and why one confronted with the Evil Inclination should pull it into the study hall. It is somewhat difficult, however, to understand the end of the Midrash, which states that immediately after one leaves the synagogue, the Evil Inclination is back in place! Does the Gemara not say that the Evil Inclination will be shattered and destroyed?

To answer, we must note that while the Gemara speaks of a study hall, the Midrash speaks of the Torah reading in a synagogue. The Torah reading, while critical in ensuring that there is a constant connection between every Jew and the Torah, does not provide the conditions to completely dissolve the stone, and can only roll it away temporarily. Only in the *beis midrash* (study hall), home of the Oral Law, where total immersion in Torah occurs, can the stone be totally dissolved; for it is the עֲמֵילוּת בַּתּוֹרָה, *toiling in Torah,* that ensures the demise of the Evil Inclination.

HALACHAH OF THE DAY

Although we learned yesterday that many *poskim* do not allow the initial combining of the liquid and dry components of a thick mixture on the Sabbath even when employing a modification in the order of combination, in cases of necessity, one may rely upon those opinions that do allow this. Cases of necessity would include food which may spoil if combined prior to the onset of the Sabbath, or food required for a young child or ill person that was not prepared before Shabbos. [It should be noted that even in these cases, a thick mixture should be formed only if a loose mixture will not suffice to fill the need at hand.]

The *melachah* of *kneading* is not limited to the formation of new mixtures, but applies also to the improvement of existing mixtures. Let us explain:

The mixing in of additional solids into a previously formed mixture is considered *kneading,* because when adding the additional substance, one must work it in to the existing mixture in order to properly combine all the ingredients into one mass. Thus, to add dry cereal mix into a previously mixed bowl of baby cereal is problematic, since the new cereal will be kneaded into the existing mix. In order for this addition to be permissible, one must once again employ a *shinui,* forming the new mixture in an unusual manner. The type of *shinui* to be employed will once again depend on the density of the new mixture being created, as well as the density of the existing ingredients being worked with.

TUESDAY

PARASHAS VAYEITZEI

If the original mixture is of a very loose consistency and one desires to thicken it somewhat, one must first reverse the order in which the ingredients are added, and then change the manner of mixing that he will use. For example, when thickening previously mixed baby cereal, one must first place the dry cereal in a bowl, and then add the loose, mixed cereal into the bowl. [This would constitute a change in the typical order.] After doing so, he must employ a *shinui* in the method he will use to mix the cereal — for example, by using the crisscross method described earlier. [This is permitted only if the final, thickened mixture will still be loose enough to be considered a "loose" mixture as defined earlier. If the resultant mixture will be "thick," such thickening of the mixture would be permitted only in cases of great necessity, as explained above.]

A CLOSER LOOK AT THE SIDDUR

Above, in *A Mussar Thought for the Day,* we discussed the importance of עֲמֵילוּת, *toil,* in Torah study. We find an allusion to this each morning at the beginning of *Shacharis,* in the wording of the first blessing we recite upon the study of Torah.

Actually, we recite three blessings upon the Study of Torah: (1) לַעֲסוֹק בְּדִבְרֵי תוֹרָה (2) וְהַעֲרֶב (3) אֲשֶׁר בָּחַר בָּנוּ. Before these blessings are recited, one may not study or recite verses of Torah. Since these blessings are considered בִּרְכוֹת הַמִּצְוָה, *blessings made before performing a mitzvah,* we immediately follow them by saying portions from the various branches of Torah: *Bircas Kohanim* from the Torah, *Eilu Devarim* from the Mishnah, and the Baraisa of *Eilu Devarim* from the Gemara. [Portions from the Torah, Mishnah and Gemara are also found in the section of *Korbanos* — see *Abudraham* in the name of *R' Zerachia HaLevi.*]

Beis Yosef (*Orach Chaim* §47) states that although these blessings are *Birchos HaMitzvah,* one need not repeat them each time he studies Torah during the day, for the commandment to study Torah is ever

פרשת ויצא
TUESDAY
PARASHAS VAYEITZEI

present, and all other activities are viewed merely as interruptions of one's learning.

Although many *Rishonim* (particularly those in Spain) had a text of the first blessing that ended: עַל דִּבְרֵי תוֹרָה, *upon the words of Torah,* the accepted version is לַעֲסוֹק בְּדִבְרֵי תוֹרָה, *to involve ourselves in Torah. Iyun Tefillah, Yaavetz* and others explain that since this blessing refers to the Oral Law, לַעֲסוֹק is the correct reading, as it implies toil and serious, in-depth engagement with the subject. They explain that one can grasp the principles and halachos of Torah only by being completely engrossed therein, questioning and answering, flexing and expanding one's reason and intellect.

The second blessing begins with: . . . וְהַעֲרֶב נָא, *Please, Hashem, our God, sweeten the words of Your Torah in our mouth. Yaavetz* suggests that we pray for "sweetening" of the Torah because so much of the Mishnah is "closed," in the sense that the reasoning behind the halachos is not provided, and we need wisdom and determination to pursue its study and truly understand its concepts.

Iyun Tefillah suggests, in a historical context, that the heretical sects such as the Sadducees (*tzedukim*), who did not accept the Oral Law, constantly waged battles against the traditional schools, and attempted to denigrate the Oral Law and Rabbinic authority. The blessing of וְהַעֲרֶב נָא, *Please sweeten,* was formulated as a plea to Hashem to help the traditionalists find the Oral Law sweet, and to encourage them to stand fast against the "embittering" concepts and onslaughts of those sects.

Rabbi Shamshon Raphael Hirsch describes beautifully the message that the blessing וְהַעֲרֶב נָא, *Please sweeten,* carries. "May the heart and mind find sweet nourishment through this occupation with Torah. May it be spiritual food which will be appropriate for the heart and mind, enlightening and ennobling both, so that this pursuit may become for us the most loved and happiest activity, and our enthusiasm for it be passed to our children and children's children."

QUESTION OF THE DAY:
Who else in the Torah met his future wife at a well?

For the answer, see page 176.

A TORAH THOUGHT FOR THE DAY

פרשת ויצא

WEDNESDAY
PARASHAS VAYEITZEI

וַיִּהְיוּ בְעֵינָיו כְּיָמִים אֲחָדִים בְּאַהֲבָתוֹ אֹתָהּ
... and they seemed to [Yaakov] to be as but a few days, because of his love for [Rachel] (Bereishis 29:20).

The verse tells us that although Yaakov had to work for seven years before Lavan would allow him to marry Rachel, this delay did not seem long to him; rather, it seemed merely to take a few days. This would seem somewhat counterintuitive, for we know that human nature causes even a short delay in acquiring that which one longs for to seem interminably long! How is it that the seven years passed for Yaakov it what seemed to be only days?

The commentators offer various interpretations of this verse. *Mizrachi* is of the opinion that the verse is not referring to how long the time period seemed to last; rather, it is addressing why Yaakov consented to work for so long, when Rivkah had specifically told him that he was to go to Charan and remain there for *a few days* (see above, 27:44). [Indeed, we find that Yaakov was punished for remaining away from his parents for twenty-two years (not counting the years spent at the yeshivah of Ever, for which he was *not* punished), in that his son Yosef was separated from him for an equivalent length of time.] According to *Mizrachi,* the verse provides us with the reason Yaakov felt it was okay to consent to such a long term of service; the seven years seemed to him to be nothing more than the *few days* that his mother had authorized. [Indeed, the commentators explain that Yaakov was punished for the entire twenty-year period he was with Lavan only because he tarried unduly on his return trip, instead of returning as quickly as he could.]

Tur, in his commentary on the Torah, offers another approach. He states that the verse is not speaking of how the *passage* of time felt to Yaakov; rather, it speaks of his appreciation of Rachel's true worth. *Tur* draws an analogy to one who pays a tremendous price for a flawless jewel, yet considers it a great bargain, because he knows that the jewel is worth many times more than the large sum he paid. Thus, while Yaakov may have keenly felt the passage of each day of the seven years that he worked for Rachel, they seemed to him as but a few days — because he knew that it would have been worthwhile to work even seventy years to acquire such a worthy mate (see *Sforno* and *Chizkuni* for similar ideas).

Tzeidah LaDerech, however, interprets the verse to be saying that the time indeed went by exceedingly *slowly* for Yaakov. In his opinion, the

WEDNESDAY

PARASHAS VAYEITZEI

sense of the statement that the years were *as but a few days* is that Yaakov, due to his great love for Rachel, did not even feel that the end of the term was getting closer with each passing day. Rather, the remainder of his term always loomed before him interminably, as if *but a few days* had already passed.

MISHNAH OF THE DAY: SHABBOS 7:3

The following Mishnah begins a series of Mishnayos, stretching over several chapters, that discuss the details of the *avos melachos* enumerated in the preceding Mishnah. As is often the case, these discussions begin with an analysis of the last-mentioned law, in this case, the *melachah* of *one who takes out from domain to domain*:

וְעוֹד כְּלָל אַחֵר אָמְרוּ — The Rabbis **stated yet another general rule** concerning liability to a *chatas* for violation of the Sabbath, in addition to the rule mentioned at the beginning of this chapter. This rule concerns the minimum amount of a substance that one must transfer from one domain to another to be liable to a *chatas*:[1] כֹּל הַכָּשֵׁר לְהַצְנִיעַ — **Whatever** quantity of a substance **is fit to store**,[2] וּמַצְנִיעִין כָּמוֹהוּ — **and** people **store such** a quantity of that substance,[3] וְהוֹצִיאוֹ בְּשַׁבָּת — **and one took it out on the Sabbath** in that quantity,[4] חַיָּב עָלָיו חַטָּאת — **he is liable to a *chatas* for** taking **it** out.[5]

NOTES
---

1. The Mishnah here proceeds to establish the general rule for determining a minimum amount for *any* given substance. All rulings in the subsequent Mishnahs, which offer specific minimums for specific substances, derive from this general rule (as those Mishnahs serve only to identify the minimum amounts of various substances that satisfy the rule taught here).

2. I.e., a substance that most people normally use for their needs (*Rav; Rashi*).

3. I.e., an amount that most people would consider worth keeping (*Rav; Rashi*). Thus, for a person to be liable to a *chatas,* the substance must meet two criteria: (a) It must be a substance that most people would normally use; and (b) it must be an amount of the substance that most people would normally store (*Tiferes Yisrael; Tos. R' Akiva Eiger*).

4. I.e., he carried it from one domain to another. [The same rule applies to transporting an item four *amos* in a public domain.]

5. The principle taught by our Mishnah is that a person who takes out a substance that meets these criteria is liable to a *chatas* even if he is wealthy, and this substance in this amount is of no significance to him (*Tiferes Yisrael*). [The halachic significance of the item derives from the fact that *most* people consider it significant in this amount. Note, however, that the reverse is *not* true, as the Mishnah teaches below — see note 8.]

פרשת ויצא

WEDNESDAY
PARASHAS VAYEITZEI

וְכֹל שֶׁאֵינוֹ כָּשֵׁר לְהַצְנִיעַ — **But whatever is not fit to store,**[6] וְאֵין מַצְנִיעִין כָּמוֹהוּ — or most people **do not store such** a quantity of it,[7] וְהוֹצִיאוּ בְשַׁבָּת — **and one carried it out** in that quantity **on the Sabbath,** אֵינוֹ חַיָּב אֶלָּא הַמַּצְנִיעוֹ — **only a person who stores it** in such a quantity **is liable** to a chatas for doing so.[8]

———————— NOTES ————————

6. I.e., a substance that is not normally used by people. [This does not mean to preclude very valuable or rare items, which are infrequently used. Rather, it precludes items that, although commonly available, are not considered fit for use.]

7. I.e., even if the substance is one that is normally used by people, but the quantity is so small that people normally do not consider it worth storing (*Tos. R' Akiva Eiger*).

8. The Mishnah teaches that if a specific person took a liking to a certain substance and stored some of it, then even if it is a substance that people do not normally use, or even if it is a small amount that people do not normally store, he personally would be liable to a *chatas,* since for him this item is significant — even though anyone else would be exempt, since for other people the substance or the quantity renders the item insignificant (*Rav; Rashi*). [Thus, although the item is halachically insignificant with regard to everyone else, it can still be rendered significant by a person with respect to himself, if he treats it as a significant item by storing it away.]

GEMS FROM THE GEMARA

Our Mishnah taught that *anyone* who takes out an item (or items) of a type that most people store in an amount that most people store is liable to a *chatas*. Thus, even a wealthy person, who does not consider the minimum size or amount useful, is also liable.

The Gemara (75b) cites R' Yose bar Chanina, who posits that this ruling of the Mishnah is not in accordance with the opinion of R' Shimon cited in another Mishnah (below, 8:1). R' Shimon's opinion is that all the listed minimum sizes and amounts apply only to those who actually store these sizes and amounts — i.e., they apply only to an average person, who normally stores such a size or amount. A wealthy person, however, would not be liable for carrying out an item (or items) of these types in these sizes and amounts.

Our Mishnah also stated that if someone stored something that most people would not see fit to store, then only he — the one who stored it — would be liable to a *chatas,* but if another person took it out, he would remain exempt from punishment.

פרשת ויצא

WEDNESDAY

PARASHAS VAYEITZEI

Concerning this ruling of the Mishnah, the Gemara (76a) cites R' Elazar, who said that it is not in accordance with R' Shimon ben Elazar, who taught in a Baraisa that even something that is generally not fit to store, or is generally not stored in such a minute amount, but was nonetheless stored by a particular person, becomes significant enough that even *another* person who comes and takes it out is liable on account of the intention of the particular person who stored it. According to R' Shimon ben Elazar, once the item is awarded halachic significance because it was stored away by one person, it is considered significant with respect to all.

A MUSSAR THOUGHT FOR THE DAY

R' *Aharon Kotler* noted that the plan to work seven years for Rachel's hand originated with *Yaakov*, not with Lavan (see 29:19). He asks: Why did Yaakov suggest this arrangement, without even waiting to hear Lavan's price? Certainly, Lavan would have demanded an exorbitant payment (and Yaakov was penniless, having lost all of his possessions to Elifaz the son of Eisav, as we learned earlier), but Yaakov was a resourceful person, and surely could have sent an emissary back to Yitzchak for whatever funds were needed. Just as Lavan and Besuel could not prevent Rivkah from leaving to become the wife of Yitzchak, Rachel would have gladly consented to marry Yaakov. Why was it necessary to wait seven years?

R' Aharon answers that Yaakov offered the seven-year term because he knew that he was not yet ready to marry and begin producing the twelve *shevatim* that would become Klal Yisrael. Just as he had prepared for his stay in Lavan's house by studying for fourteen years in the yeshivah of Ever, so too he needed to spend years tending Lavan's sheep in the most difficult of circumstances, exercising the highest standards of scrupulous honesty and integrity even in the face of the blatant trickery and deceit that was Lavan's hallmark. Yaakov knew that these standards had to become second nature to him so that they could be passed on to his children, becoming part of the fabric of every Jew. The years of learning Torah in Yitzchak's house had not provided him with this vital experience. Even the years at Ever's yeshivah, though they provided him with the knowledge of how to learn Torah in exile, still had not fortified him with respect to direct interaction with evil men. This lesson had to be learned in Lavan's employ, before Yaakov was married.

For this reason, explains R' Aharon, Yaakov was able to regard the seven long years he waited to marry Rachel as being but a few days. Had Yaakov been engaged in some senseless pursuit, he would have indeed felt that each day was an eternity in his longing for Rachel. But that was not the case. As he tended Lavan's sheep, he was preparing for their marriage — this, too, was a part of his mission. Thus, *in spite* of his intense love for Rachel, the days passed quickly — because they were filled with purpose.

פרשת ויצא

WEDNESDAY
PARASHAS VAYEITZEI

HALACHAH OF THE DAY

If one wishes to add solids to an existing thick mixture, it is not necessary to reverse the order in which the ingredients are added to the mix. This is because the binding agent being used to blend in the new additions is not a liquid (rather, it is the existing thick mixture, which has the status of a solid), and therefore no bonding will take place until the mixture is stirred. [This is similar to using mayonnaise when making tuna salad.] One must, however, use one of the recommended *shinuim* — i.e., stirring in a crisscross fashion or barehanded — when mixing in the new ingredients, to avoid transgressing the *melachah* of *kneading*. For example, if one has a bowl of tuna salad into which he now wishes to introduce some diced vegetables (see the *melachah* of *grinding* above regarding how finely such vegetables may be diced), he must stir the vegetable bits into the salad using a *shinui*.

We have defined the *melachah* of *kneading* as the binding together of disparate particles in order to form one mass. To cause a completed mixture to lose density and become more loose is, therefore, the opposite of *kneading*, and is thus permitted. For this reason, it is permissible for one to add liquids to a previously combined mixture on Shabbos without the use of any *shinuim*.

There is, though, one caveat to this rule. This holds true as long as the mixture had already been thoroughly kneaded prior to the addition of the newly introduced liquids. If, however, there still remain particles in the mixture that have not been fully combined, the additional liquid will have the effect of causing these unmixed particles to blend. This would be a transgression of the *melachah* of kneading, and therefore necessitates the use of a *shinui* in both the initial pouring in of

פרשת ויצא
WEDNESDAY
PARASHAS VAYEITZEI

the fresh liquid and the stirring of the new combination.

For example, if one wishes to add more milk into a cereal mix that is too thick, he must first take note of whether the dry mix is fully combined with the liquid. If it is, he may add the fresh milk without *shinuim*. If, however, there is still unmixed dry cereal in the bowl, *shinuim* must be employed when thinning the mix.

A CLOSER LOOK AT THE SIDDUR

This week, we will continue our discussion of the sixth of the Thirteen Fundamental Principles (י״ג עיקרים) enumerated by *Rambam*, which states:

אֲנִי מַאֲמִין בֶּאֱמוּנָה שְׁלֵמָה שֶׁכָּל דִּבְרֵי נְבִיאִים אֱמֶת

I believe with perfect faith that all the words of the nevi'im (prophets) are true.

We may ask a fundamental question: Why is it so important for us to believe that Hashem speaks to prophets? After all, we have not merited to have *nevi'im* in our midst for many centuries. Why is belief in their existence so important?

One answer is that *nevuah* points to an important truth; when Hashem created the world, He did not simply do so and then abandon His creation to exist without His guidance. Rather, He continues to control and guide even the minutest details in all of Creation. This belief is bolstered by the belief that He speaks to man, to convey His wishes and His decrees.

Moreover, lack of belief in prophecy opens the door to false beliefs such as idolatry. When Hashem spoke to all the Jews at Har Sinai, He demonstrated conclusively to the entire nation that He was their King and the Master of the World; this, indeed, is the tradition that is passed down, father to son, through the generations. *Nevuah* served to strengthen this tradition, by providing clear proof to any dissenter. Indeed, *Zohar* writes that when the Sages succeeded in eradicating the powerful inclination toward idolatry that existed in ancient times (see *Sanhedrin* 64a), *nevuah* ceased. *Zohar* explains that the two events were linked; with the powerful urge to idolatry gone, the proof provided by the *nevi'im* was no longer critical.

Rambam, in the seventh chapter of his *Hilchos Yesodei HaTorah,* explains that not all *nevi'im* prophesied on the same level. Nevertheless, there were certain attributes common to all *nevi'im* (other than

WEDNESDAY

PARASHAS VAYEITZEI

Moses, whose prophecy will be discussed in the seventh principle). All *nevi'im* received their prophecy through a vision or a dream (see *Bamidbar* 12:6); all *nevi'im* were affected by bodily weakness of one type or another during their *nevuah* (see, for example, *Bereishis* 15:12); all *nevi'im* received their *nevuah* through an intermediary (such as an angel) rather than directly from Hashem; and no *navi* was able to initiate *nevuah* at will. The sole exception to this was Moses, as will be discussed below.

It is important to note that while a *navi* can prophesy for many reasons — to foretell what Hashem plans to do, or to deliver rebuke from Hashem to forestall disaster (as in the case of Yonah) — the *navi* does *not* have the authority to start a new religion, or to add or subtract from the laws of the Torah. [For details regarding how to tell whether a prophet is genuine, see *Rambam* ibid.]

QUESTION OF THE DAY:

How many years did Yaakov actually work for Rachel's hand?

For the answer, see page 176.

פרשת ויצא

A TORAH THOUGHT FOR THE DAY

THURSDAY

PARASHAS VAYEITZEI

וַתִּקְרָא שְׁמוֹ רְאוּבֵן . . . כִּי עַתָּה יֶאֱהָבַנִי אִישִׁי . . .
וַתֹּאמֶר כִּי־שָׁמַע ה׳ כִּי־שְׂנוּאָה אָנֹכִי . . . וַתֹּאמֶר עַתָּה
הַפַּעַם יִלָּוֶה אִישִׁי אֵלַי . . . וַתֹּאמֶר הַפַּעַם אוֹדֶה אֶת־ה׳ . . .

*And she called his name Reuven . . .
"for now my husband will love me." . . . And she declared,
"Because* HASHEM *has heard that I am unloved" . . .
And she declared, "This time my husband will
become attached to me" . . . And she declared,
"This time let me gratefully praise* HASHEM*" (Bereishis 29:32-35).*

The verses tells us that Leah named her first son Reuven to express the hope that she would now be loved, and her second son Shimon to indicate that she would no longer be hated. *Ohr HaChaim* asks: Surely, logic dictates that the order should have been reversed! Moreover, an earlier verse (v. 31) explicitly states that Hashem blessed Leah with Reuven because she was hated, not because she was less beloved.

Ohr HaChaim explains that in fact, Leah was not hated by Yaakov. He bases this on the Gemara in *Bava Basra* (123a) that states that Leah's eyes were tender because she cried to be spared from marrying Eisav, who was known as the "hated one"; and she was also known as שְׂנוּאָה ("hated one") because they were destined to be married, according to the custom of the day — the older daughter of Lavan to the older son of Yitzchak. When the previous verse states that Hashem saw that she was hated, it actually means that Hashem saw that her only wish was to be the wife of a *tzaddik* rather than the wife of a *rasha,* and so He opened her womb.

Nevertheless, Leah did feel less loved than Rachel, for whom Yaakov had toiled so many years. With the birth of Reuven, Leah hoped to gain Yaakov's love on an equal par with Rachel, and this is why she declared upon his birth, *". . . for now my husband will love me."* However, when she had a second son, while Rachel still had none, she began to doubt her original assessment (that she was merely *less loved* than Rachel). Perhaps, she reasoned, Hashem heard (i.e., understood) what I did not understand — that Yaakov not only loves me less than Rachel (for my deceit on the night of the wedding), he actually hates me! Her new assumption was that the reason Hashem had given her two sons was so that one would remove the indignity of her being a despised wife, and the second would increase the love between her and Yaakov. Thus, it was her *second* son whom she named Shimon, for it was only then that she realized that she might actually have been hated by Yaakov.

פרשת ויצא

THURSDAY

PARASHAS VAYEITZEI

Ohr HaChaim notes further that when Leah had her third son, she named him Levi, declaring, *" 'This time' my husband will become attached to me."* He explains that Leah was not wishing for anything specific, because Yaakov was already attached to her; rather, she was stating that Levi's birth shed light on the propriety of her marriage. Thus, she declared: *This time* — i.e., this birth is proof that my marriage to Yaakov was just and proper *from the outset.* For if the sons born to me were only for the purpose of removing hatred and increasing love, it would have sufficed for me to have two sons. Having three sons (three being a *chazakah,* which legally provides proof of ownership in many instances) shows that I am Yaakov's rightful partner by Hashem's decree, and that he is attached to me as my rightful husband.

Ohr HaChaim does not address why the verse at the naming of Yehudah also uses the term הַפַּעַם, *this time. Rav Shimon Schwab* offers the following insight: Until this point, mankind understood that one must pray to Hashem and be grateful for His favors. And one was expected to offer thanksgiving for receiving something tangible, which had value and purpose. Leah, too, until this point ascribed the "presents" she had received as each having accomplished or proven something (although, according to *Ohr HaChaim,* she had not interpreted correctly, as we have explained). However, when Yehudah was born, no specific reason why Leah had to have a fourth child was apparent. Thus, *this time* Leah thanked Hashem simply for the gift of a son, thus teaching that the underlying reason for thanksgiving should be to acknowledge that one has merited receiving something from the Creator, without dwelling upon the importance of the item itself.

Rav Schwab offers a parable to elucidate this concept. If one receives a present from a king, his joy will be boundless simply because the king honored him with a gift, and not because of the value of the item. This recognition came to Leah with the birth of Yehudah. Indeed, *Chidushei HaRim* notes that this understanding became a hallmark of the Jewish people, who are called יְהוּדִים — those who are always grateful to Hashem.

QUESTION OF THE DAY:

Which two of Yaakov's children have names that derive from similar roots?

For the answer, see page 176.

פרשת ויצא

THURSDAY
PARASHAS VAYEITZEI

MISHNAH OF THE DAY: SHABBOS 7:4

The previous Mishnah taught us that a person is not liable to a *chatas* for transferring from one domain to another unless he takes out a substance that most people consider significant, in an amount that most people consider significant. The following Mishnah begins to list the precise minimum amounts of various commonly used substances. This particular Mishnah discusses items used for animal feed:

הַמּוֹצִיא תֶבֶן — *One who takes out straw*[1] from one domain to another, or takes it a distance of four *amos* in a public domain, כִּמְלֹא פִי פָרָה — is liable to a *chatas* if he takes out *as much as a cow's mouthful;*[2] עֵצָה בִּמְלֹא פִי גָמָל — if he takes out *tough straw,* he is liable to a *chatas* if he takes out *as much as a camel's mouthful;*[3] עָמִיר בִּמְלֹא פִי טָלֶה — if he takes out *soft straw,* he is liable to a *chatas* if he takes out *as much as a lamb's mouthful;*[4] עֲשָׂבִים בִּמְלֹא פִי גְדִי — if he takes out *grasses,* he is liable to a *chatas* if he takes out *as much as a kid goat's mouthful;*[5] עֲלֵי שׁוּם וַעֲלֵי בְצָלִים — if he takes out *leaves of garlic and leaves of onion,*[6] לַחִים בִּגְרוֹגֶרֶת — if they are *fresh,* he is liable to a *chatas* if he takes out *the equivalent of a dried fig;*[7] יְבֵשִׁים כִּמְלֹא פִי

NOTES
---

1. The straw being discussed here is produced by crushing cut stalks of grain (*Rashi* to 140a).

2. Since straw is commonly eaten by cows, a cow's mouthful is the prescribed minimum amount. A person who takes out this amount of straw is liable even if he takes it out to feed a camel, for whom this amount is insignificant (*Meiri* from Gemara 76a).

3. *Etzah,* derived from עֵץ, *wood,* refers to tough straw. Since this harder straw is not generally fit for bovine consumption, one is not liable to a *chatas* for taking out a cow's mouthful. He becomes liable only when he takes out the equivalent of a camel's mouthful, since *etzah* is commonly fed to camels. This measure is larger than a cow's mouthful (*Rav; Rashi*).

4. *Amir* is a softer straw, which is fit for the consumption of smaller animals (*Tiferes Yisrael*). Since it is softer, it is suitable for lamb fodder. Hence, a person who takes out *amir* is liable even if he takes out only the equivalent of a lamb's mouthful, the measure of which is smaller than a cow's mouthful.

5. A kid goat's mouthful is smaller than a lamb's mouthful. Since even soft straw is still too hard for a kid, one is not liable unless he takes out at least a lamb's mouthful. However, for taking out grasses, which are fit for both lambs and kids, one is liable for the smaller measure of the equivalent of a kid's mouthful (*Rav; Rashi*).

6. These leaves, by which the onion can be picked, are the shoots that grow from the bulb of the onion and sprout above the ground (*Tos. Yom Tov*).

7. Since these leaves are fit for human consumption, the minimum measure is the equivalent of a dried fig (i.e., an amount of leaves equal in volume to a dried fig; this

THURSDAY
PARASHAS VAYEITZEI

גְּדִי — if they are *dry*, he is liable to a *chatas* if he takes out *as much as a kid goat's mouthful*. [8] וְאֵין מִצְטָרְפִין זֶה עִם זֶה — *And these* types of feed *cannot be combined with one another,* [9] מִפְּנֵי שֶׁלֹּא שָׁווּ בְּשִׁיעוּרֵיהֶן — *because they are not alike in their prescribed measures.* [10] הַמּוֹצִיא אוֹכָלִים — *One who takes out foodstuffs,* [11] בִּגְרוֹגֶרֶת חַיָּיב — if he takes out as much *as the equivalent of a dried fig,* [12] *he is liable.* וּמִצְטָרְפִין זֶה עִם זֶה — *And they do combine with one another,* מִפְּנֵי שֶׁשָּׁווּ בְּשִׁיעוּרֵיהֶן — *because they are alike in their prescribed measures,* [13] חוּץ מִקְּלִפֵּיהֶן וְגַרְעִינֵיהֶן וְעֻקְצֵיהֶן — *excluding their shells, and their pits, and their stems,* [14] וְסוּבָּן — *and their coarse bran,* [15] וּמוּרְסָנָן — *and their fine bran.* [16]

---- NOTES ----

is the minimum measure generally used for all foodstuffs). Hence, if he takes out the smaller amount of a goat kid's mouthful, he is exempt from a *chatas*, because fresh garlic and onion leaves are not fit for kid's fare (*Rav; Rashi*).

8. Dry garlic and onion leaves are not fit for human consumption, but are eaten by goat kids. Therefore, if one takes out a kid's mouthful of dry leaves, he is liable (see *Meiri*).

9. For example, if one takes out one-half of a cow's mouthful of crushed straw and one-half of a camel's mouthful of *etzah*, he is not liable (*Tiferes Yisrael*).

10. Since the minimum amount to be liable for taking out tough straw is higher than the minimum amount to be liable for taking out regular straw, tough straw cannot be combined with regular straw to complete the minimum amount of regular straw.

However, if one takes out less than the minimum amount of tough straw, but completes that minimum amount (of a camel's mouthful) by adding regular straw, he *is* liable. This is because the law of regular straw is more stringent than the law of tough straw. Therefore, regular straw combines with tough straw to make up the minimum amount (*Tiferes Yisrael; Tos. R' Akiva Eiger* from *Gemara* 76a; see further in *Gems from the Gemara*).

11. I.e., any foodstuffs fit for human consumption (*Tiferes Yisrael*).

12. This minimum is a הֲלָכָה לְמשֶׁה מִסִּינַי, *an Oral Law taught to Moshe at Sinai,* that is not explicit in the Written Torah (*Eruvin* 4b).

13. Since all foodstuffs that are fit for human consumption have the same minimum amount, they all combine with each other to make up that minimum amount of the equivalent of a dried fig (*Rav; Rashi*). Human foodstuffs thus differ from the animal feeds discussed above, which have varying minimums, because they are intended for different types of animals.

14. None of these are edible food, and therefore they do not count toward the minimum amount (*Rav; Rashi*).

15. This is the outer shell of the wheat kernel, which falls off when the wheat is pounded (*Rav; Rashi*).

16. This is the bran that is found in the sifter after sifting the flour (*Rav; Rashi;* cf. *Rambam Commentary*). Although bran is eaten along with the grain, it is not considered a foodstuff in and of itself, and therefore is not counted toward the minimum amount (*Tos. Yom Tov*).

פרשת ויצא

THURSDAY

PARASHAS VAYEITZEI

רַבִּי יְהוּדָה אוֹמֵר — *R' Yehudah says:* חוּץ מִקְּלִיפֵּי עֲדָשִׁין — No shells combine to count toward a minimum measure, *except for the shells of lentils,*[17] which do combine, שֶׁמִּתְבַּשְּׁלוֹת עִמָּהֶן — *because they are cooked with* the lentils.[18]

———— NOTES ————

17. R' Yehudah holds that the shells of lentils do count toward the measure of a dried fig to render one liable to a *chatas* (*Rav; Rashi*).

18. Since people cook lentils without first shelling them and then eat the peels as well, the peels are considered part of the lentil and can be counted toward making up the minimum. However, this is not the case with the outer shell, in which the lentil grows, because that shell falls off at harvest time, and is not eaten (*Rav; Rashi* from Gemara 76b).

GEMS FROM THE GEMARA

The Mishnah states that we cannot combine the various feeds that it mentions, because they are not alike in their prescribed amounts. The Gemara (76a), in the name of R' Yose bar Chanina, qualifies this ruling (see note 10 above): We cannot combine them to make up a more stringent prescribed amount, but we can combine them to make up a more lenient prescribed amount. [A feed whose minimum amount is large is considered "lenient," and is not considered significant enough to be combined with a "stringent" feed — one whose minimum amount is smaller — to create liability.] For example, tough straw [of which one must take out a camel's mouthful to be liable] cannot be combined and complete the [smaller] minimum amount for soft straw [i.e., a cow's mouthful]. On the other hand, a more "stringent" feed does combine with a more "lenient" feed to complete that feed's greater minimum amount. Therefore, we can combine soft straw with tough straw to complete the [larger] minimum amount for tough straw [i.e., a camel's mouthful].

The Gemara then challenges R' Yose's assertion: Can things that are not alike in their prescribed minimum measurements be combined to equal even a larger minimum measurement!? The Mishnah states (*Keilim* 27:2): The minimum size of cloth that can contract *tumah* is three *tefachim* by three *tefachim;* the minimum size of sackcloth that can contract *tumah* is four by four *tefachim;* a hide, five by five *tefachim;* a mat, six by six *tefachim;* and although a Baraisa taught that cloth and sack, sack and hide, hide and mat, all combine with one another to complete the [larger] minimum amount for *tumah,* R' Shimon explains that the only reason we can combine those materials is that they all share the same minimum size with respect to being able to contract *tumah* when certain *tamei* persons

פרשת ויצא

THURSDAY
PARASHAS VAYEITZEI

sit upon them [even without touching them] (this is known as *tumas midras;* see further, *Rashi* to *Succah* 17b). We see from R' Shimon's explanation that if they would not have identical minimums with respect to *midras,* they would not combine even to form a *larger* minimum. Why, then, do the different types of feed combine to create liability for carrying on the Sabbath?

The Gemara (76b) answers, in the name of Rava, that here too, we find an instance where the various feeds are equal, for even different types of feed are fit to be combined to make up a display sample. I.e., someone who sells various types of feed will pile them together in front of his window to display his stock. [Indeed, he prefers to combine them in this manner, for if he piles them separately, the wind will blow away the smaller piles.] Since there is a circumstance in which combining is useful for different types of feed (and all of them are equal in this situation), we can also combine them to complete the [larger] minimum amount for liability. A "stringent" feed can therefore combine and complete the minimum amount of a more "lenient" feed.

A MUSSAR THOUGHT FOR THE DAY

Rashi, citing the Midrash, explains that Leah thanked Hashem when Yehudah was born because, as a prophetess, she knew that Yaakov would have four wives and twelve sons. Since this was her fourth son, she was particularly grateful, for she realized that she had received more than her equitable share. [Clearly, *Rashi* does not mean to imply that a person need not thank Hashem unless he was given something extraordinary — he means only that for this reason, the gratitude was exceptionally significant, such that a child was given a name to commemorate it.]

In a similar vein, the Midrash says that Leah had assumed that her descendants would be privileged to lead the nation either as priests or as kings, but not both. When she gave birth to Yehudah, whose tribe would assume the crown of kingship, after already having given birth to Levi, from whom the priests of the nation would arise, she was exceptionally grateful for this honor.

R' Yerucham Levovitz (*Daas Torah, Bereishis* 1:184) points out that Leah's special acknowledgment of Hashem at this time is illustrative of the concept that one should increase his devotion and gratitude to Hashem as his perception of the goodness showered upon him grows. Indeed, this is the theme of the sixth chapter of *Chovos HaLevavos*

פרשת ויצא

THURSDAY

PARASHAS VAYEITZEI

(*Shaar Avodas Elokim*). After explaining the general categories for which one must be thankful, *Chovos HaLevavos* delineates three areas in a person's thinking which mar his ability to properly acknowledge and express his thankfulness to Hashem, though he recognizes that Hashem is the source of his life and bounty: (1) excessive self-love, and a desire to obtain and increase one's gratification; (2) a lack of understanding that Hashem's beneficence is based on His desire to bestow His goodness upon someone, and is not the result of a particular supplication; and (3) the mistaken belief that one is deserving of the good he receives from Hashem, in return for the services one provides to Hashem. In truth, of course, Hashem of His own volition seeks and knows what is best for each person, and freely showers us with good even though we are undeserving.

The Gemara in *Berachos* (7b) states that until Leah's naming of Yehudah, no one had praised Hashem for the bounty they had received. This raises the apparent difficulty: Did the *Avos* not understand and comply with the tenets laid forth in *Chovos HaLevavos*? What was novel about Leah's gratitude?

An explanation might be suggested based upon the words of *Chovos HaLevavos* in Chapter 7, where he enumerates ten conditions of requisite thought in properly discharging one's minimal obligations of service and acknowledgment of Hashem. The fifth is that one should not be proud or boastful of his fortune, ascribing it to his own strength or wisdom or any other personal quality. It would seem that the greatest danger of this failing arises when one's success surpasses that which might be construed as normal or expected. It is then that the tendency to take credit is most prevalent. The antidote to this feeling is the forceful and open declaration that one understands that this "extra" beneficence is attributable only to Hashem's kindness. This was first done by Leah. At the very time she was shown that she was to be the mother of a larger share of the *shevatim* than she could have expected, she took no credit, but thanked Hashem for the [undeserved] gift. Thus, Leah meant to say, "[Especially] at this time, I [declare] acknowledgment of Hashem."

HALACHAH OF THE DAY

It is permissible to mix and knead together two fully combined mixtures that are of the same consistency. Since all the particles in each mixture have already been blended, combining the two mixtures is not an act of kneading.

פרשת ויצא

THURSDAY
PARASHAS VAYEITZEI

For example, one may mix egg salad with chopped liver or with tuna salad, as all of these are thick mixtures. Similarly, one may combine applesauce with another fruit puree, as these are both loose mixtures.

However, in cases where one of the mixtures is loose and the other is thick, it is possible for one to transgress the prohibition of kneading by causing the particles contained in the loose mixture to become more tightly bound together through the addition of the thick mixture. Therefore, when blending a thick mixture with a thin one, one must take note of what the final result will be. If the final mixture will be loose, the blending may be done with the employ of a proper *shinui*. If, however, the final result will be a thick mixture, it is prohibited (even with a *shinui*) except in cases of necessity.

We will close our discussions of the melachah of *kneading* with some commonplace applications of this *melachah*.

Chopped eggs or tuna may be combined with mayonnaise without reversing the order in which the ingredients are added to one another. As we explained above, since the mayonnaise is a heavy, thick substance, we are not concerned that the solids will begin to combine prior to their being mixed. However, after adding the ingredients together, the mixing must be done with a *shinui,* i.e., mixing in a crisscross fashion or with a bare hand.

Egg salad in which oil is used as a binder (in a situation where the finished product is a true mixture, rather than moistened clumps that fall apart readily) should preferably be prepared prior to the onset of Shabbos. If this is not possible, one may prepare it on Shabbos by adding the ingredients together in the reverse of the usual manner, and then mixing it with a *shinui.*

Loose baby cereal may be prepared on Shabbos as long as the proper *shinuim* are used. One must first reverse the order in which the ingredients are added, and the stirring must be done in an irregular manner. [One should take care to add a large amount of the liquid in the first pour, to avoid creating a thick mixture initially.]

Thick baby cereal may be prepared only in cases of necessity, for example, for a baby who will not eat loosely mixed cereal. The order of adding the ingredients must be reversed, and the stirring must be done with a *shinui* — such as crisscross or with a bare hand. Stirring such a mixture with a knife or with the handle of a utensil is forbidden.

Powdered baby formula may be prepared on Shabbos. However, one must be careful to start mixing the liquid and the powder with a large quantity of liquid so that it does not form a paste initially.

We have now concluded our discussions of the *melachah* of *kneading.*

פרשת ויצא

THURSDAY

PARASHAS VAYEITZEI

A CLOSER LOOK AT THE SIDDUR

In every *Shemoneh Esrei*, we say the blessing of מוֹדִים אֲנַחְנוּ לָךְ ..., *We thank you, Hashem ...*, as the penultimate blessing, after the blessing of עֲבוֹדָה, *service*, and prior to the blessing for שָׁלוֹם, *peace*.

The fundamental concept of *hodaah*, thanking Hashem, is beautifully illuminated by *Rabbi Shamshom Raphael Hirsch*. He states: "It reminds us of the great debt of gratitude which we owe to our Maker even now for all the things which He has given us in the past, and for all the favors that we still receive at every moment of the present. *Hodaah* is not mere verbal thanksgiving. The word מוֹדִים derives from the root ידה, from which is also derived יד, the Hebrew word for *hand*. Thus, it actually means 'to give one's hand to Hashem.' It is homage deriving from our awareness of what we owe Him ... In fact, our very hands belong to Hashem for it is from Him alone that we have whatever strength and ability we possess."

This blessing begins with a direct acknowledgment of Hashem as our God and the God of our fathers, as well as our Savior and Protector. We then offer particular thanks for specific benefits for which we are grateful. These are: (1) our lives, that are committed to His Hands; (2) our souls, that are entrusted to Him (every evening as we sleep); and (3) the many miracles (נִסִּים) that are with us every day, and the wonders (נִפְלָאוֹת) and benefits that He constantly performs, at all times, for our benefit.

Iyun Tefillah explains that the word נֵס, *miracle*, can be used both for miraculous events which defy nature, as well as for common events, which by virtue of their regularity are not recognized as miraculous. The light of the sun and moon and the harmonious operation of the world are no less wondrous and majestic workings of Hashem than the perceived supernatural miracles, and both are alluded to in our thanks.

Akin to this lesson, *Siach Yitzchak* and *Eitz Yosef* say that the *wonders* (נִפְלָאוֹת) referred to in this blessing are the natural laws that keep us alive (such as gravity, respiration, and the like). For this reason, the wonders are described as being with us *at all times*, while the miracles are not.

After declaring that we acknowledge Hashem at all times — evening, morning, and afternoon — the prayer continues with הַטּוֹב כִּי לֹא כָלוּ רַחֲמֶיךָ, *the Beneficent One, for Your compassion is never exhausted;* וְהַמְרַחֵם כִּי לֹא תַמּוּ חֲסָדֶיךָ, *and the Compassionate One, for Your Kind-*

THURSDAY

PARASHAS VAYEITZEI

nesses never ended; מֵעוֹלָם קִוִּינוּ לָךְ, *always have we put our hope in You.* These seemingly repetitive phrases are interpreted by *Siach Yitzchak.* He explains that one may have the wonderful quality of compassion (רַחֲמִים), but it is not open-ended, and there are situations where he will not feel compassionate. And even one who has a great capacity for compassion is limited in his ability to effectively bring that compassion to fruition (חֶסֶד). Hashem, however, has a boundless desire to be compassionate, and a limitless capability of bestowing that compassion on man.

פרשת ויצא — A TORAH THOUGHT FOR THE DAY

FRIDAY
PARASHAS VAYEITZEI

וְלָבָן הָלַךְ לִגְזֹז אֶת־צֹאנוֹ וַתִּגְנֹב רָחֵל אֶת־הַתְּרָפִים אֲשֶׁר לְאָבִיהָ
Lavan had gone to shear his sheep, and Rachel stole the teraphim (idols) that were her father's (Bereishis 31:19).

The commentaries are bothered by the problem of how Rachel was permitted to take Lavan's *teraphim*. Although the Midrash (cited by *Rashi*) explains that Rachel's intent was a noble one — to prevent her father from worshiping idols — taking something that belongs to somebody else is theft, and it is prohibited even if one has the best intentions. Another question that is raised (see *R' Eliyahu Mizrachi*) addresses the seemingly overly wordy style in which the verse is written. Since the verse begins by noting that Lavan was absent, it could have continued simply by stating וַתִּגְנֹב רָחֵל אֶת תְּרָפָיו, *and Rachel stole his teraphim*, or even וַתִּגְנֹב רָחֵל אֶת תְּרָפֵי אָבִיהָ, *and Rachel stole her father's teraphim*. Instead, the Torah chooses to use a longer, seemingly unnecessary phrase: וַתִּגְנֹב רָחֵל אֶת הַתְּרָפִים אֲשֶׁר לְאָבִיהָ, which literally translates as: *and Rachel stole the teraphim that were to her father*.

In answer to the first question of how Rachel was allowed to take her father's possessions, *Chavatzeles HaSharon*, quoting *Shevus Yaakov* (3:38), points out that since the *teraphim* were idols, Lavan, like everyone else, was forbidden to worship them. More importantly, as *Rambam* in *Hilchos Avodah Zarah* (7:2) — apparently quoting the Gemara *Yerushalmi Avodah Zarah* 5:12 — states, beyond the prohibition to worship an idol, a person must not benefit from it in any way whatsoever, and in fact, we have an obligation to destroy any form of idolatry.

Many commentators (see, for example, *Tosafos* to *Sanhedrin* 79a), maintain that an item has no value if it may not be used. In addition, they conclude that such an item cannot be owned. Ownership is essentially the right to derive benefit from an object without needing anyone else's permission. If no one is allowed to use a certain object, then the person who happens to be holding onto it at the moment has no more rights to it than anyone else. This implies that the *teraphim* in Lavan's house — like all *issurei hanaah*, items from which one is forbidden to derive any benefit — in addition to being intrinsically worthless, were also ownerless. For this reason, the Torah refers to them not as "Lavan's *teraphim*" — for indeed, they were not legally his — but rather as "the *teraphim* that were to her father"; that is, the *teraphim* that he was holding, without really owning them.

פרשת ויצא

FRIDAY

PARASHAS VAYEITZEI

Therefore, *Shevus Yaakov* explains, Rachel did nothing wrong by taking the *teraphim*. In a proper case of "theft," the owner loses his ability to use and enjoy his object. This was not true in regard to the *teraphim;* since the Torah forbids deriving any benefit from them, the *teraphim*, like all idols, had no value and were legally ownerless. As such, Lavan did not actually lose anything (since the idols were not his to begin with). Understanding this, Rachel, wanting to stop Lavan from continuing his idolatrous ways, took these *teraphim* with her when leaving.

R' Yaakov Kamenetsky, bothered by what the Torah means to teach us in recounting Rachel's theft of her father's *teraphim* and Lavan's relentless hunt to find them, suggests that we may use this episode to better appreciate the flawless integrity of Yaakov and his family. Even after thoroughly searching through the belongings of Yaakov's family in search of his idols, Lavan was forced to concede to Yaakov's angry retort of: כִּי־מִשַּׁשְׁתָּ אֶת־כָּל־כֵּלַי מַה־מָּצָאתָ מִכֹּל כְּלֵי־בֵיתֶךָ, *When you rummaged through all of my things, what did you find of all of your household objects?* (31:37). Even after twenty years of living with Lavan, Yaakov and his family had been so careful not to take what was not theirs that Lavan was unable to find a single thing that belonged to him among all of their possessions! Perhaps this insight into the integrity of Yaakov and his family is even stronger in light of *Shevus Yaakov's* explanation; even when driven by the pure desire to prevent her father from sinning, Rachel acted only because she knew that her actions would not violate the prohibition against thievery.

MISHNAH OF THE DAY: SHABBOS 8:1

The previous chapter concluded with a discussion of the minimum amounts of various foodstuffs that one must take out on the Sabbath in order to be liable to a *chatas*. This chapter continues the topic, discussing various beverages, liquids, and other substances:

הַמּוֹצִיא יַיִן — *One who takes out wine*[1] from one domain to another on the Sabbath, or carries it a distance of four *amos* in a public domain,

---
NOTES

1. The Mishnah refers to pure, undiluted wine (*Rav; Rashi*). [In Talmudic times, raw wine was very concentrated and had to be mixed with water before it was suitable for drinking.]

FRIDAY

PARASHAS VAYEITZEI

בְּדֵי מְזִיגַת הַכּוֹס — is liable to a *chatas* if he takes out **enough to mix a cup**;[2] חָלָב — if he takes out **milk,** בְּדֵי גְמִיעָה — he is liable to a *chatas* if he takes out **enough for a swallow;**[3] דְּבַשׁ — if he takes out **honey,** בְּדֵי לִיתֵּן עַל הַכָּתִית — he is liable to a *chatas* if he takes out **enough to place** it as ointment **upon a sore;**[4] שֶׁמֶן — if he takes out olive **oil,** בְּדֵי לָסוּךְ אֵבֶר קָטָן — he is liable to a *chatas* if he takes out **enough to anoint a small limb;**[5] מַיִם — if he takes out **water,** בְּדֵי לָשׁוּף בָּהֶם אֶת הַקִּילוֹר — he is liable to a *chatas* if he takes out **enough to rub** on **an eye salve;**[6] וּשְׁאָר כָּל הַמַּשְׁקִין בִּרְבִיעִית — **and** if he takes out **any other beverages,** he is liable to a *chatas* if he takes out a

---- NOTES ----

2. I.e., the amount of pure wine that, when mixed with the proper amount of water, yields enough wine for mixing the cup used for reciting *Bircas HaMazon* — the Grace After Meals. This amount is 1/16 of a *log*. This figure is arrived at as follows: Raw wine was customarily diluted with water in the proportion of one part wine to three parts of water. [This is what is meant by *mixing* a cup — i.e., mixing the necessary amount of wine with the proper proportion of water to form one cupful.] Now, the minimum size of the cup used for *Bircas HaMazon* and other mitzvos that require a cup of wine is one-quarter of a *log*, known as a רְבִיעִית, *revi'is*. Thus, the amount of wine actually used in such a cup was one-quarter of the total volume of the cup. This comes to 1/16 of a *log* (*Rav* from *Gemara* 76b).

3. This is the amount of milk that a person can consume in a single gulp (*Rav; Rambam Commentary*).

4. The sore in question is a type of blister that often forms on the backs of horses and camels, due to the constant rubbing of the burdens that they bear (*Rav; Rashi;* see their alternative interpretations). Now, it is true that honey is used mainly as a foodstuff, and therefore we might have expected the minimum amount to be the same as that of all other foodstuffs — viz., the equivalent of a dried fig (as in Mishnah 7:4). Nevertheless, it is also *commonly* used for medicinal purposes. Hence, even a person who takes out the smaller amount that can be used as an ointment is liable to a *chatas* (*Rav, Meiri* from *Gemara* 78a).

5. The *Gemara* (77b, 78a) explains that this is an amount sufficient to anoint the smallest limb of a newborn infant. Some explain this as the infant's little toe (*Rav; Rambam*); others as a joint of its little finger (*Rashi*).

6. One is liable for taking out water only if it is an amount at least sufficient to rub on an eye plaster. Just as is the case with honey, although water is used mostly for drinking, its alternative use on an eye plaster was also a common use. Hence, even a person who takes out the smaller amount that is used to rub on an eye plaster is liable to a *chatas*. [Although other liquids are also suitable for this purpose, generally water was used, since other liquids would form a crust and impair the vision of the person who was using the plaster. Therefore, only in the case of water is one liable for this smaller amount; the minimum amount of other liquids is the amount suitable for drinking (*Tos. R' Akiva Eiger* from *Gemara* 78a; see next note).]

PARASHAS VAYEITZEI — FRIDAY

revi'is;[7] וְכָל הַשּׁוֹפָכִין בִּרְבִיעִית — *and if he takes out any waste water,* he is also liable to a *chatas* if he takes out *a revi'is.*[8]

The Mishnah cites a dissenting view: רַבִּי שִׁמְעוֹן אוֹמֵר — כּוּלָן בִּרְבִיעִית — *R' Shimon says:* The minimum amount for *all of these* substances is a *revi'is;*[9] וְלֹא נֶאֶמְרוּ כָּל הַשִּׁעוּרִין הַלָּלוּ — *and all of these* smaller *measurements* given by the previous Tanna *were not stated* אֶלָּא לְמַצְנִיעֵיהֶן — *except for those who store* these substances in small quantities.[10]

―――――― NOTES ――――――

7. Other beverages are normally not used for medicinal purposes, but for drinking. Hence, one is liable only if he takes out the normal amount for drinking a cupful — i.e., a רְבִיעִית, a quarter-*log* — the equivalent of the volume of one-and-a-half hen's eggs (*Rav*; *Rashi*). [Modern authorities differ as to the contemporary equivalent of a *revi'is*; opinions range between 2.9 and 5.2 ounces.]

8. Dirty or fouled water is fit neither for rubbing on an eye plaster nor for drinking. Nevertheless, one is liable for taking out a quarter-*log*, since that amount is suitable for kneading clay (*Rav* from Gemara 78a).

9. R' Shimon disagrees with the Tanna Kamma of the Mishnah, and maintains that wine, milk and honey are to be treated as beverages, and therefore one is liable only if he takes out a *revi'is* (*Rav*; *Rashi*). [*Rav* and *Rashi* imply that R' Shimon does *not* dispute the rulings of the Tanna Kamma with respect to oil or water. *Tiferes Yisrael* suggests that in the case of olive oil this is because it is not used as a beverage. Therefore, it cannot be categorized as a beverage. Consequently, its common use — viz., anointing — defines its minimum amount. In the case of water, its alternative use for an eye plaster was more common than the alternative use of wine, milk and honey, and therefore even R' Shimon agrees that its minimum amount is defined by its alternative use.]

10. According to R' Shimon, while the smaller amounts mentioned by the first Tanna of the Mishnah do not apply to all persons, they do apply to someone who had previously stored such small amounts of these substances and then took them out on the Sabbath. This is in line with the Gemara's statement (on 75b) that R' Shimon disagrees with the rule of the Mishnah (7:3) that a person who stores even a minute amount of a substance is liable if he subsequently takes it out. In his opinion, even one who stores a substance is liable for taking it out only if it is an amount that is *occasionally* stored by most people (*Rav*; *Rashi*).

QUESTION OF THE DAY:
Why were the idols of Lavan called terafim?

For the answer, see page 176.

פרשת ויצא

GEMS FROM THE GEMARA

FRIDAY
PARASHAS VAYEITZEI

The Mishnah stated that one is liable to a *chatas* for taking out honey if he took out enough honey to place on a sore. The Gemara (77b) cites a statement that mentions another treatment for sores:

Rav Yehudah said in the name of Rav: "In all that the Holy One, Blessed is He, created in His world, He did not create even one thing needlessly."

Rav Yehudah illustrates his point by enumerating uses for several seemingly useless creations: Hashem created the slug as a remedy for a sore; He created the fly to crush and use as a salve for the sting of a hornet; He created the gnat to use as a salve for the bite of a snake; He created the snake to be used as a salve for certain types of boils; and He created a spider to be used as a salve for the sting of a scorpion. Thus, even creatures that are seemingly purposeless serve as valuable remedies.

Subsequently, the Gemara cites a Baraisa that notes five instances of fears where the fear of the weak is upon the strong. The Baraisa mentions several of the insects discussed by Rav Yehudah:

(1) The fear of a small beast called a *mafgia* upon the lion. The *mafgia* has an exceedingly powerful cry, and when it screams, the lion fears that a great beast is coming to challenge it, and it flees.

(2) The fear of the gnat upon the elephant. [The gnat enters the trunk of the elephant, and the elephant cannot dislodge it.]

(3) The fear of the spider upon the scorpion. [The spider enters the body of the scorpion via its ear, and the scorpion cannot dislodge it.]

(4) The fear of the swallow upon the eagle. [The swallow enters beneath the wings of the eagle, and, once ensconced there, prevents the eagle from spreading its wings.]

(5) The fear of a small creeping creature called the *kilbis* upon the great Leviathan fish of the sea. [The *kilbis* kills larger fish by burrowing into their ears.]

Rav Yehudah in the name of Rav cites a Scriptural source for these phenomena: What verse is there that refers to such relationships in nature? It is the verse that proclaims (*Amos* 5:9): *He who causes the weak to triumph over the powerful.*

Thus, the Gemara demonstrates that besides the medicinal uses mentioned by Rav Yehudah, all creatures can be used as instruments of God to exact retribution from the wicked, even if they seem to be insignificant creations of no purpose. Hence, a person should never arrogantly assume that his power is such that he cannot be punished, for God can summon even the lowliest of creatures to triumph over him (see *Maharsha;* for an example of such retribution, see *Gittin* 57a).

פרשת ויצא

FRIDAY

PARASHAS VAYEITZEI

A MUSSAR THOUGHT FOR THE DAY

Although, as we explained in *A Torah Thought for the Day,* a person is precluded from enjoying and even owning *issurei hanaah,* items from which one is forbidden to derive any benefit, a quick overview of the list of forbidden items reveals something very interesting: there are no items that are permanently forbidden when found in their natural state. For example, milk and meat, or wool and linen, when enjoyed individually, may be eaten or worn; it is only when they are combined that the new mixture becomes forbidden for use and for enjoyment. Similarly, the raw materials used to make Lavan's *teraphim,* or any *avodah zarah,* may be used for the myriad of purposes to which wood, stone or metal may be put. Use of this material becomes forbidden only when man designates the material or something constructed from it as an idol. Even items that are forbidden in their natural state, such as *chametz* on Pesach, are not *permanently* proscribed; after the forbidden window of time has passed, the restriction is lifted, and the *chametz* is Biblically permitted for use. [However, *chametz* that remained in a Jew's possession on Pesach is *Rabbinically* prohibited, to ensure that people do not inadvertently transgress the Torah prohibition of actually owning *chametz* on Pesach.]

From this we can derive an important lesson: Hashem did not create anything in nature which man is not allowed to use in some way or another (see *A Closer Look at the Siddur*). Moreover, many forbidden items (such as milk and meat that were cooked together, idols, or *shaatnez* mixtures) come about only because something was done to them by a person — it was he who combined them or designated an item as an idol. Although the *reason* why each individual *issur hanaah* is forbidden to be used is often unique unto itself, only one thing can actually *make* these items forbidden — man's actions.

פרשת ויצא

FRIDAY

PARASHAS VAYEITZEI

With this in mind, the laws of *issurei hanaah* serve as a powerful reminder of the *mussar* principle of *gadlus ha'adam*, man's inherent greatness. Through his every deed, a person affects spiritual worlds to an extent far beyond that which he can tangibly appreciate. It is only through the latent power in man's actions that a previously permitted item of Hashem's creation, with all of its potential for use, growth, and development, can in an instant become totally worthless and forbidden, to the extent that a person will even be punished for using this item. [Of course, man's inner potential for greatness through the ramifications of his actions does not mean only that he has the potential to destroy. More importantly, he has the means, and therefore the duty, to use his abilities to build, by spiritually improving the world through performing mitzvos wherever possible.]

The Alter of Slabodka reveals in *Ohr HaTzafun* (vol. 2, p. 72) what it is about a person that gives him the great power to affect lofty spiritual worlds: man — or more specifically, his *neshamah* — is created *b'tzelem Elokim*, in God's Image. This, explains the Alter, means that from of all of creation, only man was granted *bechirah*, the ability of choice, allowing him the freedom to actually make a decision and change part of creation, in emulation of Hashem Himself. Another similarity between man's abilities and those of Hashem is that a person's decisions and actions do not only affect himself. Rather, man's position as the only one able to serve Hashem through choice allows him to use all of creation as the stage in which to do so. As a result, any action — good or bad — that a person does affects all of creation.

The *mashgiach* of the prewar Slabodka Yeshivah, *R' Avraham Grodzenski*, emphasizes in his *Toras Avraham* that a person must constantly remember his inherent greatness, for only when realizing that every mitzvah that he does improves the world and any misdeed damages it, will he be sufficiently motivated to use his great potential to perform only good. A person who forgets what he can achieve through his actions will often sin, by rationalizing that he really isn't doing anything wrong. It is only by maintaining an awareness of man's inherent greatness through *mussar* teachings and tangible examples that a person will realize the great privilege and responsibility that Hashem has given him.

HALACHAH OF THE DAY

פרשת ויצא

FRIDAY

PARASHAS VAYEITZEI

At the outset of our discussions of the thirty-nine forbidden labors of Shabbos, we mentioned that the first eleven of these forbidden activities are at times referred to as the *Sedura D'Pas*, the *order of baking bread*. They are so called because they comprise the labors necessary to bring raw materials from their natural raw state to the point where they are fully prepared for consumption. Having covered the first ten labors in this group, we now arrive at one of the forbidden *melachos* that is the most applicable in the kitchen on an ordinary Shabbos — the *melachah* of בִּשּׁוּל, *cooking*.

Although the literal translation of the word בִּשּׁוּל is *cooking*, bishul is a general term used to include all methods of food preparation that employ the application of heat. This includes baking, frying, broiling, and roasting.

The halachic definition of *cooking* is to effect a change in the properties of a substance through the application of heat. Thus, cooking raw foods, melting hard substances, or baking substances in order to harden them are all forms of the forbidden labor of *cooking*.

While the *melachah* applies to food as well as non-food items, we will limit our discussion to *bishul* as it applies to the preparation of food.

This prohibition applies to all foods, both solid or liquid. Even foods that are edible in their raw state, for instance many fruits and vegetables, may not be cooked on Shabbos. Similarly, liquids that are fit for drinking while cold are still subject to this prohibition, and may not be heated on Shabbos.

It is forbidden to cook on or near any source of heat on Shabbos. A flame, an electric heating element, hot plate or urn are all forms of heat sources that may not be used for cooking on Shabbos. Cooking with a microwave oven is likewise forbidden on Shabbos. [However, some of these forms of *bishul* are forbidden by Biblical law, while others are forbidden Rabbinically.]

The *melachah* of *cooking* is separate and distinct from the *melachah* of הַבְעָרָה, *kindling*. One may not cook on Shabbos even over a flame that has been kindled prior to the onset of Shabbos.

The degree to which an item must be heated or changed through the application of heat varies depending on the item in question. Tomorrow, we will begin to discuss this issue in detail.

פרשת ויצא — A CLOSER LOOK AT THE SIDDUR

FRIDAY
PARASHAS VAYEITZEI

As we noted in *A Mussar Thought for the Day*, the many types of *issurei hanaah*, items from which one is forbidden to derive any benefit, have one thing in common: None of Hashem's creations are completely forbidden for benefit in their natural state. While it true that the Torah will forbid certain uses of an item, nothing is completely forbidden. While horses or rabbits, for example, may not be eaten, they may certainly be used for their furs, hides, or as beasts of burden. There is nothing that Hashem created that may not be enjoyed in some way. It is only after man *misuses* an item, and effectively ruins it to the extent that any further use will do more harm than good, that the Torah precludes further use by designating it as forbidden for further benefit.

This observation is easily understood when seen in light of the *Mesillas Yesharim's* statement that Hashem created the world to give pleasure to man. It is unquestionably true, as the *Mesillas Yesharim* goes on to explain, that the ultimate place where this pleasure will be given is in the spiritual bliss of *Olam Haba;* the present world is the place to perform mitzvos in order to earn this ultimate delight. *Sefer HaChinuch* (*Mitzvah* 430, see also *Mitzvos* 62 and 92) points out that, albeit to a lesser degree, the Divine wish to provide pleasure is the reason for the vast array of beauty and enjoyment that may be easily appreciated in *Olam Hazeh* as well. [See also *Ohr HaTzafun,* end of vol. 3.] Everything that Hashem, the ultimate Doer of *chesed,* created, from health to pleasant-tasting fruits to the beautiful spectacle of a sunset, was not created to provide for Hashem's needs, for He needs nothing; rather, it was all intended for man's enjoyment. With this insight for the reason behind all of the world's magnificence and opportunity in mind, it makes sense why there is nothing in nature that man may not use; why would Hashem create a world that is only there for man's benefit, and then forbid him to use part of that world?

R' Yosef Brown points out that the message that the world and all its bounty was created only for man's enjoyment is seen in the *Tur's* (*Orach Chaim* 207) explanation of a phrase in the *berachah* of *Borei Nefashos*. After partaking of a snack, we thank Hashem, *Who creates numerous living things with their deficiencies, and for all that You have created* **to enliven the existence of every being.**

Tur (see also *Shulchan Aruch HaRav*) explains that the phrase *Who creates numerous living things with their deficiencies* means that Hashem, in addition to creating man, took into account all of man's needs, such as food and shelter, and in His great kindness, created the materials needed to make up these *deficiencies* as well. In the continuation of the *berachah*, we thank Hashem for *all that You have created to enliven the existence of every being.* Tur explains that this phrase refers to all the other things in the world that man does not absolutely need, which would not be lacking if they were not available. These "extras" were nonetheless created by Hashem for the singular purpose of bestowing added pleasure and enjoyment upon mankind — *to enliven the existence of every being.*

A TASTE OF LOMDUS

Several commentators, including *Noda BiYehudah* (*Mahadura Kamma, Orach Chaim* §19), ask an interesting question: If forbidden items are both worthless and ownerless, as *Shevus Yaakov* explains in regard to Lavan's *teraphim* (see *A Torah Thought for the Day*), it would seem that a person who "buys" *chametz* on Pesach should not transgress the prohibition against owning *chametz*! For, as was explained above, an object that is *assur b'hanaah,* totally forbidden for benefit, is intrinsically worthless, and in effect cannot be owned. Thus, a Jew should not be able to legally complete such a purchase during Pesach. If he tries to buy *chametz* from another Jew, the transaction would be meaningless, since the seller does not actually own the forbidden *chametz*, and he cannot sell what he does not own. And even a non-Jew, who definitely owns his *chametz* during Pesach (since halachah places no restrictions on what a non-Jew may own on Pesach), will not be able to complete a sale of *chametz* to a Jew. For from the Jew's perspective, this *chametz* still falls under the category of *issurei hanaah,* and since he cannot eat or use it, there should be no way for him to become the legal owner of the *chametz*, as there is nothing about it for him to acquire. Yet, we find that *Rambam* (*Hilchos Chametz U'Matzah* 1:3) clearly rules that a person is liable for purchasing *chametz* on Pesach!

Now, it is true that the Gemara (*Pesachim* 6b) comments that *chametz* is unique in that a person can be held responsible for its "possession" even without owning it. Indeed, from a halachic standpoint, *chametz* is considered to belong to a person as long as he failed to destroy it before the onset of the *chametz* prohibition. One may argue, however, that this rule applies only to *chametz* that the person actually owned at some point before Pesach. Everyone agrees that the Torah requires a person

פרשת ויצא

FRIDAY

PARASHAS VAYEITZEI

to rid his house of *chametz,* and that he is liable for any of "his" *chametz* that remains once the festival begins. However, since he never owns or even acquires *chametz* that he buys *on* Pesach, perhaps there is no justification for holding him accountable for its possession, since it was never legally "his." Thus, *Rambam's* ruling still requires explanation.

Many commentators struggle to explain the legal mechanics that render a person who tries to purchase *chametz* on Pesach halachically liable, despite the fact that he never owns the *chametz. Chedvas Yaakov* (1:136) offers an ingenious explanation, based on a ruling of *Ritva* (brought in *Nesivos HaMishpat* 232). *Ritva* states that a buyer who discovers that his purchase is defective, although he is entitled to a full refund, is still considered a *shomer sachar,* a paid custodian, with respect to the object. Although the seller has not actually paid the buyer to guard the merchandise, the laws governing a paid custodian apply to anyone who derives benefit from his custodial responsibilities. Since the buyer can get his money back only if he returns the item in its original condition, and any theft or damage to the object will result in the loss of his refund, he obviously has a personal interest in guarding the merchandise well. *Chedvas Yaakov* observes that a person who pays for *chametz* on Pesach would also be considered a paid custodian. Although he cannot legally acquire or own the *chametz,* he nonetheless maintains a financial interest in ensuring that the *chametz* stays in good condition, because otherwise he will not be able to get a refund.

With this in mind, *Chedvas Yaakov* explains why one who buys *chametz* on Pesach is liable for owning *chametz,* although he is unable to acquire it. The buyer gains from the *chametz,* in the sense that his responsibility to properly watch the article gives him a financial interest in it; this limited involvement in *chametz* is also prohibited on Pesach. A person who attempts to buy *chametz* will therefore be liable — not for buying it per se, but for enjoying financial gain from it on Pesach.

A TORAH THOUGHT FOR THE DAY

פרשת ויצא

SHABBOS
PARASHAS VAYEITZEI

הָיִיתִי בַיּוֹם אֲכָלַנִי חֹרֶב וְקֶרַח בַּלָּיְלָה וַתִּדַּד שְׁנָתִי מֵעֵינָי.
זֶה־לִּי עֶשְׂרִים שָׁנָה בְּבֵיתֶךָ עֲבַדְתִּיךָ אַרְבַּע־עֶשְׂרֵה שָׁנָה בִּשְׁתֵּי
בְנֹתֶיךָ וְשֵׁשׁ שָׁנִים בְּצֹאנֶךָ וַתַּחֲלֵף אֶת־מַשְׂכֻּרְתִּי עֲשֶׂרֶת מֹנִים

This is how I was: By day scorching heat consumed me,
and frost by night; my sleep drifted from my eyes.
This is my twenty years in your household.
I served you fourteen years for your two daughters,
and six years for your flocks, and you changed
my wage a hundred times (Bereishis 31:40-41).

Many commentators address the question of why it was necessary for Yaakov to repeat, *"This is my twenty years ...,"* when he had just said to Lavan, *These twenty years I have been with you* (v. 38). Furthermore, why does the verse here interject the word לִי (*my* twenty years) in Yaakov's argument?

Kli Yakar explains that Yaakov was contrasting his behavior during those twenty years with Lavan's, as if to say, "Whereas I worked for you for twenty years diligently and honestly, and you prospered, you in turn treated me badly, by changing the terms of compensation ten times." This interpretation, adds *Kli Yakar*, explains why the first verse (v. 38) says עִמָּךְ, *with you,* while the latter verse (v. 41) says לִי, *my* or *to me.*

Rabbeinu Bachya understands the two verses in essentially the same way, but adds a Kabbalistic interpretation. He states that for purposes of Yaakov's rejoinder to Lavan, the first verse alone would have sufficed. The latter verse, however, was meant as a veiled reference to Hashem's Presence (which occurred לִי — for *my* benefit alone) during the twenty years that Yaakov was in Lavan's employ. This also explains why, in the very next verse (v. 42), Yaakov explicitly acknowledges Hashem's intervention as being responsible for his success.

Netziv (in *Haamek Davar*), too, agrees that only the first verse was necessary for Yaakov's argument. In the second verse, however, Yaakov is explaining why Lavan was so suspicious. Yaakov declared: "I toiled for you for twenty years with impeccable honesty, and shepherded your flocks to a degree far beyond the norm — yet, you accuse me of theft. The reason for your mistrust is that although 'for twenty years I worked for you,' you were nevertheless crooked and deceitful toward me, and you assumed that your wicked nature and behavior must be mirrored in mine."

SHABBOS

PARASHAS VAYEITZEI

This is based on the psychological truism, says the *Netziv*, that one who is lax or guilty of some misdeed is suspicious of others being so as well; as the Gemara notes in *Kiddushin* (70a), one who denigrates others is likely to accuse them of possessing those very failings that he himself possesses.

Malbim, however, explains that both verses are necessary, as two components of Yaakov's argument: "If you have chased after me because you suspect me of having stolen something from your house, 'you have rummaged through all my things' and found nothing. And if you accuse me of shortchanging you as your shepherd, 'These twenty years I have been with you,' performing every aspect of shepherding to the utmost degree, and you suffered no losses. Perhaps you came after me because you felt that you shortchanged me in some way, and wished to make restitution? But that is illogical, because in this, my twenty years in your household, you have dealt with me only with trickery and thievery, both while I worked for your daughters and while I worked for your sheep. And had not Hashem been with me, you would surely have sent me away empty-handed even now. So why are you here?" [For a similar explanation, see *Abarbanel*.]

MISHNAH OF THE DAY: SHABBOS 8:2

The following Mishnah continues the discussion of the minimum amounts of various substances that one would need to take out on the Sabbath in order to be liable to a *chatas*:

הַמּוֹצִיא חֶבֶל — **One who takes out rope** from one domain to another, or carries it a distance of four *amos* in a public domain, כְּדֵי לַעֲשׂוֹת אוֹזֶן לְקוּפָּה — is liable to a *chatas* if he takes out **enough to make a handle for a basket;**[1] גֶּמִי — if he takes out **reed-grass,** כְּדֵי לַעֲשׂוֹת תְּלַאי לְנָפָה וְלִכְבָרָה — he is liable to a *chatas* if he takes out **enough to make a hanging loop for a sifter or a sieve.**[2] רַבִּי יְהוּדָה אוֹמֵר — *R' Yehudah*

NOTES

1. A קוּפָּה is a large basket or barrel (*Tiferes Yisrael*). Since rope is coarse, it is useful only for heavy utensils such as large baskets or barrels. Lightweight or thin utensils may be damaged by a coarse rope. Consequently, only a large enough amount of rope to make a basket handle will make a person liable (Gemara 78b; see next note).

2. A תְּלַאי is a kind of handle by which to hang a sifter or a sieve. This is a smaller minimum amount than the minimum amount of rope necessary to make a handle for a basket (*Rav*). [A sifter has fine holes, and is used to sift flour to rid it of bran. A sieve has large holes, and is used to separate kernels of grain from pebbles.]

SHABBOS

PARASHAS VAYEITZEI

says: בְּדֵי לִיטוֹל מִמֶּנּוּ מִדַּת מִנְעָל לְקָטָן — **He is liable to** a *chatas* if he takes out **enough to take the measure of a child's foot** for a shoe **with it.** [3] נְיָיר — **If he takes out *paper*,** בְּדֵי לִכְתּוֹב עָלָיו קֶשֶׁר מוֹכְסִין — **he is liable** to a *chatas* if he takes out **enough to write a tax collector's receipt on it;** [4] וְהַמּוֹצִיא קֶשֶׁר מוֹכְסִין חַיָּיב — **and one who takes out a tax-collector's receipt is liable** to a *chatas.* [5] נְיָיר מָחוּק — **If one takes out previously *erased paper*,** בְּדֵי לִכְרוֹךְ עַל צְלוֹחִית קְטַנָּה שֶׁל פְּלָיָיטוֹן — **he is liable to a *chatas* if he takes out enough to wrap around the mouth of a small flask of balsam oil.** [6]

---— NOTES ---—

3. Grass-reed was cut to measure the length of a child's foot, to show a cobbler so that he would make shoes of the proper size (*Rashi; Rav*). This is a smaller amount than that prescribed by the first Tanna (*Rav; Meiri*).

4. Toll collectors on one side of a river would issue receipts to be shown on the other side of the river as proof of payment. The receipt was a piece of paper with the collector's seal stamped on it. The seal generally consisted of two larger-than-usual letters (*Rav; Rashi*).

5. The Mishnah states this seemingly superfluous ruling to teach that even if the tax receipt was written on parchment or hide, for which minimum sizes are larger if they are blank (see the next Mishnah), one is still liable if he takes out a small piece of parchment or hide on which a tax receipt was written, because the receipt written upon it renders it significant (*Tosafos*).

6. Paper that has been written on and then erased is no longer suitable for writing upon. Therefore, the minimum size for such paper is larger than the small size needed for a tax collector's receipt — namely, the size required to wrap around the mouth of a small bottle of perfume as a stopper (*Rav; Rashi; Meiri*).

GEMS FROM THE GEMARA

The Mishnah stated that one who takes out a tax collector's receipt is liable. The Gemara (78b) cites a Baraisa that elaborates upon this ruling. The Tanna Kamma states that if one takes out a tax collector's receipt, the law is as follows: If he has not yet shown it to the tax collector, he is liable for taking it out; but once he has shown it to the tax collector, he is exempt, for he no longer has use for the receipt. R' Yehudah, however, disagrees, stating that even once he has shown it to the tax collector, he is still liable, because he still needs it.

The Gemara offers three explanations of the dispute between the Tanna Kamma and R' Yehudah:

(1) Abaye says that at issue is whether the person will wish to retain the

SHABBOS

PARASHAS VAYEITZEI

receipt to show to the tax collector's runners. R' Yehudah holds that he will, while the Tanna Kamma maintains that he will not keep it for that purpose. [*Rashi* explains that the tax collectors would occasionally send runners after people to check if they had paid the taxes, and these runners would bring back anyone who could not prove that he had already paid the official. R' Yehudah holds that a person would retain the receipt to avoid this, while the Tanna Kamma holds that a person resigns himself to returning if the runners call him.]

(2) Rava says that at issue is whether he will wish to retain the receipt in a situation where there are a chief tax collector and a subordinate tax collector. R' Yehudah maintains that even after the taxpayer has shown the receipt to the chief official, he will retain it to show to the subordinate official, while the Tanna Kamma holds that he will not. [*Rashi* explains that the Tanna Kamma and R' Yehudah dispute whether a person who has already paid the tax and has an official receipt to this effect will keep his receipt to show to the minor official. R' Yehudah maintains that he will; thus, one who takes it out is liable. The Tanna Kamma, however, maintains that the person will not want to show the chief tax collector's receipt to a minor official; rather, the senior official (who knows that he paid the tax) will have given him a verbal code or password that he can use to pass the minor official. Thus, the receipt is no longer valuable to him.]

(3) Rav Ashi said that the dispute concerns a case in which there is but a single tax collector in this vicinity. R' Yehudah holds that, nevertheless, the taxpayer will retain the receipt to show it to some future tax collector at another location, for he will want to produce the receipt and say to him, "See that I am a man who pays his taxes." [*Rashi* explains that both the Tanna Kamma and R' Yehudah agree that the tax receipt will not be used to prove that he has paid *this* tax. They differ only about whether he will wish to retain it so that he can prove his veracity and avoid being persecuted at another place and time by some other tax collector.]

QUESTION OF THE DAY:

Where in this parashah do we find words in the Torah that are not Hebrew?

For the answer, see page 176.

A MUSSAR THOUGHT FOR THE DAY

פרשת
ויצא

SHABBOS
PARASHAS
VAYEITZEI

The *Mesillas Yesharim*, in his discussion of *Middas Nekius* (Ch. 11), points out that although most people are not overt thieves, many have a "taste" of dishonesty in their business dealings, enjoying illegal gains at another's expense and rationalizing their behavior as acceptable for profit. One of the many types of dealings he discusses is the responsibilities of a worker to his employer. Citing the verse spoken by Yaakov Avinu to Lavan (*By day scorching heat consumed me, and frost by night; my sleep drifted from my eyes*), *Mesillas Yesharim* asks: "What can those who indulge in their private pleasures or needs during their work time answer to this?" Indeed, the obligation of a worker to utilize his full time and energy during the period for which he was hired is so strong that the Sages exempted him from saying a blessing on bread, and from reciting parts of *Krias Shema* and *Bircas HaMazon,* lest it interfere with his work. If so, how can a worker possibly imagine that it is permissible to cavalierly engage in his private activities? [It should be noted that nowadays these restrictions do not apply, as workers are generally hired with the understanding that they will be given time to make blessings and pray. In Talmudic times, however, this was not the case.]

Mesillas Yesharim further states that even if the worker engages in a mitzvah during his work time, it is not to his credit, but is deemed a sin. In his discussion of this point, *Mesillas Yesharim* points out that it is akin to the *Yerushalmi* (*Succah* 3:1) that says, in reference to one who stole a *lulav*, "Woe is to him, for his defender (mitzvah) has become his prosecutor." He explains that just as when one steals a mitzvah article, we say "Woe is to him . . ." rather than giving him credit for doing the mitzvah, so too when one steals time to do a mitzvah.

[*Rav Avraham Pam* (in *Atarah LaMelech* §125) adds that a teacher who comes late to class because of a custom to pray slowly and at length is also guilty of theft. Nor may he forego breakfast in order to be on time, for then he is performing his work in a weakened, hence less than optimal, state.]

In showing to what lengths a worker should go to be honest with his employer, *Mesillas Yesharim* cites the Gemara in *Taanis* (23b). The Gemara relates that when the world was in need of rain, the Rabbis would ask Abba Chilkiya, a grandson of Choni HaMe'agel, to pray and he would be answered. One time scholars were dispatched to him with this request, and they found him tending a field. They greeted him, but he took no notice of them. When they questioned him later about this strange

SHABBOS

PARASHAS VAYEITZEI

behavior, he told them that he was a day laborer, and he could not be distracted from his work.

Commenting on this story, R' Eliyahu Lopian (*Lev Eliyahu* 2:92) notes that it was specifically to such a person that the Rabbis entrusted the task of praying for rain, for he is close to God, as it says, *My eyes are upon the faithful* (trustworthy) *of the land, that they may dwell with me* (*Psalms* 101:6). In recounting the entire episode of Abba Chilkiya, the Gemara highlights his honesty, humility and decency, and not his wisdom or intellectual prowess. This is the type of person who can petition Hashem for rain, for the *Shechinah* rests upon him.

HALACHAH OF THE DAY

The Torah forbids one to cook a solid food on Shabbos to even a minimal degree of edibility. The Talmud defines minimal edibility as food that has been prepared *"like the food of Ben Derusai."* Ben Derusai was a thief who was constantly on the run due to the danger of his being apprehended, and as a result he was in the habit of cooking his foods quickly, bringing them only to the point of being barely edible. It is this degree of cooking that is prohibited on Shabbos.

There is a question among the *poskim* about how to precisely quantify this level of cooking. One opinion is that when the food has been cooked for one-third of its standard cooking time, it has reached the requirement of *Ben Derusai;* the other opinion requires the food to be half-cooked to reach this level. We follow the stringent view; it therefore follows that cooking food to one-third of its fully-cooked point is a violation of the Biblical prohibition against *cooking* on Shabbos.

While a food that has been one-third cooked is seen by halachah as being cooked in regard to transgressing the violation of *cooking,* it is nevertheless still forbidden to take such a food and cook it further, thereby bringing it to a greater degree of edibility on Shabbos. This will be discussed in greater detail further on.

In order to prevent any possible transgression of the Biblical prohibition of this *melachah,* the Sages added an additional prohibition as a safeguard. It is therefore forbidden by Rabbinic decree to place any uncooked item in a hot area where it could eventually become cooked. This decree applies even if one wishes to place the item in such a location for only a short time, during which it could not possibly become cooked. This decree was enacted out of concern that a person might forget to

פָּרָשַׁת
וַיֵּצֵא

SHABBOS

PARASHAS VAYEITZEI

remove the food before it becomes cooked, thus transgressing the Biblical prohibition discussed above.

Heating any liquid to its boiling point is considered cooking. Furthermore, as with solid foods, the Biblical prohibition forbids cooking liquids even to a minimal degree. The minimum level of cooking liquids is attained when the liquid is heated to a point referred to as *yad soledes bo,* the temperature at which *the hand will recoil.* We will discuss this measure in more detail tomorrow.

A CLOSER LOOK AT THE SIDDUR

This week, we will continue our study of the *V'Shomru* prayer, which is recited on Friday night immediately preceding the *Shemoneh Esrei* of *Maariv.*

In this prayer, we identify the Sabbath as *a sign* between Hashem and the Children of Israel. This is an allusion to the fact that only Israel is commanded to observe the Sabbath (indeed, a non-Jew is *forbidden* to do so), although the testimony that Sabbath observance offers — that Hashem created the world in six days and rested on the seventh — obviously has import with respect to all of mankind. Only Israel is commanded to commemorate this, because it is only Israel that can claim to be the *cause* of Creation; as *Rashi* (*Bereishis* 1:1) states, the word בְּרֵאשִׁית is expounded to mean *because of Israel, who are called* רֵאשִׁית.

In the Talmud, we find several expositions of the verses (*Shemos* 31:16-17) that comprise the *V'Shomru* prayer. The Gemara in *Eruvin* (96a) discusses the requirement to don *tefillin* every day. R' Akiva said: One might think that it is proper to don *tefillin* even on the Sabbath. But this is not the case, for the Torah refers to *tefillin* as a *sign* (אוֹת) in the verse (*Shemos* 13:9): *And it shall be for you as a sign* (אוֹת) *upon your hand* . . . This teaches us that only on ordinary days, which need a "sign," must one wear *tefillin.* But on the Sabbath, which itself is a "sign" (as indicated in our verse (v. 17) — *For it is a sign between Me and them* . . .), *tefillin* are not worn.

Rashi (*Eruvin* ibid.) explains: The wearing of *tefillin* is a sign that the wearer is upholding Hashem's Torah; this is a sign that should be worn every day. But the Sabbath itself is an expression of the special bond between Hashem and the Jewish nation, and thus no secondary sign of *tefillin* is necessary on it.

Another exposition can be found in the Gemara in *Yoma* (85a-b). The Gemara asks: From where do we know that it is permitted to desecrate the Sabbath (by performing forbidden labor) in order to save a life? R' Shimon

SHABBOS

PARASHAS VAYEITZEI

ben Menasya says: It is derived from the verse (ibid. v. 16): *And the Bnei Yisrael shall keep the Sabbath*. The Torah teaches us: It is permitted to desecrate one Sabbath for the purpose of keeping a person alive, so that he will be able to keep many more Sabbaths. According to this exposition, the verse is not simply commanding us to keep the Sabbath (this commandment is found several other times in the Torah); rather, it is instructing us that we must ensure that the Jews will be able to keep *many* Sabbaths, even if this means that occasionally, one Sabbath will be desecrated to save a life.

ANSWERS TO QUESTIONS OF THE DAY

Sunday:
Fourteen years and one day. He spent fourteen years studying in the yeshivah of Ever, and then traveled to Charan in a single day.

Monday:
One example is the verse in *Parashas Mishpatim* (*Shemos* 22:24): *When you lend money to My people* . . . It is a positive commandment to extend loans to those in need, not an option.

Tuesday:
Moshe met the daughters of Yisro at the well (see *Shemos* 2:18), and married Tzipporah.

Wednesday:
Fourteen years. The verse states (29:27) that after seven years passed and Lavan tricked Yaakov into marrying Leah, he offered to give him Rachel as well, in return for seven more years of labor. Thus, Yaakov labored the entire fourteen years for Rachel.

Thursday:
Dan and Dinah. Both derive from the word דִּין, *judgment*.

Friday:
Ramban states that the word derives from the root רפה, which means *weak*; this is an allusion to their total lack of any power.

Shabbos:
The verse (31:47) states that Lavan called the pile of stones that Yaakov and he set up as a witness to their covenant, "Yegar Sahadusa." These words mean *mound of witness* in Aramaic.

פרשת וישלח
Parashas Vayishlach

פרשת וישלח

A TORAH THOUGHT FOR THE DAY

SUNDAY

PARASHAS VAYISHLACH

וַיִּשְׁלַח יַעֲקֹב מַלְאָכִים לְפָנָיו אֶל־עֵשָׂו אָחִיו אַרְצָה שֵׂעִיר שְׂדֵה אֱדוֹם. וַיְצַו אֹתָם לֵאמֹר כֹּה תֹאמְרוּן לַאדֹנִי לְעֵשָׂו כֹּה אָמַר עַבְדְּךָ יַעֲקֹב עִם־לָבָן גַּרְתִּי וָאֵחַר עַד־עָתָּה. וַיְהִי־לִי שׁוֹר וַחֲמוֹר צֹאן וְעֶבֶד וְשִׁפְחָה וָאֶשְׁלְחָה לְהַגִּיד לַאדֹנִי לִמְצֹא־חֵן בְּעֵינֶיךָ. וַיָּשֻׁבוּ הַמַּלְאָכִים אֶל־יַעֲקֹב לֵאמֹר בָּאנוּ אֶל־אָחִיךָ אֶל־עֵשָׂו וְגַם הֹלֵךְ לִקְרָאתְךָ וְאַרְבַּע־מֵאוֹת אִישׁ עִמּוֹ

Then Yaakov sent angels ahead of him to Eisav his brother to the land of Seir, the field of Edom. He instructed them, saying, "Thus shall you say, 'To my lord, to Eisav, so said your servant Yaakov: I have sojourned with Lavan, and have lingered until now. I have acquired oxen and donkeys, flocks, servants and maidservants, and I am sending them to my lord to find favor in your eyes.'"
The angels returned to Yaakov, saying, "We came to your brother, to Eisav; moreover, he is heading toward you, and four hundred men are with him" (Bereishis 32:4-7).

The commentators ask: Why, after the Torah describes the content of Yaakov's message to Eisav, does the Torah not mention that the angels actually carried out their mission, and conveyed Yaakov's words to Eisav? Also puzzling is the Torah's description of the angels' return to Yaakov; instead of just stating the content of their message — that Eisav was heading toward Yaakov with four hundred armed men — the Torah emphasizes the angels' apparently superfluous description of how they had carried out their mission, by stating, *We came to your brother, to Eisav . . .*

It appears from *Midrash HaBeur* (cited in *Torah Sheleimah*) that the second question in fact answers the first, for the Midrash learns from the Torah's retelling of what the angels said upon returning to Yaakov that a messenger, upon completing his mission, has an obligation to return to the person who sent him, to inform him that the job for which he was dispatched was successfully completed (see *A Taste of Lomdus;* see also *Rashi* to *Shemos* 19:8, where a similar idea is taught). This being the case, the Torah did not have to state explicitly that the angels accomplished their mission; this point is made clear by the verse telling us that the angels, in keeping with the guidelines of proper conduct, *returned* to Yaakov to tell him that they had done as he had instructed. After reporting to Yaakov that they had carried out their job, the angels described Eisav's actions of preparing for war.

פרשת וישלח
SUNDAY
PARASHAS VAYISHLACH

Panim Yafos offers an original answer to the questions we raised, by mentioning another point: When recounting Yaakov's instructions to the angels, the Torah states: *He instructed them, saying, "Thus shall you say, 'To my lord, to Eisav, so said your servant Yaakov.'"* The word לֵאמֹר, *saying,* appears redundant; the verse could simply have stated what Yaakov instructed them to say! *Panim Yafos* gleans from this that the angels were not told to give their message to Eisav directly; rather, they were to transfer the message to another party, who would in turn give it to Eisav. He explains that since Yaakov's messengers were celestial angels, they (as *Rashi* explains at the beginning [28:12] and end [32:3] of *Parashas Vayeitzei*) were not allowed to leave Eretz Yisrael. Thus, the only way Yaakov was able to appoint them to deliver a message to Eisav, who lived in *the fields of Edom,* outside of Eretz Yisrael, was by instructing these angels of Eretz Yisrael to tell the angels of outside the Land (who had escorted Yaakov until the Jordan River and were not permitted to enter Eretz Yisrael) to deliver this message on his behalf. *Panim Yafos* thus translates the verse as follows: "*He instructed them* (the first set of angels) *to say* (to the other set of angels), *"Thus shall you say, 'To my lord, to Eisav, so said your servant Yaakov . . .'"*

In line with this novel interpretation, *Panim Yafos* explains the angels' reply: *The angels* that Yaakov sent *returned to Yaakov, saying*: *We came to your brother, to Eisav.* We did not have to inform the other angels to deliver the message outside of Eretz Yisrael, as you directed us, because *he is heading toward you* — he is already in Eretz Yisrael, on the way to wage war with you. When we saw this, the angels said, we did not fulfill the mission with which you charged us, fearing that once Eisav had already made up his mind to attack you, delivering the message that you gave us would not change his mind, and our speaking with him could only prove detrimental, by allowing him to determine your exact location. Thus, concluded the angels, since *we* ourselves *came to your brother, to Eisav,* we returned to warn you that *he is heading toward you, and four hundred men are with him.*

QUESTION OF THE DAY:
From where in the Torah can it be inferred that the messengers Yaakov sent to Eisav were actual angels?

For the answer, see page 227

פרשת וישלח

SUNDAY
PARASHAS VAYISHLACH

MISHNAH OF THE DAY: SHABBOS 8:3

The following Mishnah continues to list the minimum amounts of various substances that, when taken out on the Sabbath, will render a person liable to a *chatas*:

עוֹר — One who takes out a *hide*[1] from one domain to another, or carries it a distance of four *amos* in a public domain, כְּדֵי לַעֲשׂוֹת קָמִיעַ — is liable to a *chatas* if he takes out **enough to make an amulet;**[2] קְלָף — if he takes out **parchment,**[3] כְּדֵי לִכְתּוֹב עָלָיו פָּרָשָׁה קְטַנָּה שֶׁבַּתְּפִילִּין — he is liable to a *chatas* if he takes out **enough to write the smallest passage** found **in tefillin upon it,**[4] שֶׁהִיא ״שְׁמַע יִשְׂרָאֵל״ — **which is** the passage of **Shema Yisrael.** דְּיוֹ — If he takes out **ink,** כְּדֵי לִכְתּוֹב שְׁתֵּי אוֹתִיּוֹת — he is liable to a *chatas* if he takes out **enough to write two letters;**[5] כְּחוֹל — if he takes out **eye paint,** כְּדֵי לִכְחוֹל עַיִן אַחַת — he is liable to a *chatas* if he takes out **enough to paint one eye.**[6]

NOTES

1. The hide being discussed in this Mishnah is an animal skin that is only partially tanned — i.e., it has been salted, but not yet treated with flour or gallnut juice (*Tos. Yom Tov* from Gemara 79a).

2. Amulets, consisting either of pieces of parchment with various verses of the Torah written upon them, or of bundles of herbs (see above, 6:2), were worn to cure diseases or to ward off disease. These parchments and bundles were often wrapped in pieces of partially tanned hide. The Mishnah teaches that the minimum significant size of such hide is enough to wrap an amulet therein (*Rav; Rambam Commentary;* cf. *Chidushei HaRan* to 79a).

3. The parchment called קְלָף is made from the outer layer of the animal hide, and it is used for writing *tefillin* and *mezuzos*.

4. Since parchment is expensive, it is not used for writing tax collector's receipts (unlike the paper mentioned in the previous Mishnah). Consequently, one is not liable for taking out such a small size, but only for taking out a size sufficient for writing the smallest section of the *tefillin* (*Rav; Rashi*).

5. Two letters were often written on two adjoining sections of a utensil or sections of a wall, so that they could be matched together. Thus, enough ink to write two characters is deemed a significant amount (*Rav; Rashi*).

6. Modest women would go out in the street with veils over their face, leaving only one eye exposed. They would therefore paint only that one eye [and enough eye paint to paint one eye is therefore significant] (*Rav* from Gemara 80a).

GEMS FROM THE GEMARA

פרשת
וישלח

SUNDAY
PARASHAS VAYISHLACH

The Gemara (80a) cites a Baraisa that amplifies the Mishnah's ruling. The Baraisa rules that one is liable for taking out two letters' worth of dried ink, or two letters' worth of ink in a quill, or two letters' worth of ink in an inkwell. *Rashi* explains that the novelty of the Baraisa is that the minimum amount of ink is constant — it remains at two letters' worth — no matter where the ink is located. We do not say that ink that is in the inkwell or the pen is more significant, and therefore requires a minimum of less than two letters' worth.

The Gemara then cites Rava, who asks: If one were to take out one letter's worth of dried ink, and one letter's worth of ink in a quill, or one letter's worth of ink in an inkwell, what is the law? Do the inks that are in different places combine to comprise a minimum measurement to render him liable to a *chatas,* or do we say that since the inks are not in one location, they cannot combine? The Gemara offers no resolution to this question, and concludes: *Teiku* — Let [the question] stand.

Rashi (ibid.) deals with an obvious difficulty. If the ink is in a quill or an inkwell, then why is the person not liable for taking out the quill or inkwell, even if there is not sufficient ink to be liable? *Rashi* explains that the person is not liable for taking out the quill or the inkwell themselves, although they are inherently significant items, because when he takes them out filled with ink (even partially) they are subordinate to the ink that they contain, and they are not deemed significant in their own right. [A Mishnah (below, 10:5) teaches this law, stating that if a person takes out less than the minimum measurement of a food in a utensil, he is exempt both for taking out the food and for taking out the utensil.]

A MUSSAR THOUGHT FOR THE DAY

Rabbeinu Yonah devotes the second section of his *mussar* classic, *Shaarei Teshuvah,* to suggestions on how a person should focus to bring himself to return to Hashem through *teshuvah* (repentance); and, in a broader sense, how to enable himself to focus on serving Hashem throughout his everyday life. One idea found there (2:21) is learned from Shlomo HaMelech's wisdom in *Mishlei* (22:19-21): *Let your trust remain with Hashem etc., to teach you the veracity of true words, so that you may answer words of truth to He who sent you.* Rabbeinu Yonah understands these verses to be teaching that a person was placed on earth

פרשת וישלח

SUNDAY

PARASHAS VAYISHLACH

only to act as a *shliach* — a *representative* of Hashem.

This perspective on a person's lifelong mission goes beyond the suggestions *Rabbeinu Yonah* mentions earlier in the chapter (for example, constantly pursuing mitzvos, understanding the scrutiny of Hashem's judgment, and realizing that the present world is a temporal existence where the only value of all its beauty is for use in *avodas Hashem*). All these awarenesses will no doubt inspire a person to become closer to Hashem and make him more aware of the need to constantly fulfill Hashem's desire. He will actually be "convinced" of the need to perform mitzvos, since the reward given for carrying out Hashem's commandments is simply so much greater than the effort or material setback that doing them entails. It will become obvious, when the matter is seriously contemplated, that it makes sense to do mitzvos.

A *shliach* of Hashem, however, is different. He does not carry out his mission because he will be rewarded, or even because this action makes so much more sense to him than any other alternative. Rather, the reason that a messenger sent on assignment to a faraway land carries out his mission is because this is the only reason he was sent to this particular place. Similarly, while it is true that a lifetime of successful mitzvah performance is the safest and most rewarding accomplishment that a person can achieve, *Rabbeinu Yonah* is pointing out that this is not the ultimate reason to do mitzvos; rather, since fulfilling Hashem's commandments is the only reason a person exists, it is obvious that this is what he must do. Although someone without this elevated awareness may also follow Hashem's directive, every time he is challenged he must convince himself not to sin because in the long run, it will be better for him to follow Hashem's word. A *shliach* with single-minded devotion to his mission, however, avoids enticement and the need to overcome it; he will not be tempted to begin with. A loyal *shliach* realizes that he has a job to fulfill, and it does not include sinning!

HALACHAH OF THE DAY

As we learned earlier, a liquid is considered to have been cooked when it has been heated to the degree of *yad soledes bo*. Literally translated, this means: *[a degree of heat] from which the hand recoils.* Simply explained, it means a temperature so hot that a person's hand will reflexively withdraw when brought into contact with the heated liquid. The Sages further quantify this level of heat as the temperature at which the heated water would scald a baby's abdomen.

The precise temperature of *yad soledes bo* is subject to dispute. *Rav Moshe Feinstein* ruled that due to uncertainty, a temperature of 110 degrees Fahrenheit must be considered as the minimum heat for *yad soledes bo.* He further states, however, that only temperatures of 160 Fahrenheit or higher may be considered as **definitely** exceeding the level of *yad soledes bo.* Thus, on a case-by-case basis, we must always follow the temperature which presents us with the greater stringency. While in most cases the adoption of the lower temperature would seem to generate the greater stringency, we will find, as we continue exploring the intricacies of the *melachah* of *bishul,* that there are times when the opposite holds true.

SUNDAY
PARASHAS VAYISHLACH

While liquids are considered to be cooked once they have reached the temperature of *yad soledes bo,* most *poskim* agree that to heat liquids already at this temperature to the even higher temperature of their boiling point is also forbidden under the Biblical prohibition against cooking on Shabbos.

In order to protect against possible violation of the Biblical prohibition, the Sages forbade *any* warming up of liquids on a heat source that is *capable* of eventually heating them to the level of *yad soledes bo,* even if they are being warmed only slightly. It is therefore forbidden for one to place a liquid near such a source of heat even momentarily, if that heat source is powerful enough to cause, over time, such a significant temperature change in the liquid.

Thus, we may summarize as follows: The Biblical prohibition of *bishul* forbids cooking solid foods to the level of *Ben Derusai* — one-third cooked — and liquids to the point of *yad soledes bo* — either 110 degrees Fahrenheit or 160 degrees Fahrenheit. In practice, however, it is forbidden, by Rabbinic decree, to place any uncooked item — even momentarily — near a heat source capable of bringing the item in question to its minimal "cooked" state.

A CLOSER LOOK AT THE SIDDUR

In *A Mussar Thought for the Day,* we mentioned the concept that one must realize that he is a *shliach,* agent, of Hashem. There is a principle that applies to the legal rules of agency *(shlichus),* which states that part of an agent's mission is to return to the person who sent him and report that the job was carried out successfully; one who is unable to do so cannot act as a *shliach* (for further discussion of this principle, see *A Taste of Lomdus*). R' *Yosef Engel (Gilyonei HaShas* to *Gittin* 24a) explains

פרשת וישלח
SUNDAY
PARASHAS VAYISHLACH

that this is necessary because a person who appoints a messenger to represent him is in effect using this person to allow himself to move beyond his own limited boundaries. An agent who is legally unable to return to the person who sent him, however, is in effect being sent away with no possibility of further relationship; thus, he cannot be considered one who extends the sender's reach. The impossibility of reporting back home shows that there is no longer any connection between these two people, precluding the agent's ability to function as a legal *shliach*.

It has been noted that the Hebrew root שלח gives rise to two verbs, identical in spelling and differing only in vowelization, that have two very different meanings. The word וַיִּשְׁלַח means simply *and he sent;* this implies the sending of a message or an agent, as an extension of one's self. The word וַיְשַׁלַּח, on the other hand, means *and he sent away;* this implies a severance of the connection between the sender and the object or person being dispatched.

We find examples of both these usages in our daily prayers. The *tefillah* of *Az Yashir,* the Song at the Sea, contains the phrase, תְּשַׁלַּח חֲרֹנְךָ יֹאכְלֵמוֹ כַּקַּשׁ, *You sent forth Your anger, and consumed [the Egyptians] like straw.* When Hashem punishes evildoers, He does not associate with them directly; rather, He sends *forth* His anger to deal with them (see *Tosafos* to *Taanis* 3a, who state: אֵין הקב״ה מַזְכִּיר שְׁמוֹ עַל הָרָעָה, *Hashem does not associate His Name with evil*). Similarly, we find that when Yonah was told to carry the word of impending destruction to Ninevei, Hashem simply said to him, "לֵךְ, *go,* " and did not refer to him as a *shliach.*

R' Chaim Vital uses this idea to better understand a *pasuk* in *Tehillim* that is included in *Pesukei D'Zimrah*: הַשֹּׁלֵחַ אִמְרָתוֹ אָרֶץ עַד־מְהֵרָה יָרוּץ דְּבָרוֹ, *He who sends forth His utterance earthward; His spoken word runs swiftly* (*Tehillim* 147:15). This verse speaks of Hashem's commands being fulfilled by reaching mankind in two ways; the first half of the verse states that Hashem sends forth His utterance, while the verse's close does not mention Hashem directly, and simply speaks about the instructions themselves. *R' Chaim Vital* points out that the key to understanding the verse's apparent repetition, is, as *Rashi* (*Shemos* 19:3) explains, that the root אמר is used to describe pleasant or positive directives, while דבר refers to a harsher statement. Thus, in line with the idea that Hashem does not associate his name with evil, that verse states that Hashem is הַשֹּׁלֵחַ אִמְרָתוֹ, *He who sends forth His utterance* — the good that He sends is directly linked to His Name. Misfortune, however, is described at the end of the verse as יָרוּץ דְּבָרוֹ, *His spoken word runs* — as if by itself, without direct association with Hashem.

A TASTE OF LOMDUS

פרשת וישלח

**SUNDAY
PARASHAS VAYISHLACH**

We explained in *A Torah Thought for the Day* that *Midrash HaBeur* (cited in *Torah Sheleimah*) understands from the Torah's description of the angels' report to Yaakov that a *shliach*, agent, must return to the person who sent him, to report that he successfully accomplished his mission.

Rashi (*Gittin* 63b) explains that according to one opinion mentioned in the Gemara there, a person may not legally become a *shliach* unless he has the *ability* to report back to the sender. The Gemara discusses an example of a case in which the *shliach* would be unable to fulfill this condition: A husband wishes to divorce his wife but, being unable to personally deliver the *get* (bill of divorce) to his wife, designates another person as an agent to give her the document. Before the agent hands the *get* to the man's wife, however, she appoints him to be *her* agent to *accept* the *get*. Since a *shliach* is a legal extension of the person who sent him, the Gemara is in doubt about whether or not a *shliach* who accepts a responsibility that diametrically opposes his initial mission (e.g., when his first job requires him to *give* the *get*, while his second job entails *receiving* it), can continue to represent the person who sent him originally.

Other commentaries, some of which are cited in *Ritva*, explain the issue in the Gemara as relating to laws that are particular to the giving of a *get*. *Rashi*, however, explains that the agent may no longer represent the husband because by becoming the woman's delegate to accept the *get*, he makes himself ineligible to complete his mission. An agent for one side of a contract cannot continue to represent the other. This inability to report back to the husband, explains *Rashi*, prevents the person from continuing to serve as a *shliach* for him.

Many commentators wonder about *Rashi's* source and his reasoning. After all, the *get* seems to have been transferred from the husband's possession into the wife's; the mission is ostensibly completed. Why should it make any halachic difference whether or not the *shliach* may then report home?

According to the *Midrash HaBeur* cited above, a possible source may be drawn from the instructions implicit in the description of the angels' discussion with Yaakov, as explained above. *Rashi* concludes from here that the directive to report back is a necessary part of a *shliach's* mission, not merely an appropriate way for the agent to comport himself once he discharges his duty. The *shliach's* job is not over when he carries out the sender's will. He is also required to inform the sender that the job has been done. Therefore, a person who, for whatever reason, is unable to give a report, is unable to fulfill the Torah's requirements, and may

פרשת וישלח

SUNDAY

PARASHAS VAYISHLACH

not serve as a *shliach*. [Although a *shliach* who can, but does not, inform the person who sent him, would still be valid, the lack of ability from the outset to perform any, even non-essential, part of the mission, means that the appointment was never valid to begin with.]

Rashba uses this requirement — that a *shliach* must be able to report home once he completes his mission, whether or not he actually does so (see also *Chasam Sofer* to *Gittin* 24a and *Avnei Miluim* 141:1) — to explain a difficult contradiction between two Gemaras. In *Gittin* (24a) we find a case in which a husband insists that divorce proceedings take place in front of a specific *beis din*, yet he is unable to travel there. Thus, he appoints his wife to be his *shliach* to bring her own *get* to this place. When she arrives, he instructs her to accept the *get* from herself. The Gemara rules that it is halachically unacceptable for the woman to act as a *shliach* for her husband to bring a *get* to herself, for a prerequisite for a *shliach* is the ability to return to the sender, and this woman, since she will ultimately *accept* the bill of divorce, putting her on the other side of the transaction, is unable to continue to act as a representative of her ex-husband. She will therefore be unable to report back to him that the mission was successful. *Rashba* asks: When a husband tries to make his wife a *shliach* to "deliver" her own *get*, the Gemara is *certain* that her inability to report back invalidates her designation as his *shliach*. But when one *shliach* was appointed by both the husband and the wife, the Gemara (ibid. 63b, cited above) is *unsure* whether or not this rule rightly applies. What is the difference between these cases? Why should the Gemara see them in two different lights?

Rashba answers that in order to be a fitting *shliach*, a person must be able, in principle, to complete every aspect of the job. It is obvious from the outset that a woman charged as her husband's agent to deliver her *get* will be unable to report back upon receiving it; she no longer is the *shliach*, or legal extension of, the sender. The Gemara therefore rules unambiguously that the original appointment was invalid. However, when a husband instructs another person to deliver the *get*, he has no reason to suppose that his wife will appoint the same person to be her *shliach* to receive it. Thus, one opinion in the Gemara reasons that since the *shliach* was able to do the job *as of his appointment*, the fact that he becomes unable to do so later is immaterial; while the other holds that this subsequent inability can also invalidate the *shlichus*. All agree, however, with the basic principle that a person who will be unable to complete every aspect of his (or her) mission may not be appointed to represent another person as a *shliach*.

A TORAH THOUGHT FOR THE DAY

פרשת וישלח

MONDAY
PARASHAS VAYISHLACH

הַצִּילֵנִי נָא מִיַּד אָחִי מִיַּד עֵשָׂו
Rescue me, please, from the hand of my brother, the hand of Eisav (Bereishis 32:12).

Ramban opens his commentary to this *parashah* with an introductory note about the lessons we can learn from it. One of the concepts, the famous idea of מַעֲשֵׂה אָבוֹת סִימָן לַבָּנִים, *the actions of the forefathers are signposts for the children,* is a lesson that *Ramban* mentions several times in *Sefer Bereishis.* Everything that occurred to our forefather Yaakov before and during his confrontation with Eisav will continually recur between Eisav's descendants and us. It is therefore fitting for us to hold fast to the path of our righteous forefather Yaakov. We should prepare ourselves for confrontation in the three ways he prepared himself: prayer, gifts to appease Eisav, and preparation for battle if necessary.

At the conclusion of Yaakov's encounter with Eisav, the *Ramban* again notes that the Sages used this *parashah* as a guide in dealing with Eisav's descendants. He cites a Midrash that states that before Rav Yannai would have dealings with the government, he would study this *parashah,* to prepare himself, because this *parashah* is the "chapter of exile," i.e., the source of information for proper conduct in exile.

Let us focus upon one lesson that the *Beis HaLevi* gleans from the actions of Yaakov, which is relevant in all periods of *galus.*

Yaakov prayed to Hashem: *"Rescue me, please, from the hand of my brother, the hand of Eisav, for I fear him, lest he come and strike me down, mother and children."* Why, asks *Beis HaLevi,* must Yaakov repeat the word מִיַּד, *from the hand,* a second time? Yaakov could simply have said, "Rescue me from the hand of my brother Eisav!"

According to the *Beis HaLevi,* Yaakov understood that Eisav's approach presented two separate dangers, and that he needed protection from both of them. First, he saw the imminent danger of Eisav waging war with him and attempting to kill him. But Yaakov knew that even if Eisav could somehow be appeased and his anger assuaged, he would still present a danger. For if Eisav were to start treating Yaakov with brotherly love, this too would pose a threat, as good feelings and love from Eisav would constitute a spiritual danger to Yaakov.

Thus, Yaakov made two separate requests of Hashem: Rescue me from the hands of Eisav the wicked one, who is coming to kill me. But I also beseech You to rescue me from my "brother" — from the loving, caring behavior that Eisav might adopt.

MONDAY

PARASHAS VAYISHLACH

We see that both of Yaakov's prayers were accepted. When Eisav came to attack and destroy Yaakov's entire family, Hashem caused Eisav to be appeased. Then, Eisav tried a new tactic, offering to remain with Yaakov and accompany him on his journey. Yaakov insisted that he could not travel together with Eisav, and was successful in convincing Eisav to leave.

The *Beis HaLevi* concludes by noting how these two "hands" of Eisav have continually appeared during our lengthy exile. First, nations would issue harsh decrees against the Jews, and inflict pain and death on them. Then, Hashem has mercy and saves us from their wicked hands. Later, the nations try to befriend us and give us equal rights, offering to "travel together" with us. We must realize that these overtures of friendship are all too often only a ploy, meant to detach us from our strong commitment to the Torah. We must constantly remember that both of these "hands" pose equal danger to the continued existence of the Jew.

MISHNAH OF THE DAY: SHABBOS 8:4

The following Mishnah continues to list the minimum amounts of various substances that, when taken out on the Sabbath, will render a person liable to a *chatas*:

דֶּבֶק — One who takes out **glue** from one domain to another, or carries it a distance of four *amos* in a public domain, כְּדֵי לִיתֵּן בְּרֹאשׁ הַשַּׁבְשֶׁבֶת — is liable to a *chatas* if he takes out **enough to place on the head of a bird hunter's board;**[1] זֶפֶת וְגָפְרִית — if he takes out **pitch or sulfur,** כְּדֵי לַעֲשׂוֹת נֶקֶב (קָטָן) — he is liable to a *chatas* if he takes out **enough to make a** seal for a **(small) hole;**[2] שַׁעֲוָה — if he takes out

---
NOTES

1. Hunters would attach a small board to the end of a stick, upon which they would put glue. A bird alighting upon it would be caught. The amount of glue necessary to hold the bird fast to the board suffices to render a person who takes out the glue liable to a *chatas* (*Rav, Rashi* 80a).

2. [This wording is found in *Rav* and *Rashi*. In our editions, as well as *Meiri's*, the word קָטָן, *small*, does not appear.] This refers to a vial in which mercury is kept. Its opening is sealed with pitch or sulphur. A small hole is then made in the seal, through which the mercury can be removed without danger of its spilling. The hole is then sealed again with pitch or sulfur. It is the amount needed to seal the hole to which the Mishnah refers (see *Rashi* and *Chidushei HaRan* to 79a; see also *Tiferes Yisrael;* cf. *Meiri*).

MONDAY

PARASHAS VAYISHLACH

wax, כְּדֵי לִתֵּן עַל פִּי נֶקֶב קָטָן — he is liable to a *chatas* if he takes out **enough to place on the opening of a small hole;** [3] חַרְסִית — if he takes out **crushed brick,** כְּדֵי לַעֲשׂוֹת פִּי כּוּר שֶׁל צוֹרְפֵי זָהָב — he is liable to a *chatas* if he takes out **enough to make an opening for the crucible of gold refiners.** [4] רַבִּי יְהוּדָה אוֹמֵר — *R' Yehudah says:* כְּדֵי לַעֲשׂוֹת פִּיטְפּוּט — Even **enough to make a tripod.** [5] סוּבִּין — If he takes out **bran,** כְּדֵי לִיתֵּן עַל פִּי כּוּר שֶׁל צוֹרְפֵי זָהָב — he is liable to a *chatas* if he takes out **enough to place on the opening of the crucible of gold refiners.** [6] סִיד — If he takes out **lime,** כְּדֵי לָסוּד קְטַנָּה שֶׁבַּבָּנוֹת — he is liable to a *chatas* if he takes out **enough to spread** upon **a girl's smallest** limb. [7] כְּדֵי לַעֲשׂוֹת בִּלְבֵּל — **Enough** רַבִּי יְהוּדָה אוֹמֵר — *R' Yehudah says:* **to make** the hair on **the temples** lay flat. [8] רַבִּי נְחֶמְיָה אוֹמֵר — *R' Nechemyah says:* כְּדֵי לָסוּד אוּנְדְּפֵי — **Enough for a** forehead **plaster.** [9]

NOTES

3. The Gemara explains that the Mishnah here refers [not to the small hole just mentioned, but rather] to a small hole in a wine barrel. The Gemara notes further that wine flows through a very small hole, as opposed to more viscous liquids, such as oil and honey, which require a larger hole (*Tos. Yom Tov* from *Rashi* 80a).

4. I.e., to seal the hole in the crucible. A crucible is a vessel used to heat metals to an intense heat, in order to refine or fuse them. There is a hole into which the bellows is inserted to fan the fire. Crushed brick would be placed around the bellows to seal the hole (*Rav; Rashi; Tiferes Yisrael*).

5. I.e., the amount of cracked brick sufficient to plaster the cracks of a tripod made to support a small stove (*Shenos Eliyahu; Tos. Chadashim* from Gemara 80a; cf. *Rav; Rashi; Rambam Commentary*). Although crushed brick is used more often to make an opening for a crucible than to repair the tripod of an oven, R' Yehudah regards the smaller amount necessary for this repair as sufficient for liability, since crushed brick is sometimes used for this purpose. On the other hand, the first Tanna determines the minimum amount on the basis of the more common use (*Ran;* see *Tos. R' Akiva Eiger* from Gemara ibid.).

6. In places where charcoal is scarce, gold refiners smelt gold using bran as a fuel (*Rav; Rashi*).

7. Various reasons are given for this practice: to give a ruddy hue to the skin (*Rashi* 80b); as a depilatory (*Rashi* ibid.); as a skin whitener (*Tos.* ibid.); to bring on the menstrual cycle of a pubescent girl (*Rav*). The lime had to be applied to large parts of the body, but it could not safely be applied all at once (Gemara ibid.). Therefore, the lime was applied to only one limb at a time. Thus, this Tanna rules that one who takes out enough for even the smallest limb of a girl is liable.

8. [The translation follows *Rav, Rashi.*]

9. Lime was plastered to the forehead to give it a ruddy hue (*Rashi* ibid.; *Tiferes Yisrael; Tos. Chadashim;* cf. *Rav*).

פרשת וישלח

MONDAY
PARASHAS VAYISHLACH

GEMS FROM THE GEMARA

In the Mishnah, we explained that according to R' Yehudah, the minimum measure of lime that one must take out (to be liable to a *chatas*) is enough to flatten the hair upon a girl's temples (כִּלְבֵּל). Initially, the Gemara assumed that R' Nechemyah also based the minimum measure of lime upon its use as a grooming aid. According to this initial assumption, the difference between R' Yehudah and R' Nechemyah is only that R' Yehudah maintains that the lime was used to flatten the hair of the temples, while R' Nechemyah bases his identification of the minimum measure on the amount of lime that was used to remove the short hairs *beneath* the temples. However, the Gemara challenges this from a Baraisa, which cites Rebbi (R' Yehudah HaNasi) as stating that R' Yehudah's measure appears to be the correct one when the substance being carried out is *dissolved* lime, while R' Nechemyah's measure appears to be the correct one when the substance being carried out is kneaded, solid lime. Now, the lime used as a grooming aid, both to flatten the hair of the temples and to remove the hair beneath the temples, was generally dissolved lime. Thus, obviously R' Nechemyah's minimum measure of אוּנְדְּפֵי, which Rebbi understood as appropriate for kneaded lime, was *not* based upon its use as a grooming aid!

To resolve this difficulty, the Gemara offers several other interpretations of אוּנְדְּפֵי. R' Yitzchak suggested that R' Nechemyah referred to the quantity used to seal the *two spigots* of a wine barrel (with אוּנְדְּפֵי meaning *two mouths*). The Gemara dismisses this possibility, however, for no one would use lime to seal a wine barrel, as wine would dissolve the seal, and the wine would be lost. R' Kahana then explains that אוּנְדְּפֵי means the lime markings that were used to indicate incremental measurements on a measuring vessel (it is unclear how the word אוּנְדְּפֵי carries this meaning). Finally, the Gemara offers as another alternative the meaning that we offered in the Mishnah — that according to R' Nechemyah, the lime was placed upon the forehead as a plaster. [According to this explanation, the word אוּנְדְּפֵי means *forehead;* the Gemara concludes by citing another place where this meaning of the word is found.]

QUESTION OF THE DAY:

What can we learn from the fact that Yaakov asked to be saved "from my brother, from Eisav"?

For the answer, see page 227.

A MUSSAR THOUGHT FOR THE DAY

פרשת וישלח

MONDAY
PARASHAS VAYISHLACH

In *A Torah Thought for the Day*, we discussed the two dangers that Eisav can pose for the Jews in *galus:* the physical danger of being harmed or killed, and the spiritual danger that can be caused by his friendly behavior toward us. What Eisav really has in mind with his "friendship" is to find a way to somehow integrate the Jewish nation and the other nations in society, and to do away with those commandments that separate us from the other nations.

The truth is that the *yetzer hara* also uses both of these tactics, but it is more successful when it approaches as a friend. *Chovos HaLevavos* (*Yichud HaMaaseh* Ch. 5) describes at length the dangerous power that the *yetzer hara* possesses: "A person must realize that his biggest enemy in this world is his *yetzer hara,* which is well connected to his character and is mixed into his personality. It is a partner in all of a person's spiritual and physical aspirations. It gives advice on all of one's movements, the revealed ones and the concealed ones, and lies in ambush to persuade one to sin at all times. Even while sleeping, one is not safe; the *yetzer hara* is always wide awake, seeking to harm. A person may forget about it, but it never forgets. It masquerades as a friend and a close confidant; indeed, with its shrewdness it tries to be considered a most loyal and trusted friend. The *yetzer hara* is so convincing that a person might think that it is running to fulfill his every wish. But in truth, it is shooting dangerous, deadly arrows, to uproot the person from the World to Come."

Chovos HaLevavos notes that this trap is a very dangerous one that has captured many in its net. He continues to explain that just as in wartime, one cannot begin to think of victory until he realizes the danger posed by the enemy, one must clearly identify the *yetzer hara* as his implacable foe, and be prepared for all its tactics and familiar with its entire arsenal.

The *yetzer hara* employs the same tricks that were tried by Eisav. Hashem listened to Yaakov's prayers, and he was saved. We must also pray to Hashem to save us from the wiles of the *yetzer hara.* As the Gemara states (*Kiddushin* 30b), every day the *yetzer hara* sees a person and wishes to kill him (i.e., to cause him to sin to the extent that he will deserve death), and without help from Heaven, a person is not able to stand up against it.

HALACHAH OF THE DAY

MONDAY
PARASHAS VAYISHLACH

Accelerating the cooking process, so that an item will reach the point at which it is cooked more quickly, is also a violation of the *melachah* of cooking. Therefore, one may not do anything to cause an item that was already on a flame before Shabbos to cook faster. While it is obviously forbidden for one to increase the size of a flame on Shabbos (this would result in the violation of two prohibitions — the *melachah* of cooking as well as the *melachah* of kindling), there are various other methods of accelerating cooking times that are forbidden on Shabbos, as we will see.

Moving a pot of food closer to a heat source causes the food in the pot to cook faster. Therefore, any food which is not yet fully cooked may not be brought closer to the flame on Shabbos. [In the context of this halachah, an item is deemed "fully cooked" if it is cooked to the point at which most people would normally eat it without cooking it further.] This holds true even for a pot that has been placed on a stovetop covered with a *blech* (the tin sheet often used to cover flames on Shabbos) prior to the onset of Shabbos. [We will discuss the intricacies of repositioning pots of fully cooked foods on the *blech* further along in our discussions of this *melachah*.] To reposition a pot on Shabbos in this manner is a violation of the Torah prohibition against cooking on Shabbos.

Reducing the volume of food in a pot is another action which results in diminished cooking time, and is therefore also forbidden on Shabbos. Thus, if there is a pot of food that is not fully cooked on the flame on Shabbos, he may not remove any of its contents, because by doing so he will cause the remaining food in the pot to cook faster. For example, if one has a pot of cholent that is already cooked to the point where it is edible, but it has not yet reached the point of being fully cooked, he may not remove a portion from the pot on Friday night. Since removing this portion will cause the rest of the cholent to reach the fully-cooked stage faster, this will be in violation of the *melachah* of cooking.

It is important to note that the above prohibition applies even to a pot that has been removed from the stovetop, as long as it still retains the temperature of *yad soledes bo*.

A CLOSER LOOK AT THE SIDDUR

פרשת וישלח

MONDAY
PARASHAS VAYISHLACH

Yaakov Avinu prepared himself with three essential tools to protect himself from the hands of Eisav: He offered presents to appease him; prepared to defend himself if necessary, and harnessed the power of prayer. *Maalos HaTefillah* points out that just as the first two tools work as natural remedies [עַל פִּי טֶבַע], so too prayer is a natural protection from any danger.

This concept helps us better understand the true power of prayer. We know that, on the one hand, the Gemara says: אֵין סוֹמְכִין עַל הַנֵּס, *one cannot relay on a miracle,* and must do whatever he can to protect himself naturally. On the other hand, the Gemara (*Berachos* 10a) tells us that even when a sharp sword is placed upon the neck of a person, he should not give up hope, but rather he should pray for mercy from Hashem. How do we reconcile these mixed messages?

The answer is that prayer is also a natural power built into Creation. A person cannot fight with a lion while unarmed and trust that Hashem will help him and a miracle will occur, or eat something poisonous and rely on Hashem. This is because Hashem established a system called טֶבַע, *nature,* and will usually not disturb or change its workings (unless there is a special reason to make a miracle in a specific instance). But a person *can* expect to achieve goals with prayer. This is not a miracle, but follows the same system that allows trees to grow and food to give nourishment. When one prays, Hashem will give him what he needs.

We find this concept in the *Maharsha* in *Kiddushin* (30b). The Gemara relates an incident about a study hall that contained a *mazik* (a dangerous creature of some sort) that was so dangerous that even if two people would go into the study hall together during the day, they would both be attacked. Abaye suggested that matters should be arranged so that Rav Acha, who was a great and pious person, would be forced to stay overnight in the study hall. He would then pray there, and his prayer would surely chase away this *mazik*. The stratagem was successful; but the next morning, when Rav Acha realized what had occurred, he declared: "If not for the miracle, my life would have been put in danger!"

Maharsha asks: How was Abaye allowed to expose Rav Acha to danger and rely on a miracle to save him? Being saved through a miracle would automatically cause a reduction in Rav Acha's merit in the World to Come.

Maharsha answers that Abaye was fully confident that the great Rav Acha's prayer would help to chase away the *mazik* without a miracle, because the power of prayer is woven into Creation. It is as natural as planting or eating and drinking, and even more so, because everything in this world needs the help of prayer to allow it to function.

פרשת וישלח

A TORAH THOUGHT FOR THE DAY

TUESDAY
PARASHAS VAYISHLACH

וַיָּקָם בַּלַּיְלָה הוּא וַיִּקַּח אֶת־שְׁתֵּי נָשָׁיו וְאֶת־שְׁתֵּי שִׁפְחֹתָיו וְאֶת־אַחַד עָשָׂר יְלָדָיו וַיַּעֲבֹר אֵת מַעֲבַר יַבֹּק

And [Yaakov] got up that night and took his two wives, and his two handmaids and his eleven children, and crossed the ford on the Yabbok (Bereishis 32:23).

Rashi asks: Where was Dinah, Yaakov's daughter? He cites the Midrash that says that Yaakov placed her in a chest and closed it over her, so that Eisav should not set his eyes upon her and want to marry her. The Midrash notes that Yaakov was punished for withholding Dinah from his brother in this way, because she may have caused him to repent; she therefore fell into the hands of Shechem.

Gra asks: Why does the Midrash assume that Dinah was the missing child? The verse states only that Yaakov took eleven *children* across the Yabbok. Perhaps one of the brothers was missing, and Dinah was included in the eleven children!

To address this difficulty, *Gra* cites the *Targum Sheni* on *Megillas Esther*, which relates that Haman tried to convince Mordechai to bow down to him by citing the example of Mordechai's ancestor Yaakov, telling him that Yaakov his grandfather had bowed down to Haman's grandfather, Eisav, and therefore there was no reason why Mordechai should not bow down to him. Mordechai answered, "It is true that Yaakov bowed to Eisav. But I trace my lineage back to Binyamin, who had not yet been born at the time of the confrontation with Eisav. Thus, Binyamin never bowed down to any human. I, Mordechai, follow the practice of my ancestor Binyamin!"

The *Targum* continues, stating that Binyamin's reward for never having bowed to another human was that the *Beis HaMikdash*, where everyone comes to bow down to Hashem, was built mostly in his portion of Eretz Yisrael. *Gra* explains that this *Targum* indicates that Binyamin must have been the only one of the *shevatim* that did not bow to Eisav — for if another brother had also been absent, and thus had not bowed to Eisav, he should have merited having the *Beis HaMikdash* in his portion as well! Why would Binyamin have been rewarded more than another brother?

Thus, it is clear that all of the eleven other brothers were there, and bowed down to Eisav together with Yaakov. Therefore, the one child who could have been missing was Dinah (who, as a daughter, did not receive her own portion of Eretz Yisrael). This, says *Gra*, is how the Midrash knew that Dinah was the missing child. [See there for another explanation as well.]

MISHNAH OF THE DAY: SHABBOS 8:5

פרשת וישלח

TUESDAY
PARASHAS VAYISHLACH

The following Mishnah continues to list the minimum amounts of various substances that, when taken out on the Sabbath, will render a person liable to a *chatas*: אֲדָמָה — One who takes out *earth*,[1] כְּחוֹתַם הַמַּרְצְפִין — is liable to a *chatas* if he takes out *enough for the seal of cargo sacks*;[2] דִּבְרֵי רַבִּי עֲקִיבָא — these are *the words of R' Akiva*. וַחֲכָמִים אוֹמְרִים — *But the Sages say:* כְּחוֹתַם הָאִיגְּרוֹת — He is liable to a *chatas* even if he takes out only *enough for the seal of letters*.[3] זֶבֶל וְחוֹל הַדַּק — If he takes out *fertilizer or fine sand,* כְּדֵי לְזַבֵּל קֶלַח שֶׁל כְּרוּב — he is liable to a *chatas* if he takes out *enough to fertilize a* single *cabbage stalk*;[4] דִּבְרֵי רַבִּי עֲקִיבָא — these are the *words of R' Akiva*. וַחֲכָמִים אוֹמְרִים — *But the Sages say:* כְּדֵי לְזַבֵּל כְּרֵישָׁא — He is liable to a *chatas* even if he takes out only *enough to fertilize a* single *leek*;[5] חוֹל הַגַּס — if he takes out *coarse sand,* כְּדֵי לִיתֵּן עַל מְלֹא כַף סִיד — he is liable to a *chatas* if he takes out *enough to put on a full trowel of lime*;[6] קָנֶה — if he takes out *a reed,* כְּדֵי לַעֲשׂוֹת קוּלְמוֹס — he is liable to a *chatas* if he takes out *enough to make a pen*;[7] וְאִם הָיָה עָבֶה אוֹ מְרוּסָּס — *but if it was thick*[8] *or cracked,* and thus unsuitable as a pen, כְּדֵי לְבַשֵּׁל בּוֹ בֵּיצָה קַלָּה שֶׁבַּבֵּיצִים — he is liable only if he takes out *enough to cook the most easily cooked of eggs,* טְרוּפָה וּנְתוּנָה בָּאִילְפָּס — when it has already been *beaten and placed in a pot.*[9]

NOTES

1. The earth that is being discussed here is a type of red clay that was used for making seals (*Rav*).

2. These sacks were used for holding cargo in ships. It was the practice to place seals on these sacks (*Rav; Rashi*).

3. Letters were sealed so they would not be read by persons for whom they were not intended. This amount of clay is a smaller amount than the amount required by R' Akiva (*Rav*).

4. Even a single plant is considered significant in this regard (Gemara 79a).

5. The amount required to fertilize a leek is less than that required to fertilize a cabbage stalk (*Rav; Rashi*).

6. I.e., enough to fill a plasterer's trowel (*Rav* from Gemara 80b).

7. Reeds were used as pens, in the same fashion as quills. The length of the reed had to be sufficient to fashion from it a pen long enough to reach the middle joint of the finger (*Rav; Tiferes Yisrael*).

8. I.e., if the reed was too thick to be used for writing (*Rav*). [A thick reed cannot be used for writing, since its hollow interior holds too much ink, and it will smear as one writes.]

9. I.e., a skillet. [*Cooking* in this context means *frying*.] Since the reed is not suitable for writing, it is treated as firewood, and one is liable only if he takes out a sufficient quantity to fuel a fire to cook an egg [as in Mishnah 9:5] (*Meiri*). The amount of egg

TUESDAY

PARASHAS VAYISHLACH

––––––––––– NOTES –––––––––––

cooked must be equal to the size of a dried fig [the minimum amount for all foodstuffs; see above, Mishnah 7:4]. This is less than a whole egg (*Rashi* 80b). The most easily cooked of eggs is a chicken egg, which cooks faster than all other eggs (*Rav* from Gemara).

GEMS FROM THE GEMARA

Our Mishnah indicates that the custom was to add sand to lime. The Gemara (80b) therefore asks: Who is the Tanna of our Mishnah, who holds that mixing sand into lime is beneficial?

Rav Chisda responds that it is R' Yehudah. He bases this on a Baraisa that teaches that after the destruction of the Temple, as a sign of mourning for that destruction, one is forbidden to plaster his house with white lime in a decorative manner. The Tanna Kamma states that this is so only if he did not mix straw or sand into the lime. However, if straw or sand are mixed into the lime, the lime is no longer as pure as it was, and it may be used for such plastering.

R' Yehudah, on the other hand, says that if one mixed straw into the lime, it may be used to plaster a house; but if one mixed in sand, it may not be used, because this mixture makes for a stronger plaster. [R' Yehudah holds that the enhanced strength of the plaster offsets the loss of its brightness. Such plaster is also considered beautiful (see *Maharshal*); thus, plastering with it is equally forbidden.] Thus, this Baraisa states that according to R' Yehudah, the addition of sand is beneficial to lime, and our Mishnah is in accordance with his view.

The Gemara then cites Rava's interpretation, according to which we can reconcile our Mishnah with both of the Tannaic views expressed in the Baraisa: Rava maintained that it is even possible that the Mishnah accords with the view of the Sages; for since they permit the adding of sand to lime with respect to building in the post-Temple era, it emerges that "its ruination is its remedy" — i.e., although the sand impairs the appearance of the lime, it is nevertheless considered an improvement to the lime, for it allows the lime to be used. Accordingly, even the Sages agree that the amount of sand that is added to lime is considered significant, and it suffices to render a person who takes that amount out on the Sabbath liable to a *chatas*.

A MUSSAR THOUGHT FOR THE DAY

פָּרָשַׁת וַיִּשְׁלַח

TUESDAY
PARASHAS VAYISHLACH

From the *Rashi* that we discussed in *A Torah Thought for the Day*, we can derive a powerful message. The *Mesillas Yesharim,* in the fourth *perek,* discusses the severity of Heavenly judgment, and notes that the greater the person being judged, the more stringent the judgment is.

One of the examples he offers is the punishment Yaakov received for placing Dinah in a chest in order to protect her from Eisav. Although, he says, Yaakov definitely had a proper intention — to protect his daughter from the evil Eisav — nevertheless, because he withheld a good opportunity for *teshuvah* from his brother, he was punished. As the Midrash states, Hashem said, "You withheld kindness from your brother, and you didn't want Dinah to marry an uncircumcised man; she will be taken by someone who is not circumcised. You did not want to marry her off legitimately; she will be taken away by force."

It is still not clear, however, what exactly Yaakov did wrong. How could the Torah expect Yaakov to allow Dinah to marry his brother, the *rasha* Eisav, and mete out such a severe punishment for his failure to do so? Indeed, the Gemara states that someone who lets his daughter marry an ignoramus (עַם הָאָרֶץ) is viewed as if he tied her up and threw her into a lions' den. So what was Yaakov's misdeed?

The *Alter of Slabodka* says that the words of the Midrash, וַיִּנְעַל בְּפָנֶיהָ, *and he closed [the chest] upon her,* is where the fault lies. The Alter explains that while Yaakov was closing up the box, he gave an extra bang of the hammer, which, on his great level, betrayed some slight satisfaction that Eisav would have no access to Dinah. For this, he was punished.

To understand this a bit better, we may turn to the approach of *Rav Shach.* He notes that if Yaakov had been expected to give Dinah to Eisav for a wife, why was he blamed only now? All the years before his encounter with Eisav, he would also have been expected to let Dinah marry Eisav, to cause him to repent. Thus, it is clear that he was *not* expected to do so. Rather, Yaakov was blamed because, in his calculations regarding whether he should hide Dinah, he did not even *consider* the possibility that she might be able to save Eisav. He should have thought about his brother — who was now close to 100 years old and still living like a *rasha* — perhaps he can repent, and maybe now is the time! Although the final verdict might have been that it was indeed correct to place her in the chest, Yaakov was held liable for not thinking enough about his brother's welfare.

פרשת וישלח

TUESDAY

PARASHAS VAYISHLACH

The Torah is teaching us an important lesson here. Just as Hashem always leaves the door open for sinners to repent, we must never "close the chest" all the way, barring a sinner's road home without at least considering every possible option. This will allow people who have turned away from the path of Torah to repent and return to their heritage.

HALACHAH OF THE DAY

As we learned yesterday, any action that will result in speeding up the process of cooking is forbidden on Shabbos. Yesterday we discussed two examples of actions forbidden as a result of this halachah. Today we will continue our discussion with some additional manifestations of this rule.

Stirring a pot of food that is not yet fully cooked tends to accelerate the cooking process. Therefore, it is forbidden for one to stir a pot of partially cooked food or liquid. [The stirring of fully cooked foods will be discussed later.] This halachah, too, pertains even to foods that have been removed from the stove, as long as the food is still at or above the temperature of *yad soledes bo*.

Placing a cover on top of a pot is another method of hastening the cooking of a pot's contents. It is therefore forbidden for one to place a cover on top of a pot of partially cooked foods or liquids that is on the fire (or at the temperature of *yad soledes bo*). This holds true even if the pot was previously covered and then subsequently became uncovered. Even if one merely lifted the cover off a pot for a moment in order to inspect its contents, the cover may not be replaced unless the food has reached the point of being fully cooked. Practically speaking, one should exercise care before lifting the cover off any pot (that he wishes to remain covered) unless he is certain that the contents are fully cooked.

We have seen so far that the Torah forbids one to cook an uncooked food even to the degree of minimal edibility as represented by the stages of *Ben Derusai* and *yad soledes bo* for solids and liquids respectively. It is also Biblically prohibited to then heat a food from its point of minimum edibility to a fully cooked state — the point at which most people would normally eat it without requiring additional cooking. Tomorrow we will discuss the *melachah* of *bishul* as it pertains to the question of reheating foods that have already been fully cooked, but have since cooled down. We must stress that the question of the permissibility of reheating pertains only to foods that have previously been fully cooked. Foods that have been only partially cooked prior to being allowed to cool may never be reheated.

פרשת וישלח

TUESDAY

PARASHAS VAYISHLACH

A CLOSER LOOK AT THE SIDDUR

The sixth blessing of the weekday *Shemoneh Esrei* states:

הֲשִׁיבֵנוּ אָבִינוּ לְתוֹרָתֶךָ . . . וְהַחֲזִירֵנוּ בִּתְשׁוּבָה שְׁלֵמָה לְפָנֶיךָ. בָּרוּךְ אַתָּה ה׳ הָרוֹצֶה בִּתְשׁוּבָה

Return us, our Father, to Your Torah . . . and bring us back, in complete repentance, before You. Blessed are You, HASHEM, Who desires repentance.

In this blessing, we ask Hashem to help us repent. As in most of the prayers, we speak in plural terms, to include all of Klal Yisrael — even wicked sinners — in our request. As the Gemara says, even though a Jew has sinned, he is still part of Klal Yisrael, and there is always hope. [The exceptions to this rule are a select few great sinners, against whom the gates of repentance are closed. In a different blessing of *Shemoneh Esrei*, the blessing of וְלַמַּלְשִׁינִים (which speaks of slanderers who attempt to have Jews killed, or those who cause others to stray from the way of Torah) we pray for their total demise.]

As we learned in *A Mussar Thought for the Day*, the Torah requires us never to give up hope for sinners; we must hope for and look forward to their return. Even a *rasha* like Eisav should be given an opening to be able to repent, and Yaakov was punished for not considering such a possibility.

The Gemara in *Berachos* (10a) relates the following incident: There was a gang of cruel men who used to antagonize R' Meir. He prayed that they should die, until his wife Beruriah pointed out to him the verse in *Tehillim* (104:35): יִתַּמּוּ חַטָּאִים מִן־הָאָרֶץ, *Let sinners cease from the earth*. She noted that the verse does not say חוֹטְאִים, which would mean the sinners themselves should die. Rather, it says חַטָּאִים, meaning the *sins* should cease to be. This tells us that we are to pray that sinners should repent; and then the end of the verse: וּרְשָׁעִים עוֹד אֵינָם, *there will be wicked ones no more*, will be fulfilled. The Gemara says

פרשת וישלח

TUESDAY

PARASHAS VAYISHLACH

that R' Meir followed his wife's instructions, and the men repented and stopped bothering R' Meir.

The *Maharsha* (ibid.) asks: How can one pray that someone else should repent? Don't we have a rule that everything is in the hands of Heaven except for fear of Heaven, which means that man's free choice will determine what path he takes, and this cannot be influenced by prayer or help from Above?

In his discussion, *Maharsha* differentiates between praying for oneself and praying for another. To pray for oneself is not a violation of the above rule, because one can choose to pray, and prayer bears results. One can even include others in his prayers, as we do in *Shemoneh Esrei*. But to pray exclusively for others to repent, as R' Meir apparently did, would seem to be a contradiction to the above rule!

The *Chazon Ish* (*Hosafos* to *Taharos*), however, is of the opinion that even praying exclusively for someone else is not a contradiction to this rule, because anything accomplished through the prayer of a human being is not considered "in the hands of Heaven." Just as one can talk to his fellow and convince him to repent, and that would not be a contradiction to free choice (because it is done through the actions of someone with free choice), so too, if one prays for someone else and Hashem listens to the prayer, this is considered as having been effected by the one who prayed, because it was his prayer that bore those results.

[See also *Igros Moshe, Orach Chaim* vol. 4 p. 65.]

QUESTION OF THE DAY:
Which children of Yaakov did not bow down to Eisav?

For the answer, see page 227.

A TORAH THOUGHT FOR THE DAY

פרשת וישלח

WEDNESDAY
PARASHAS VAYISHLACH

וַיִּוָּתֵר יַעֲקֹב לְבַדּוֹ וַיֵּאָבֵק אִישׁ עִמּוֹ עַד עֲלוֹת הַשָּׁחַר
And Yaakov was left alone, and a man wrestled with him until the break of dawn (Bereishis 32:25).

Rashi states Yaakov was alone because he had forgotten some small jars, and went back to get them. From here we see that the righteous treat their property with care. The Gemara in *Chullin* (91a) states that we see that *tzaddikim* treat their money with more care than they treat their own bodies, for Yaakov put his own life in danger by going back himself to retrieve some small jars. The Gemara asks: Why do *tzaddikim* attach such importance to their money? Because they do not allow themselves to derive enjoyment from any money that is not their own; even insignificant objects are cherished by them.

It seems somewhat amazing that *tzaddikim* would have such love for their money, even to the point of endangering their own lives for its sake.

Rabbeinu Bachya cites a *Chazal* that expounds the word לְבַדּוֹ (*alone*) in the verse as if it read לְכַדּוֹ, *for his jar,* thus finding an allusion in the verse to the reason Yaakov went back. He then advances an original idea — Yaakov went back for those small jars because they were the baby bottles from which the infants would drink. Had he been missing those cheap bottles, he would be endangering the lives of the children. He went back, endangering his own life for the sake of his children, and that is when he encountered the angel.

The *Taam VeDaas* explains that the Gemara does not mean literally that *tzaddikim* love money more than their bodies, for it is obvious that anyone would give whatever he owns to save and protect himself. The righteous, however, understand that any money given to them is a present from Hashem and was given to them for a purpose. Its loss is therefore not to be taken lightly.

The *Kli Yakar* also says later in the *parashah* that Yaakov did not have a lust for money, but rather viewed all money that comes through his hard and honest toil as a blessing from Hashem. One must be careful not to abuse or misuse such a blessing. Yaakov understood that if he had been blessed even with something as insignificant as small jars, they too must have had a purpose, and should not be left behind to be wasted. When the Gemara says that *tzaddikim* love money יוֹתֵר מִגּוּפָם, *more than their bodies,* it means that just as everyone understands that our bodies are a gift from Hashem that must not be abused, so too do the righteous view and appreciate their money. Each man's possessions must therefore be treated royally, as befitting a present from the king. [The term

פרשת וישלח

WEDNESDAY

PARASHAS VAYISHLACH

"more" than their bodies is meant only to emphasize this point.]

That is what the Gemara's continuation means: "Why to such a great degree? Because they do not steal." Since *tzaddikim* truly understand that every man's money is given to him as a gift from Hashem, they are unable to even contemplate stealing, for how can they steal Hashem's gift to another?! Thus, they treasure their own gifts all the more.

MISHNAH OF THE DAY: SHABBOS 8:6

The following Mishnah continues to list the minimum amounts of various substances that will render a person who takes them out on the Sabbath liable to a *chatas*:

עֶצֶם — If one takes out **bone,** כְּדֵי לַעֲשׂוֹת תָּרְוָד — he is liable to a *chatas* if he takes out **enough to make a spoon;** [1] רַבִּי יְהוּדָה אוֹמֵר — **R' Yehudah says:** כְּדֵי לַעֲשׂוֹת מִמֶּנּוּ חָף — **Enough to make a tooth of a key.** [2] זְכוּכִית — If he takes out **glass,** כְּדֵי לִגְרוֹר בּוֹ רֹאשׁ הַכַּרְכַּר — he is liable to a *chatas* if he takes out **enough to scrape the head of a weaver's pick with it.** [3] צְרוֹר אוֹ אֶבֶן — If he takes out **a pebble or a stone,** כְּדֵי לִזְרוֹק בְּעוֹף — he is liable to a *chatas* if he takes out one that is large **enough to throw at a bird.** [4] רַבִּי אֶלְעָזָר בַּר יַעֲקֹב אוֹמֵר — **R' Elazar bar Yaakov says:** כְּדֵי לִזְרוֹק בִּבְהֵמָה — He is only liable to a *chatas* if he takes out one that is large **enough to throw at an animal.** [5]

---------- NOTES ----------

1. Animal bones were often dried and then carved into spoons. A תָּרְוָד is a small measuring spoon used by doctors (*Rambam Commentary*).

2. The keys of that era were composed of separate teeth made from bone that were inserted into the main body of the key. R' Yehudah views each tooth as important in its own right. As in all previous cases, R' Yehudah's measurement is smaller than that of the Sages (*Rav*).

3. The warp threads of a loom would sometimes become entangled; the weaver had a wooden pick which he would insert between the threads to separate and align them. The pick had a pointed head, which would be kept sharp by scraping it with glass (*Rav; Rashi;* see above, Mishnah 7:2).

4. To drive away a bird, one tosses a pebble at it. To be effective, the pebble must have a certain amount of heft. A pebble that is heavy enough to drive a bird away is sufficiently significant to render a person who takes it out on the Sabbath liable to a *chatas*.

5. R' Eliezer bar Yaakov contends that using a pebble to drive away a bird is unnecessary, since it is just as easily driven away by shouting at it. Consequently, the smallest stone a person would normally bother to use is one sufficiently large to throw at an animal to drive it away (*Rav; Rashi*). In a Baraisa quoted by the Gemara (81a), R' Eliezer defines this as a stone weighing ten *zuz*.

GEMS FROM THE GEMARA

פרשת וישלח

**WEDNESDAY
PARASHAS
VAYISHLACH**

During Talmudic times, people did not use paper for cleansing after relieving themselves; rather, small, sharp-sided stones and pebbles were used for this purpose. Our Mishnah discusses the law of taking out on the Sabbath stones and pebbles that are *not* shaped to be fit for this use. The Gemara then discusses the related issue of this alternative use of stones and pebbles on the Sabbath. [Although, as a rule, stones are *muktzeh* and cannot be moved on the Sabbath, the Sages permitted the handling of stones that people used to clean themselves, out of concern for human dignity. The Gemara (81a) records several views regarding the size and number of such stones that one was permitted to take in hand on the Sabbath for this purpose.] Near the end of its discussion, the Gemara (82a) recounts an incident in which the importance of relieving oneself in the proper manner is stressed:

Rav Huna said to his son Rabbah, "What is the reason that you do not frequently sit [as a disciple] before Rav Chisda, whose teachings are incisive?" Rabbah replied to him: "Why should I go to him? Whenever I go to him, he sits me down [and tells me] about mundane matters [rather than words of Torah]! [For example,] he said to me, 'One who enters the bathroom should not sit forcefully, nor should he strain himself overly, for the rectum is supported by only three muscles, and excessive straining can cause the muscles of the rectum to become dislocated or torn, and he will be endangered.'" [If the sphincter muscles tear, the rectum itself can protrude into the opening; this is known as rectal prolapse. This condition can make it impossible to eliminate, and there is also the danger of infection.] Rav Huna then said to his son, "He [Rav Chisda] is dealing with peoples' lives, and you say that these are mundane matters!? [If he discusses such very important matters,] certainly you should go to him!"

A MUSSAR THOUGHT FOR THE DAY

With respect to the verse discussed above in *A Torah Thought for the Day* (וַיִּוָּתֵר יַעֲקֹב לְבַדּוֹ, *and Yaakov remained alone*), the Midrash draws an intriguing parallel. Just as it says regarding the ultimate redemption, וְנִשְׂגַּב ה׳ לְבַדּוֹ, HASHEM *"alone" will be exalted on that day* (*Yeshayah* 2:11), so too by Yaakov it says that *he was left "alone."* What is the meaning of this comparison?

Rav Yerucham Levovitz, the *mashgiach* of Mir, states that there is a trait

פרשת וישלח
WEDNESDAY
PARASHAS VAYISHLACH

(מִדָּה) called לְבַדּוֹ that Yaakov was following, emulating the way of Hashem. He explains that לְבַדּוֹ does not mean simply *alone*; rather, the trait of לְבַדּוֹ is referring to the ability to be self-sufficient and independent, not requiring any outside assistance. Hashem created a world with angels and people to serve Him; He set it up in a manner that would suggest that He needs the help of those that He created, as the verse states (*Tehillim* 68:35): תְּנוּ עֹז לֵאלֹהִים, *Give strength to Hashem*. But this is just an attitude that Hashem sometimes adopts. He has another attitude called לְבַדּוֹ, in which He demonstrates that He does not really need any help at all. Hashem is not lacking or deprived in any way when we do not serve Him properly. It is only we who lose.

This trait can and should be imitated by Klal Yisrael. Yaakov came to this lofty level at the point of time described in this verse. He reached the level of לְבַדּוֹ, meaning that he had whatever he needed and did not require help from any outside source. This was an exalted level of *sheleimus* (completeness) that would allow him to serve Hashem under any circumstances, with whatever means he had at his disposal.

The trait of לְבַדּוֹ is also a trait of which Klal Yisrael as a whole can be proud. As it says in *Parashas Balak*: הֶן־עָם לְבָדָד יִשְׁכֹּן וּבַגּוֹיִם לֹא יִתְחַשָּׁב, *Behold! It is a nation that will dwell in solitude, and not be reckoned among the nations* (*Bamidbar* 23:9).

Targum Yonasan explains this verse in the following manner. Klal Yisrael will eventually inherit *Olam Haba* (the World to Come) because they did not adopt any customs from the other nations. The courage not to try to emulate these customs and practices comes from this *middah* of לְבַדּוֹ. The Jews do not need to acquire anything from other nations; their tradition comes from within. People look for others to imitate only when they feel they are lacking and inadequate. Once they realize that they have all they need, they no longer feel deprived.

This, then, is the meaning of the parallel drawn by the Midrash. At the time of the ultimate redemption, it will become clear to all that Hashem is the Master of Creation, and that He has no need of anyone's assistance. This is the level that Yaakov reached at the time that he remained לְבַדּוֹ, able to stand on his own.

QUESTION OF THE DAY:
What was the nature of the injury Yaakov sustained when he wrestled with the angel?

For the answer, see page 228.

HALACHAH OF THE DAY

פרשת וישלח

WEDNESDAY
PARASHAS VAYISHLACH

The applicability of the *melachah* of *bishul* to the question of reheating foods is dependent upon the type of food being reheated, as well as upon the method of reheating being used. We will begin by discussing the halachah as it applies to solid foods.

A solid food that has been fully cooked is no longer subject to the Biblical restrictions of the *melachah* of *bishul*. This rule is known as אֵין בִּשׁוּל אַחַר בִּשׁוּל, there is no [prohibition against] cooking [an item] after [that item] has already been cooked.

Fully baked foods are also exempt from the Biblical prohibition of cooking on Shabbos, due to the rule of אֵין אֲפִיָּה אַחַר אֲפִיָּה, there is no [prohibition against] baking [an item] after [that item] has already been baked.

Thus, in accordance with these two rules, it would be permissible for one to reheat fully cooked or fully baked solid foods on Shabbos. However, in order to protect one from inadvertently transgressing the *melachah* of *bishul* on Shabbos, the Sages prohibited the placing of even fully cooked or baked items directly on the fire — or even on a *blech* — on Shabbos. Therefore, one may reheat solid foods on Shabbos only by employing an indirect method of reheating. These methods will be discussed further on.

While both cooking and baking improve the edibility of food through the application of heat, and they are therefore both subject equally to the restrictions of the *melachah* of *bishul*, they are still distinct in the qualities that they impart to the food being prepared. Boiled chicken and roast chicken are both equally edible as a result of their preparation, yet they are two distinct dishes, each possessing a flavor and texture different from the other, due to the different methods of preparation employed. For this reason, while cooking a previously cooked item or baking a previously baked item is not considered a halachically significant act, many *poskim* rule that it is forbidden to bake or roast an item that had been previously cooked in liquid, or to cook in liquid an item that had previously been roasted or baked. Since the secondary act will impart a quality to the food that it did not have after the initial preparation, it is seen as a significant act, and is therefore forbidden.

The position of these *poskim* presents us with the following rules: (1) יֵשׁ אֲפִיָּה אַחַר בִּשׁוּל, there is [a prohibition against] baking [an item] that has already been cooked; (2) and יֵשׁ צְלִי אַחַר בִּשׁוּל, there is [a prohibition against] roasting [an item] that has already been cooked; and the inverse of these rules, (3) יֵשׁ בִּשׁוּל אַחַר אֲפִיָּה / צְלִי, there is [a prohibition against] cooking [an item] that has already been baked / roasted.

We will continue the topic of reheating foods tomorrow.

A CLOSER LOOK AT THE SIDDUR

WEDNESDAY
PARASHAS VAYISHLACH

In the first chapter of the *Shema*, which we say every day and every night in our prayers, we find the verse: וְאָהַבְתָּ אֵת ה׳ אֱלֹהֶיךָ בְּכָל־לְבָבְךָ וּבְכָל־נַפְשְׁךָ וּבְכָל־מְאֹדֶךָ, *And you shall love* HASHEM, *your God, with all your heart, with all your soul, and with all your resources.*

The Gemara in *Berachos* (54a) explains that *with all your heart* means that one must love Hashem with both his *yetzer hara* and his *yetzer tov*. *With all your soul* teaches that even if a person is faced with death, he may not stop loving Hashem. *With all your resources* has two explanations: (1) with all your money, which means that a person must fulfill the commandment to love Hashem even if this will cause him to lose all his money; and (2) with every *middah* that Hashem gave you — a person must utilize all of his character traits in the service of Hashem.

Rashba states that these three forms of serving Hashem correspond to the three *Avos*. Avraham fulfilled *with all your heart* by being ready to sacrifice his most beloved treasure, Yitzchak. He quashed his natural tendencies of *chesed*, and was ready to give up his own son, all for his love of Hashem.

With all your soul includes suffering any harm or damage or pain, including losing your soul for the sake of Hashem, which clearly corresponds to Yitzchak, who agreed to be slaughtered by his father.

Yaakov exemplified *with all your resources*, for we find many times when he was ready to give up his possessions to fulfill Hashem's will. *Rashba* gives a few examples, such as: (1) Yaakov offered Eisav a pile of money to secure his place in the *Me'aras HaMachpelah*; (2) Yaakov promised to give *maaser* of his possessions to Hashem; (3) Yaakov chose a life of sitting in the tents of Torah instead of managing Yitzchak's vast riches. We can also add to this how Yaakov returned to get the small jars that he had left behind, because he understood that everything he owned was a present from Hashem and had a purpose in serving Him. So whenever it was necessary to give up possessions for Hashem's sake, it was natural for Yaakov to do so.

A TORAH THOUGHT FOR THE DAY

פרשת וישלח

THURSDAY
PARASHAS VAYISHLACH

וַיֹּאמֶר עֵשָׂו יֶשׁ־לִי רָב אָחִי יְהִי לְךָ אֲשֶׁר־לָךְ . . .
קַח־נָא אֶת־בִּרְכָתִי אֲשֶׁר הֻבָאת לָךְ
כִּי־חַנַּנִי אֱלֹהִים וְכִי יֶשׁ־לִי־כֹל וַיִּפְצַר־בּוֹ וַיִּקָּח

And Eisav said, "I have plenty, my brother;
let what you have remain yours." . . .
"Please accept my homage which was brought to you,
inasmuch as God has been gracious to me
and inasmuch as I have everything" . . .
[Yaakov] urged him and he accepted (Bereishis 33:9-11).

Rashi points out the difference between Eisav's choice of words and that of Yaakov. Yaakov says, "*I have everything* — all that I require," but Eisav speaks in a haughty language, saying, "*I have plenty,*" which implies: I have much more than I need.

The difference is not only in language; it is indicative of a totally different mind-set and approach that Yaakov and Eisav each had toward their respective places in this world. As the *Kli Yakar* says: The *rasha* is never satisfied, he never has enough. Whatever he has already attained pales in comparison to the vast arenas of pleasure and indulgence in this world that he has not yet experienced. In his mind, he has been placed in this world to derive as much pleasure as he can. Therefore, although Eisav was indeed wealthy — יֶשׁ־לִי רָב — he feels far from satisfied, because there is so much more to be had.

Yaakov, on the other hand (as we discussed earlier this week), understands that this world is only a preparation for the World to Come. It is only a stopover, where one must accumulate as much Torah and mitzvos as he can. Whatever pleasures are given to him to experience are only incidental, only instruments to be used to reach his true goal. Yaakov can easily say, "I have everything" I need to reach that goal.

Tanna D'Vei Eliyahu records an interesting dialogue between Yaakov and Eisav which brings out this point very clearly. Yaakov and Eisav made a deal. Eisav said that he would take this world with all its resources, enjoyment and pleasure, and Yaakov could have the World to Come with all its trimmings. So when Eisav saw all the presents and Yaakov's large family, he wondered out loud: מִי אֵלֶּה־לָּךְ, as *Rashi explains*: "Who are these, that they are yours?" He was accusing Yaakov of breaking their agreement. "If you agreed not to take any extra pleasures from this world, how is it that all these people and cattle belong to you?" challenged Eisav.

Yaakov replied. הַיְלָדִים אֲשֶׁר־חָנַן אֱלֹהִים אֶת־עַבְדֶּךָ, *The children whom*

THURSDAY

PARASHAS VAYISHLACH

God has graciously given to your servant. Yaakov told Eisav, "I believe that everything we own, or the large family with which I have been blessed, is a present from Hashem, and it therefore must be used only to serve Him. I am not taking pleasure for myself from this world, as you do; rather, I am using all resources at my disposal to serve Hashem and gain entrance to *Olam Haba*. Thus, whatever Hashem has chosen to give me does not constitute a violation of our pact."

MISHNAH OF THE DAY: SHABBOS 8:7

The final Mishnah of the chapter discusses the minimum measure of earthenware that a person must take out on the Sabbath to be liable to a *chatas*:

חֶרֶס — If one takes out *earthenware,* כְּדֵי לִיתֵּן בֵּין פַּצִּים לַחֲבֵרוֹ — he is liable to a *chatas* if he takes out *enough to place between one slat and another;*[1] דִּבְרֵי רַבִּי יְהוּדָה — these are *the words of R' Yehudah*. רַבִּי מֵאִיר אוֹמֵר — *R' Meir says:* כְּדֵי לַחְתּוֹת בּוֹ אֶת הָאוּר — He is liable to a *chatas* only if he takes out a piece large *enough to pick up fire with it.*[2] רַבִּי יוֹסֵי אוֹמֵר — *R' Yose says:* כְּדֵי לְקַבֵּל בּוֹ רְבִיעִית — He is liable to a *chatas* even if he takes out a piece that is only large *enough to hold in it a revi'is* of liquid.[3] אָמַר רַבִּי מֵאִיר — *R' Meir said:* אַף עַל פִּי שֶׁאֵין רְאָיָה לַדָּבָר — *Although there is no proof to the matter,* זֵכֶר לַדָּבָר — there is *an allusion to the matter,* for the verse states: וְלֹא יִמָּצֵא בִמְכִתָּתוֹ חֶרֶשׂ לַחְתּוֹת אֵשׁ מִיָּקוּד — *"And there will not be found among its pieces a shard with which to pick up fire from the hearth."*[4]

NOTES
---

1. One who stacks slats, pilings or beams of wood on the ground fills in the spaces and gaps between the pieces of wood with small pieces of earthenware. This is done to prevent the weight of the pile from compressing the pieces into the empty spaces, causing them to warp (*Rav; Rashi*).

2. I.e., a piece of earthenware that is large enough to use to move burning coals from place to place without burning one's hands. This is a larger size than that required by R' Yehudah (*Meiri, Shenos Eliyahu*).

3. This is a smaller size than that identified by R' Meir (*Meiri*).

4. Isaiah 30:14. The prophet castigates the Jews for lacking trust in God and seeking aid from the king of Egypt; he states that the metaphorical "wall" of protection that they seek will fall and shatter into nothingness, so that not even the smallest piece will be left whole (see *Radak* ad loc.). R' Meir says that although there is no conclusive proof from the verse, it does indicate that a shard large enough to pick up fire has value (*Rav; Rashi*).

THURSDAY
PARASHAS VAYISHLACH

מִשָּׁם רְאָיָה — *R' Yose said to him:* אָמַר לֵיהּ רַבִּי יוֹסֵי — *From there* you offer *proof!?* ",וְלַחְשֹׂף מַיִם מִגֶּבֶא" — But that verse itself concludes, *"or to scoop up water from a pit,"* which shows that even a smaller shard, one used to scoop up water, has significance![5]

— NOTES —

5. R' Yose understands the phrase *or to scoop up water from a pit* that ends the verse as indicating that even a smaller shard, one just large enough to scoop up water from a small pit where water has gathered, is likewise of value (*Rav*). Thus, the verse means that not only will there not remain a shard large enough to pick up burning coals, but not even one large enough to scoop up water from a pit (*Tiferes Yisrael*).

See *Gems from the Gemara* for how R' Meir will explain this verse.

GEMS FROM THE GEMARA

The Mishnah relates that R' Meir provided an allusion to his position from the verse that states: *And there will not be found among its pieces a shard with which to pick up fire from the hearth.* R' Yose retorted that the verse itself concludes: *or to scoop up water from a pit* — which shows that even a smaller shard, one used to scoop up water, also has significance.

The Gemara (82a) asks: It seems that R' Yose answered R' Meir well! Seemingly, the end of the verse is indeed proof that even a utensil that holds water is useful. What, then, was R' Meir's allusion?

The Gemara then comes to R' Meir's defense, explaining that R' Meir would contend that the prophet stated his curse in the sense of "it need not be said . . ."; that is, it need not be said that they will not be able to find anything that is considered significant by people, but they will not even be able to find anything that is not considered significant by people.

[Thus, R' Meir also agrees that the shard with which one can carry water is smaller than that required to carry a coal from a fire; he holds, however, that the shard needed to carry water is not considered a significant shard (see *Rashi*). Although the prophet mentions such a shard, he does so to strengthen his curse further by stating that the "wall" will be broken so utterly that even insignificant shards will not be found! (see *Rashi*).]

The Gemara also notes that it is clear from the Mishnah that the minimum measure of R' Meir (a shard large enough to hold fire) is understood to be larger than the minimum measure of R' Yose (a shard large enough to hold a *revi'is* of water). However, logic dictates that this is not the case, because even a very small shard can be used to pick up a coal! The

PARASHAS VAYISHLACH

THURSDAY

Gemara (82a) therefore explains that according to R' Meir, a shard is not considered useful unless it can be used to remove a burning coal from a large bonfire. To accomplish this, a larger shard is required [for one who attempts to pick up a coal with a smaller shard will be burned by coming too close to the fire].

A MUSSAR THOUGHT FOR THE DAY

One might ask: We have seen that Yaakov valued every penny given to him by Hashem. If so, when Yaakov was forced into giving this large present to Eisav to calm his anger, why is it that when Eisav refused at first to accept it, Yaakov urged him strongly to take the gift, until Eisav agreed to do so? One would think that if the desired results have been reached without the gifts, Yaakov should have taken the proffered gift back. Indeed *Rashi* notes (32:22, citing the Midrash) that Yaakov was pained that he needed to send all these items to appease Eisav. Why, then, when he had the opportunity to take them back, did he not do so?

This can be explained with a story that occurred to *Rav Chaim Brisker,* which can give us a better insight into the tactic called דורון, *presents* (better known as שַחַד, *bribery*). As the verse states in *Mishlei* (21:14): מַתָּן בַּסֵּתֶר יִכְפֶּה־אָף וְשֹׁחַד בַּחֵק חֵמָה עַזָּה, *An anonymous gift will cover up anger, and a bribe in the bosom will appease strong wrath.* The tactic of "tribute" has been used many times over the generations, in different forms and on various occasions, to abolish many harsh decrees issued against the Jews.

This particular story involved an important Russian minister who issued a decree against the Jews. It was well known that this minister was such an anti-Semite that no bribery in the world would move him. In fact, if an offer would be made to him, he would arrest that person just for the crime of daring to offer a bribe! So the Jews in Brisk and other areas were at a loss, trying to come up with a plan to influence this minister.

Rav Chaim called in the prominent citizens of the community, and asked them how much money they had raised to present to the minister. They told him the amount, but warned him that there was no point in making the attempt, as it would not change the minister's mind, and would likely result in the arrest of the presenter. Rav Chaim just smiled and said: "Do not worry. I will be fine."

It was a hot summer day, but Rav Chaim put on his heavy fur winter coat, and made his way to the minister, with the money in his hand. He sought an audience with the minister, and was told that while he would see him, trying to persuade the minister to abolish the decree would be a waste of time. Rav Chaim agreed.

As Rav Chaim was ushered into the minister's office, the minister was surprised to see Rav Chaim dressed in winter gear and sweating. He asked Rav Chaim: "Are you unwell?" Rav Chaim replied that he was feeling fine, but was dressed so unusually because of a dream he had had. He described the dream in great detail: He had seen that there would be terrible storms and winds today, and even hail and snow. It was so real to him in his dream, that he was forced to dress accordingly.

The minister burst out laughing, "Rabbi, are you insane?" he asked. "Anyone who looks at the sky can see that there is no way there will be a storm today." "Are you so sure?" asked Rav Chaim. "Yes," he replied. "Would you care to make a wager to that effect?" Rav Chaim suggested. The minister answered, "Most certainly!" They agreed on a huge sum (the exact amount that was collected). The meeting was delayed until the following day. Of course, it did not rain or snow, and Rav Chaim returned with his head bowed, wearing his light summer garb. The minister was waiting for Rav Chaim to ask him to forgive his debt, but Rav Chaim walked right up to him, delivered the money and immediately exited. He returned to his people in Brisk and told them: "The money is in his hands; now it will work by itself, and the decree will be nullified." And that is exactly what happened.

Yaakov wanted the money to stay in Eisav's hands for the same reason. Yaakov knew that as long as the bribe eventually ended up in Eisav's hands, it would work wonders and help keep his hatred at bay. Such is the power of a bribe!

HALACHAH OF THE DAY

As we explained yesterday, baking or roasting a cooked item, or cooking an item that has been previously roasted or baked, is considered a halachically significant act, and is therefore prohibited on Shabbos.

For example, chicken that has been cooked in soup is obviously a cooked item. If a pot of chicken soup is on the *blech* and the chicken is removed from the soup, one may not then place it directly on the *blech*. This is because placing the dry chicken on the *blech* is considered an act of roasting — which will result in an improvement to the food that had not been realized before.

Similarly, one may not place bread or matzah — which are baked

פרשת וישלח

THURSDAY

PARASHAS VAYISHLACH

items — into a pot of hot soup that is on the *blech*, since this would be considered cooking an item that had previously been baked. [The details of this halachah, including when one may dip *challah* into the soup that he is eating and when this is forbidden, will be discussed further as our exploration of this *melachah* progresses.]

To summarize: Completely cooked, roasted, or baked solid foods may sometimes be reheated in a manner identical to their initial preparation. That is, items that were cooked in liquid may be reheated in liquid, items baked or roasted dry may be reheated while dry. However, these items may not be placed *directly* on the flame or *blech* — they may be reheated only in an *indirect* manner, the details of which we will delineate in a future discussion. But it is forbidden to reheat any food in a manner that differs from the way the food was initially prepared. Thus, a cooked item may not be roasted or baked; a roasted or baked item may not be cooked.

We now arrive at the question of reheating liquids — a question which is the subject of much controversy. There are *poskim* who differentiate between solids and liquids, and rule that cooked liquids that have cooled may not be reheated. The reason for the distinction between liquids and solids is as follows: Solids are generally heated and cooked in order to achieve a qualitative difference in the substance being cooked. The desired effect may be the softening of the food, or there may be a change in flavor that is brought about through cooking. However, whatever the desired change may be, it is usually not reversed when the food cools. Liquids, however, are generally "cooked" simply by raising their temperature so that they may be enjoyed while hot — not to bring about any substantive change in the makeup of the liquids themselves. This being true, allowing a liquid to cool completely reverses the change that was brought about in the liquid through the cooking. To reheat the liquid is therefore in essence to "recook" the liquid — and this is forbidden the second time the same way it was forbidden the first time.

According to these *poskim*, the rule is that in regard to liquids, יֵשׁ בִּשּׁוּל אַחַר בִּשּׁוּל, *there is [a prohibition against] cooking [a liquid, even] after [that liquid] has already been cooked*, if the liquid has cooled.

QUESTION OF THE DAY:
Where is part of Yaakov's dialogue with Eisav found in Bircas HaMazon?

For the answer, see page 228.

A CLOSER LOOK AT THE SIDDUR

פָּרָשַׁת וַיִּשְׁלַח

**THURSDAY
PARASHAS VAYISHLACH**

Yaakov's humble attitude toward everything that Hashem gave him is expressed twice in this *parashah*: First when he says (32:11): *I have been diminished by all the kindness You have done*, and then again when he declares (33:11): *as God has been gracious to me, for I have everything.* Our Sages teach us that this is an essential attitude that we must adopt as an integral part of our approach toward prayer.

The Mishnah says in *Avos* (2:18): *Do not make your prayer a set routine, but rather [requests for] mercy and supplications before Hashem.*

Rabbeinu Yonah explains there that a person should pray like a poor man, who asks with his whole heart, as he knows that his very life is dependent on the fulfillment of his request. He goes on to explain the verse that is quoted in that Mishnah (*Yoel* 2:13): *For He is gracious and compassionate, slow to anger, abounding in kindness, and relentful of judgment.* This verse underscores the fact that everyone needs mercy from Heaven, for every person has sins that must be atoned for; and even a person who is comfortable with his situation in life is not being punished only because Hashem is delaying his punishment out of mercy, to afford him an opportunity to repent. But no one is guaranteed that his prosperity will continue, and thus every person must pray as if he is in great need.

In the opening *berachah* of the *Shemoneh Esrei* we say: גּוֹמֵל חֲסָדִים טוֹבִים וְקוֹנֵה הַכֹּל, *Who bestows beneficial kindnesses and creates everything.* The *Siach Yitzchak* (*Siddur HaGra*) explains that וְקוֹנֵה הַכֹּל can also be understood to mean that He *acquires* everything; through His endless kindness, He acquires everyone. He quotes the *Chovos HaLevavos*, who states that everyone must serve Hashem because we are indebted for all that Hashem has done for us — it is as if we have been "bought" by Hashem's many kindnesses and vast graciousness.

The *Magen Avraham* in *Shulchan Aruch* (§154) cites from the *Maharshal* that a person should not say, "I have more than I really deserve according to my actions," because he is implying that Hashem forgives a person even without repentance. Rather, he should say, "It is all in the merit of my fathers."

The *Magen Avraham* himself argues with this, maintaining that (as *Rabbeinu Yonah* says) everything Hashem does is kindness, and He gives every person far in excess of what he deserves. This does not mean that Hashem will wipe away one's sins without *teshuvah*. On the contrary, a person must always plead his case before Hashem, begging for forgiveness, and asking to continue receiving kindness from Him.

פרשת וישלח

A TORAH THOUGHT FOR THE DAY

FRIDAY
PARASHAS VAYISHLACH

וְיַעֲקֹב נָסַע סֻכֹּתָה וַיִּבֶן לוֹ בָּיִת וּלְמִקְנֵהוּ
עָשָׂה סֻכֹּת עַל־כֵּן קָרָא שֵׁם־הַמָּקוֹם סֻכּוֹת

Yaakov journeyed to Succos and built himself a house, and for his cattle he built shelters; therefore, he called the name of the place Succos (Bereishis 33:17).

This verse requires an explanation. Why would Yaakov name the place Succos just because he made shelters for animals there? Would it not be more appropriate to give a name that was connected to the houses he built for human habitation?

Ohr HaChaim suggests that perhaps Yaakov was the first one to show such mercy even toward animals, and build them huts to provide them with relief during the hot summer months (as *Rashi* points out). This had never been done before, and because of its uniqueness, it was commemorated in the name of the town.

HaRav Matisyahu Salomon in *Matnos Chaim* offers another explanation. He cites *Tur* (*Hilchos Rosh Chodesh*), who states that the three *Yamim Tovim* are parallel to the three *Avos*. Pesach is for Avraham, Shavuos for Yitzchak, and Succos for Yaakov, as it says *"for his cattle he built succos."* At first glance this seems perplexing — what does the festival of Succos have to do with the shelters that Yaakov built for his animals?

Rav Matisyahu also asks another question: Why is the Torah telling us that Yaakov built houses and huts, and what lessons can we learn from this?

Targum Yonasan on this verse states that Yaakov went to Succos, and remained there for eighteen months. He built himself a *beis midrash,* and for his possessions he built huts. According to this explanation, the בַּיִת, *house,* mentioned in the verse was not for people to live in, but rather was a study hall in which to learn Torah.

Yaakov wanted to teach his family and future generations that one builds a complete structure for a *beis midrash* because it is a permanent dwelling. For all other possessions and riches etc., one builds a temporary place, which is a *succah.* Yaakov implemented this idea and commemorated it in the name of the city, to declare that all we acquire in this world is not permanent.

This is the exact lesson of the Yom Tov of Succos: Go out of your permanent dwelling, and move into a temporary dwelling. This reminds a person that his house is not where his goal in life should be. Rather, a house of Torah that brings a person closer to *Olam Haba* should be his permanent address.

Rav Matisyahu cites *Sefer Niflaos HaTorah*, who writes that this town of Succos ended up in the portion of Gad, one of the tribes that requested a portion in *Eiver HaYarden* because of the large amount of cattle they owned. The Midrash says that Moshe rebuked them for giving much more attention to their possessions than necessary. It is possible that the town of Succos was placed by Hashem in their portion to remind them not to fall into the trap of getting caught up with material possessions, and instead to focus on preparing in this world for the World to Come.

פרשת וישלח
FRIDAY
PARASHAS VAYISHLACH

MISHNAH OF THE DAY: SHABBOS 9:1

The subject of the following Mishnah is the Rabbinic enactment that invested objects of idol worship with *tumah*. [For an explanation why these four Mishnayos are presented here, see *Gems from the Gemara*.]

מִנַּיִן לַעֲבוֹדָה זָרָה שֶׁמְּטַמְּאָה בְמַשָּׂא — אָמַר רַבִּי עֲקִיבָא — R' Akiva said: כְּנִדָּה — From where do we know that an **object of idolatrous worship contaminates** one who carries it **with the "tumah of carrying"**[1] just **as a niddah**[2] contaminates a person who carries her with the "*tumah* of carrying"? שֶׁנֶּאֱמַר — For it is stated: ,,תִּזְרֵם כְּמוֹ דָוָה — צֵא תֹּאמַר לוֹ" — "You will cast them away as you would a niddah; you will say to [the idol]: Leave!"[3] מַה נִּדָּה מְטַמְּאָה בְמַשָּׂא — This analogy between a *niddah* and an idol teaches us that **just as a niddah contaminates** one who carries her **with the "tumah of carrying,"** אַף עֲבוֹדָה זָרָה מְטַמְּאָה בְמַשָּׂא — **so too an object of idolatrous worship contaminates** one who carries it **with the "tumah of carrying."**

---— NOTES —

1. R' Akiva seeks Scriptural support for the Rabbinic enactment of *tumah* for objects of idol worship or their accessories, and particularly for the enactment of so stringent a form of contamination that it contaminates one who merely carries it without touching it — viz., in a bowl or a basket, without physical contact (*Rav*).

2. *A niddah* — a menstruating woman (see above, Mishnah 2:6) — in addition to transmitting *tumah* through direct contact, also transmits *tumah* to anyone who carries her, even if he does not touch her (e.g., if she is carried on a stretcher).

3. Isaiah 30:22. The prophet speaks of distancing oneself from idolatry as one distances himself from physical contact with his menstruating wife (*Rav*).

פרשת וישלח

GEMS FROM THE GEMARA

FRIDAY
PARASHAS VAYISHLACH

The grouping of unrelated topics because of verbal associations is very prevalent in Mishnah (see, for example, *Megillah* 1:4-11; *Chullin* 1:4-7 and elsewhere). This format is so integral a part of the pattern of Mishnah that about half of Tractate *Sotah* (3:7-8, 5:2-5 and all of Chs. 7, 8, and 9) consists of topics that otherwise have no connection to *Sotah* whatsoever, and are included only because of word and category associations and associations of these associations (see the second half of Ch. 9).

This phenomenon is readily explained if we bear in mind that prior to the days of *R' Yehudah HaNasi* (that is, Rebbi, the redactor of the Mishnah), the Mishnah was not written down. Even after Rebbi formalized and wrote down the text of the Mishnah, it was still the practice of scholars to memorize the entire text. These kinds of association were, therefore, a great aid to memory, and may account for the popularity of organizing topics according to word or category associations.

The seven topics discussed in the first four Mishnayos of Chapter 9 are unrelated. Six of them are not relevant to Tractate *Shabbos*, and it would be expected that they would appear in other tractates; indeed, some of them are repeated elsewhere almost verbatim. The commentators offer various reasons for their inclusion here:

(1) *Rashi* notes that the אֶמְצָעִיתָא, *intermediate clause*, of Mishnah 3 discusses the care for the incision of a circumcision on the Sabbath. Since the Mishnayos couch the other six cases in similar language [each begins with the word מִנַּיִן — *from where do we learn* — and ends with a Scriptural verse that lends support to the law stated, but that is not conclusive proof] they are included here.

(2) *Tosafos* object to this reasoning, since it presumes that this chapter is the proper place for discussing the care of a recently circumcised infant on the Sabbath. Actually, *Tosafos* note, it seems more likely that the proper place for this discussion is in Chapter 19, where the special laws of circumcision on the Sabbath are discussed. Since, according to this explanation, all the other topics are added only because of their association with the law of caring for a newly circumcised infant, Rebbi should have inserted this entire series of laws in Chapter 19, rather than here. *Tosafos* therefore explain that this chapter is added because of its association with the last Mishnah in Chapter 8. That Mishnah concludes by citing a verse that seems to lend support to the stated law, but is not conclusive proof. The Tanna then appends seven other cases that follow this pattern.

(3) Alternatively, since Chapter 8 concludes with two quotations from *Isaiah* 30:14, the Tanna goes on to expound on verse 22 of that same chapter [Mishnah 1]. He then continues with other similarly phrased Mishnayos (*Rav; Tos.*).
(4) Finally, the verse cited at the end of Chapter 8 may be interpreted homiletically as alluding to idolatry, as is the verse cited in Mishnah 1 of Chapter 9. Moreover, Mishnah 6 deals with transporting objects used for idolatry (*Meiri*).

פרשת
וישלח

FRIDAY

PARASHAS
VAYISHLACH

A MUSSAR THOUGHT FOR THE DAY

The Torah relates that after Yaakov left Succos, he traveled to Shechem:
וַיָּבֹא יַעֲקֹב שָׁלֵם עִיר שְׁכֶם אֲשֶׁר בְּאֶרֶץ כְּנַעַן בְּבֹאוֹ מִפַּדַּן אֲרָם וַיִּחַן אֶת־פְּנֵי הָעִיר,
Yaakov came intact to the city of Shechem, which is in the land of Canaan, upon his coming to Paddan-aram, and he encamped before the city (*Bereishis* 33:18).

Rashi explains that the word שָׁלֵם, *intact* or *complete*, teaches us that Yaakov was "complete" in all the areas of his life. He was intact bodily, for he was cured of the injury that he had received while struggling with the angel. Second, he was intact monetarily — he did not suffer any monetary loss as a result of the gift that he gave Eisav. Finally, he was intact with his Torah, for while he had been in Lavan's house he did not forget what he had learned from his father.

The Gemara in *Shabbos* (33b) connects this to the end of the verse, וַיִּחַן אֶת־פְּנֵי הָעִיר. *Rashi* there explains the word וַיִּחַן as a term that connotes *favor*. In other words, he did something which was favorable and accepted by the local townspeople.

There are three opinions as to exactly what Yaakov did. Either (1) he instituted new coinage; (2) he improved the marketplaces; or (3) he built bathhouses.

Why did Yaakov find it necessary to do these things at this point in time, at this place, while coming to Shechem?

Midrash Rabbah (76:6) states that from here we learn that a person must show his gratitude to any place from which he has benefited. The Gemara in *Shabbos* that we mentioned explains this benefit as the miracle that he was saved from Eisav. Although this was not a direct result of his being in that city, nevertheless because Yaakov felt grateful in that place for the miracle that just occurred, that is where he wanted to benefit the local residents.

FRIDAY

PARASHAS VAYISHLACH

The Gemara says that Rav Shimon ben Yochai was finally able to leave the cave in which he had hidden from the Romans for twelve years. He followed Yaakov's example, and looked for some way to improve the city where he had been hiding. In the end, he accomplished this by cleaning the city of Tiberias from any doubtful impurity (סְפֵק טֻמְאָה).

An important lesson can be seen here. If a person derives pleasure or some type of benefit from a place, even indirectly, he is obligated not only to verbally thank those who live there, but to actively do something or build something for the public to enjoy.

It is well known that *Rav Moshe Feinstein* would constantly say that we must show appreciation and gratitude to the American government for allowing us a safe haven in this country, where we can freely live as religious Jews. To indicate our gratitude, he said that we should actively show our respect to the country and perform our duties as local citizens. This is a perfect example of emulating the actions of Yaakov Avinu.

HALACHAH OF THE DAY

As we learned yesterday, some *poskim* rule that there is a prohibition against reheating liquids that have previously been cooked, once they have cooled. Other *poskim* do not accept the idea that there is a distinction between solids and liquids. These *poskim* therefore rule that just as solids may be reheated after they have cooled (subject to the limitations listed earlier) so too, one may reheat liquids that have cooled after they have previously been cooked.

In practice, we follow the more stringent view. Therefore, one may not reheat liquids once they have been allowed to cool *completely*. However, if they have only partially cooled, and they are still warm enough to be suitable for use as a "warm" drink, they may be reheated and brought to a higher temperature. The reason for this is that since the liquids are still warm enough to be enjoyed as a warm drink, reheating them is not a significant enough improvement to result in a prohibition.

As we mentioned earlier in regard to solid foods, there is a Rabbinic prohibition against placing even fully cooked foods directly on the fire or *blech* on Shabbos; similarly, even a warm liquid may not be reheated in such a manner on Shabbos. The allowable methods of reheating the foods which may be reheated on Shabbos will be delineated further on in our discussions of the *melachah* of *bishul*.

If the *melachah* of *bishul* was violated, either intentionally or unintentionally, it often results in a prohibition against deriving any benefit from the food that was cooked in violation of halachah. This prohibition may apply irrespective of whether it was a Torah prohibition that was violated, or a Rabbinic decree. Sometimes the prohibition against the food's use remains permanently, while in other cases the food may be prohibited only for the duration of Shabbos. In still other cases, there is no prohibition against using the food at all.

FRIDAY
PARASHAS VAYISHLACH

These halachos are very complex. Therefore, in any case where food was cooked on Shabbos in violation of halachah, a competent Rabbinic authority must be consulted to advise on the permissibility of deriving pleasure from the cooked food. Indeed, the same holds true for other Shabbos prohibitions. Wherever the laws of Shabbos have been violated, it is necessary to determine whether or not pleasure may be derived from the fruits of the forbidden activity.

A CLOSER LOOK AT THE SIDDUR

This week, we discuss the seventh of the Thirteen Fundamental Principles (י״ג עיקרים) enumerated by *Rambam*, which states:

אֲנִי מַאֲמִין בֶּאֱמוּנָה שְׁלֵמָה שֶׁנְּבוּאַת מֹשֶׁה רַבֵּנוּ עָלָיו הַשָּׁלוֹם הָיְתָה אֲמִתִּית וְשֶׁהוּא הָיָה אָב לַנְּבִיאִים לַקּוֹדְמִים לְפָנָיו וְלַבָּאִים אַחֲרָיו.

I believe with perfect faith that the prophecy of our Teacher Moshe was absolutely true, and that he was the chief of all nevi'im that preceded him and that came after him.

This principle actually has its roots in an explicit verse in the Torah (*Devarim* 34:10), which states: *Never has there arisen in Israel a prophet like Moshe, whom* HASHEM *had known face to face*. *Rambam*, both in his *Commentary to the Mishnah* and in the seventh chapter of *Hilchos Yesodei HaTorah*, explains that the prophecy of Moshe was unique in four ways:

(1) All the other *nevi'im* received their *nevuah* in a dream or in a vision. Moshe, however, was awake and alert, as the verse states (*Bamidbar* 7:89): *When Moshe arrived at the Tent of Meeting to speak with Him, he heard the voice* etc.

(2) All other *nevi'im* received their prophecy through an angel, and thus the prophecy was [often] in the form of an allegory or a riddle.

FRIDAY

PARASHAS VAYISHLACH

Moshe, however, spoke to Hashem directly, as the verse states (ibid. 12:8): *Mouth to mouth I will speak to him.* Moshe, who spoke directly to Hashem, perceived the essence of the *nevuah* itself without allegory or representative visions.

(3) Every other *navi* would be seized with fear, trembling, and weakness while receiving *nevuah*. Not so Moshe; of him the Torah states (*Shemos* 33:11): *Hashem spoke to Moshe face to face, as a man speaks to his fellow.* Just as a man is not physically weakened by speaking to his fellow, Moshe was able to speak with Hashem without ill effect.

(4) Other prophets could not receive prophecy whenever they desired. Moshe, however, was not so; any time he desired, the Divine Spirit would envelop him and *nevuah* would descend upon him. It was not necessary for Moshe to concentrate and prepare his mind for *nevuah;* he was on the level of an angel, who is always prepared to receive Hashem's Presence. Thus, the Torah quotes him as saying to those who had been unable to bring the *korban pesach* (*Bamidbar* 9:8): *Wait, and I will hear what HASHEM commands you to do.* Rambam explains that it was for this reason that Moshe, unlike other *nevi'im*, separated from his wife, for his level of constant holiness elevated him to the status of an angel. This is the meaning of what Hashem told him after the Torah was given (*Devarim* 5:27-28): *Go, say to them: "Return to your tents." But as for you, stand here with Me.*

We will continue our discussion of the uniqueness of Moshe's prophecy next week.

QUESTION OF THE DAY:
How long did Yaakov remain in Succos?

For the answer, see page 228.

A TORAH THOUGHT FOR THE DAY

פרשת וישלח

SHABBOS

PARASHAS VAYISHLACH

וַיֹּאמֶר לוֹ אֱלֹהִים שִׁמְךָ יַעֲקֹב לֹא־יִקָּרֵא שִׁמְךָ עוֹד יַעֲקֹב
כִּי אִם־יִשְׂרָאֵל יִהְיֶה שְׁמֶךָ וַיִּקְרָא אֶת־שְׁמוֹ יִשְׂרָאֵל

And God said to him, "Your name is Yaakov:
You shall not be called Yaakov anymore,
but Yisrael shall be your name";
and He called his name Yisrael (Bereishis 35:10).

This verse seems to contain an inherent contradiction. If Hashem wished to change Yaakov's name to Yisrael at this time, why did He preface His doing so with the statement "Your name is Yaakov"? Surely Yaakov was aware of his own name! Moreover, when Yaakov struggled with the angel and triumphed, the angel told him (Bereishis 32:29): *No longer will it be said that your name is Yaakov, but rather Yisrael.* Thus, it would seem that the name change had already taken place. What was Hashem adding at this time?

Ramban explains that one of these questions provides the answer to the other. Although the angel that Yaakov had vanquished had indeed told him that his name was to be Yisrael, this angel had not been given the mission to actually change Yaakov's name. Thus, at that time, the name remained Yaakov. The angel merely informed him that his name would be changed to Yisrael *in the future*. Because of this, Hashem began his statement here by saying: At this point, your name is still Yaakov, because it was not the angel's right to change your name. Now, however, I will indeed call you Yisrael.

Although the verse seems to say that Yaakov would no longer be called Yaakov, the commentators note that this is not the case. Indeed, we find a later verse (Bereishis 46:2) in which Hashem Himself refers to Yaakov by that name. In addition, although we find in reference to Avraham that once his name was changed from Avram, it was *forbidden* to call him Avram, with Yaakov that it not the case; the Sages in Tractate *Berachos* (13a) states that Yisrael became the *principal* name, while Yaakov was the *subsidiary* name.

R' David Feinstein suggests that this, too, in hinted at in Hashem's opening statement in the verse: "Your name is Yaakov." I.e., Hashem was telling Yaakov: I am not renaming you as I did Avraham, so that your original name may no longer be used. Rather, your name Yaakov is still usable; I am simply giving you another name as a principal name.

פרשת וישלח

MISHNAH OF THE DAY: SHABBOS 9:2

SHABBOS
PARASHAS VAYISHLACH

This Mishnah seeks the source for the law that contact with *tumah* does not contaminate a ship: מִנַּיִן לִסְפִינָה שֶׁהִיא טְהוֹרָה — **From where** do we know **that a ship is tahor,** i.e., not susceptible to contamination with *tumah*?[1] שֶׁנֶּאֱמַר — **For it has been stated** in a verse: "דֶּרֶךְ־אֳנִיָּה בְלֶב־יָם״, — *"Four [things] I do not know: . . .* **the path of a ship in the heart of the sea** [once it has passed]."[2] This verse teaches that a ship is like the sea — impervious to *tumah*.

The Mishnah now considers an aspect of the laws of *kilei zeraim* — the prohibition against planting an intermingled mix of different species of seeds. The Mishnah applies these laws to the planting of different vegetables in a small garden patch:

מִנַּיִן לַעֲרוּגָה שֶׁהִיא שִׁשָּׁה עַל שִׁשָּׁה טְפָחִים שֶׁזּוֹרְעִין בְּתוֹכָהּ חֲמִשָּׁה זֵרְעוֹנִין — **From where** do we know **that a garden patch that is six by six tefachim may be planted with five types of seeds,**[3] אַרְבָּעָה עַל אַרְבַּע — **four on the four sides of the patch,** רוּחוֹת הָעֲרוּגָה — וְאֶחָד בָּאֶמְצַע — **and one in the center?**[4] שֶׁנֶּאֱמַר ״כִּי כָאָרֶץ תּוֹצִיא צִמְחָהּ וּכְגַנָּה זֵרוּעֶיהָ

NOTES

1. In general, not all objects that come in contact with a source of *tumah* become *tamei*. Only three categories of things are susceptible to *tumah*: (a) people, (b) foods and beverages, (c) vessels. Plants, live animals, rivers, rocks and many other things cannot become *tamei*. Moreover, even vessels must meet certain conditions before they are considered susceptible to *tumah*. For example, for a non-metallic vessel to become *tamei* it must be a receptacle — i.e., it must possess a cavity that is capable of holding other things. A ship, however, is obviously a receptacle. Therefore the question arises, why is it not susceptible to *tumah*?

2. Proverbs 30:19. Since it is obvious that a ship travels in the midst of the sea, Scripture must be adding this seeming redundancy to teach some specific lesson. The Sages explain that the verse alludes to the following principle: Just as the sea cannot be contaminated by *tumah* [it is not susceptible to *tumah* since, on the contrary, it removes *tumah* by virtue of its being a *mikveh*], so too a ship cannot be contaminated by *tumah* (*Rav* from Gemara 83b; for another possible reason as to why a ship is not susceptible to *tumah*, see *Gems from the Gemara*).

3. What Scriptural evidence do we have for the law stated in *Kilayim* 3:1 that it is possible to sow five types of seeds in an area of six by six *tefachim* (i.e., six handbreadths, each of which is the equivalent of between three and four inches, depending upon the various opinions) and yet leave enough space between the types so that the seeds will not be considered intermingled? (*Rav; Rashi*).

4. Various authorities suggest different manners in which the patch under consideration might be planted. *Rav* and *Rashi* suggest that the case is one in which the perimeter of the patch is planted with four types of seeds, each filling a different side and stopping just short of the corner, which is left fallow, while in the center of the

"תַצְמִיחַ" — **For it has been stated** in a verse: *"For like the earth gives forth its plant, and like a garden causes its seeds to sprout"*; זֶרַע לֹא נֶאֱמַר אֶלָּא "זֵרוּעֶיהָ" — *"its seed"* **is not stated, but "its seeds."** [5]

פרשת וישלח
SHABBOS
PARASHAS VAYISHLACH

NOTES
---

patch a single seed of yet a fifth species is planted. Since the minimum measure of separation between species is three *tefachim*, the seeds on each side of the permiter are sufficiently distant from the seed in the middle (see diagram). Moreover, although the seeds of one type on each of the sides are not separated by three *tefachim* from the seeds of the other types on their adjacent sides, nevertheless, since the furrows run perpendicular to each other, and since the actual corners are left fallow [see diagram], each type appears distinct from the other types, and one is therefore permitted to plant them in this manner (*Rav, Rashi*).

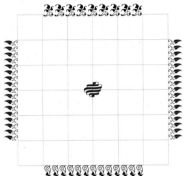

5. *Isaiah* 61:11. The Mishnah reiterates the conclusion of the verse to stress that it shifts to the plural form, thus indicating that the number of words in the verse that denote growth or vegetation is significant. This leads us to expound the entire verse as alluding to the number of types of seeds that can be sown in a single garden patch (*Pnei Yehoshua*). The Gemara (84b) explains that תוֹצִיא, *give forth*, denotes one type; צִמְחָהּ, *its plant*, denotes a second type; זֵרוּעֶיהָ, *its seeds*, being plural, denotes two more types; and תַצְמִיחַ, *it will cause to grow*, denotes a fifth type. [Although the distances between the types are not derived from the verse, the verse does indicate that there exists a manner by which five different types of seed can be planted in a single garden patch (*Tos. Yom Tov* from *Tos.* 85a; cf. *Kesef Mishneh, Hil. Kilayim* 4:16; see *Aruch HaShulchan, Yoreh Deah* 297:3-5).]

GEMS FROM THE GEMARA

In light of our Mishnah's ruling that a ship is not susceptible to *tumah*, the Gemara (83b) considers the case of a Jordan River boat. [Since the Jordan River is quite narrow and shallow, it can only accommodate small boats.] The Gemara cites a ruling of the Sages that a Jordan River boat is susceptible to *tumah*. R' Chanina the son of Akavya explains that the ruling of the Sages that a Jordan River boat is susceptible to *tumah* is due to the fact that these river boats were so small that they could be carried both while laden and while empty. [People customarily loaded them with cargo on the dry land, and then carried them to the river's edge and lowered

SHABBOS

PARASHAS VAYISHLACH

them into the water.] Chananya is of the opinion that a ship is not susceptible to *tumah* because we derive the *tumah* susceptibility of wooden utensils from an analogy between those utensils and a sack; thus, in order to be susceptible to *tumah*, they must have the characteristic of a sack, which can be carried both empty and laden. An ordinary ship is not carried when laden; thus it is not susceptible to *tumah*. The Jordan River boats, however, which *are* carried even when laden, are subject to contamination with contact-generated *tumah*.

Rav Yehudah in the name of Rav comments on R' Chanina the son of Akavya's explanation: "A person should never absent himself from the House of Study for even one moment [lest an explanation that he never heard before is propounded at that moment, and he, through his absence, would miss it]. For it was many years that this ruling of the Sages was taught in the House of Study, but we did not uncover its reasoning until R' Chanina the son of Akavya came and explained it."

The Gemara continues with a comment of a similar nature: R' Yonasan said: "A person should never absent himself from the House of Study, nor [ever refrain] from words of Torah — even at the moment of death, for it is stated (*Numbers* 19:14): *This is the Torah of a man who dies in a tent* — even at the moment of death, one should be involved with the study of Torah." [The verse translates literally as: *This is the law of a man who dies in a tent.*]

The Gemara then cites another homiletical interpretation of this verse. Reish Lakish said: "The words of Torah are not retained [by anyone], except by one who 'kills' himself [i.e., by one who 'kills' his body by refraining from physical indulgences] over the Torah. For it is stated: *This is the Torah of a man who dies in a tent.*"

A MUSSAR THOUGHT FOR THE DAY

Many interpretations have been offered as to the relative meanings of the names Yaakov and Yisrael, and the attributes they signify. The *Imrei Yosef* notes that the name Yaakov, which derives from the word עָקֵב, which means *heel*, symbolizes humility. He cites the exposition offered by the holy *Tzaddik of Lublin* (see *Yismach Moshe*) of the verse in *Devarim* (7:12): וְהָיָה עֵקֶב תִּשְׁמְעוּן, *And it will be, because* (עֵקֶב) *you will hearken*. The *Imrei Yosef* cites the Midrash (*Bereishis Rabbah* 42:3) that states that the word וְהָיָה connotes joy, and homiletically interprets the verse as teaching that Hashem experiences great joy when Jews act with

פרשת וישלח

SHABBOS

PARASHAS VAYISHLACH

the attribute of עָקֵב, *humility*, for this will cause them to realize their debt to Hashem, and motivate them to fulfill the mitzvos faithfully.

In the same vein, *Imrei Yosef* interprets Hashem's words to Yaakov as He changes his name to Yisrael. The name Yisrael connotes superiority, as the angel said to Yaakov: You will be known as Yisrael "because you have struggled with angels and men, and you have triumphed." He notes further that the letters of ישראל can be rearranged to read לי ראש, *a head for Me*; Hashem was telling Yaakov that as Yisrael, he was destined to be the head of the chosen of the nations. But in superiority there is danger, for power can lead to haughtiness, and haughtiness begets loss of one's fear of Hashem. Thus, Hashem cautions: "Your name is Yaakov!" Do not forget, even when you are successful and mighty, that you must always embody the trait for which you were named Yaakov, after the humble heel. If you retain your humility, then even in your superiority you will have your fear of Hashem.

HALACHAH OF THE DAY

We have seen thus far that the *melachah* of *bishul* prohibits cooking, accelerating the cooking process, and, in some instances, the reheating of cooked foods on Shabbos. While we have defined the term cooking as the preparing or altering of food through the application of heat, the prohibition of cooking does not apply only to cooking over a flame or some other direct source of heat. Immersing a food item in a pot of water that has been heated over a fire may cause the food to become cooked even if the pot is no longer on the fire. Even an empty pot that has been heated to a high temperature over a heat source and subsequently removed may cause food inserted into it to become cooked. For this reason, although in the above mentioned cases the food being cooked is never exposed directly to the heat *source*, such methods of cooking are also forbidden under the prohibition of *bishul*.

This aspect of the *melachah* of *bishul* is complex and affects many activities routinely performed in the kitchen. For example, mixing coffee with hot water taken from an urn, or adding seasoning to hot foods that are no longer on the fire may involve a violation of the *melachah* of *bishul*. These, as well as many similar activities, may be accomplished on Shabbos only within the guidelines and restraints we will now begin to explore.

SHABBOS

PARASHAS VAYISHLACH

When analyzing questions of cooking in vessels that are no longer on a flame or other direct heat source (such as an electric heating coil), it is necessary to first ascertain the ability of the vessel to cook an item placed inside it.

The halachah classifies vessels that have been removed from the flame into three distinct groups. These are: *kli rishon*, "the first vessel"; *kli sheni*, "the second vessel"; and *kli shelishi*, "the third vessel." Hot liquids that remain in the pot in which they were initially heated are capable of cooking any item immersed in them — even if the pot has been removed from the flame — as long as the liquids remain above the temperature of *yad soledes bo*. However, once the contents of the pot are transferred to a second pot that is not hot, the walls of this second pot begin to cool the liquid down, thereby degrading their ability to cook an item that is then immersed in it. Once the liquid is transferred to a third container, the capacity of the liquid to cook is degraded even more seriously.

Tomorrow we will begin to examine the laws pertaining to immersing foods into each category of vessel.

A CLOSER LOOK AT THE SIDDUR

This week, we will conclude our discussion of the prayer of *V'Shomru*, which is recited on Friday night before the *Maariv Shemoneh Esrei*. The *tefillah* of *V'Shomru* ends with the words, וּבַיּוֹם הַשְּׁבִיעִי שָׁבַת וַיִּנָּפַשׁ, which, literally translated, mean: *and on the seventh day, [Hashem] rested and was refreshed*. Rashi (*Shemos* 31:17) comments that this is an anthropomorphism; the verse is describing Hashem in human terms. God, of course, cannot become tired and needs no refreshment, but a man would need a day of rest to refresh himself after six days of labor. [Thus, the verse merely means that after six days, the work of Creation was completed.]

Other commentators, including *Ramban* and *R' Yehudah HaChassid*, explain that the word וַיִּנָּפַשׁ derives from the word נֶפֶשׁ, which means *soul*. They explain that the Sabbath is, in a sense, the *soul* of Creation; the Sabbath gives a new spiritual dimension to the entire universe. Thus, the verse means: *On the seventh day [Hashem] rested, and He gave a soul to the world*.

The Gemara in *Beitzah* (16a) also understands the word וַיִּנָּפַשׁ to refer to a soul; however, the Gemara states that it refers not to the soul of the

SHABBOS PARASHAS VAYISHLACH

world, but to the *neshamah yeseirah*, the *additional soul* that is given to each Jew for the duration of the Sabbath. *Rashi* (ibid.) states that the purpose of the additional soul is to enable a person to deal with the festivity and expansiveness of the Sabbath without suffering any adverse effects (such as indigestion from overindulgence, or a mental letdown after the departure of the Sabbath). *Sforno* adds that the additional soul helps a person attain greater spiritual heights on the Sabbath, a day on which Hashem is especially close to us.

Nesiv Binah cites a novel interpretation of the word וַיִּנָּפַשׁ that is offered by R' Shamshon Raphael Hirsch, who translated it to mean: *and [Hashem] withdrew into Himself* (as in the Aramaic word נַפְשֵׁיהּ, which means *himself*). He explains that Hashem designed the world as it appears today in such a way that there is no clear imprint of His Name obvious to all; He cloaked His handiwork in the laws of nature. Thus, it is necessary for us to testify, through our observance of the Sabbath, that we realize and understand that all of nature is nothing more than the workings of Hashem, and that He is the true Creator.

QUESTION OF THE DAY:
Why was Yaakov's name changed to Yisrael?

For the answer, see page 228.

ANSWERS TO QUESTIONS OF THE DAY

Sunday:
The *Midrash* states that the angels Yaakov sent were the very ones mentioned just two verses previously (at the end of *Parashas Vayeitzei*).

Monday:
Zohar derives from here that when one prays he should be as specific as possible in identifying any person mentioned in the prayer. For this reason, we use a mother's name when praying for an ill person.

Tuesday:
Dinah, who had been hidden away, and Binyamin, who was not yet born.

Wednesday:

The angel injured Yaakov's *gid hanasheh* (literally: the *displaced sinew*, commonly identified as the sciatic nerve). The Gemara (*Chullin* 90a) presents a dispute as to whether the angel injured Yaakov only on his right hip, or on both hips.

Thursday:

We ask Hashem to bless us as He blessed the *Avos*... בַּכֹּל מִכֹּל כֹּל. The word כֹּל refers to Yaakov's statement to Eisav, יֶשׁ לִי כֹל, *I have everything*.

Friday:

Rashi (33:17) states that he remained there eighteen months. This is deduced from the word בַּיִת in the verse (that implies a winter), and the two times that the verse states סֻכּוֹת (which imply two summers).

Shabbos:

Rashi (35:10) states that the name Yaakov connotes a person who comes with treachery (עָקְבָה), while Yisrael comes from the word שַׂר, which means *nobleman* (see *Chullin* 92a).

This volume is part of
THE ARTSCROLL SERIES®
an ongoing project of
translations, commentaries and expositions
on Scripture, Mishnah, Talmud, Halachah,
liturgy, history, the classic Rabbinic writings,
biographies and thought.

For a brochure of current publications
visit your local Hebrew bookseller
or contact the publisher:

Mesorah Publications, ltd
4401 Second Avenue
Brooklyn, New York 11232
(718) 921-9000
www.artscroll.com